BORN FROM ABOVE

Waking Up to Our Genesis

Dave Carringer

Merhobyah Press

Cleveland, Tennessee

~Merhobyah~

I found myself...

in the wide-open places

Merhobyah Press

Cleveland, Tennessee

Merhobyahpress@yahoo.com

BORN FROM ABOVE

Waking Up to Our Genesis

Dave Carringer -- 1st edition:

ISBN 978-1-7343546-0-7

======================================

You were *never* an ugly duckling.

You just needed a clear reflection
of who you *really* are.

The Son of Man gave you one.

======================================

~Special Thanks~

First and foremost- my wife, Kay Carringer. Anyone who's ever written and formatted a book (with no outside help), knows what a long and tedious process it is. This book wouldn't have been possible without you, Kay. Countless hours of our time together you sacrificed; not only giving me the space, but then guarding that space and helping in so many different ways to help me see this dream come true. Thank you for a love and marriage that's heaven to me. From our very first days together, we knew we would need each other to do important things we were supposed to do. You're always perfect for me in every possible way... and we are just getting started! *You're my Stuff.* I Love You!

My daughter Lea. You saved my life, literally; and then taught me what real life could be. I hope other dads and daughters may know what you and I have always enjoyed together. I couldn't be more honored or proud that you're my daughter! This book could have never existed without my Lioness of First Light. I Love You. I AM ALWAYS with you.

My mom, Frances (Lou Bell) Carringer. Your body died giving birth to me; but death couldn't hold your spirit. You came back and gave life to everyone around you till you were 92. That's who you are. You're with me every single day as I live, laugh, love, and give that same life away.

All my children who make my life so rich and full. What a joy to love you and be loved by you! Though we all may not have the same blood, our hearts are forever joined inseparably as one; and that's the most beautiful union that can ever be known. Paul, Lea, Brandon, Kelsey, Jared, Asia, Salem, Meredith, Austin, and Alexis. Each of you are uniquely and creatively beautiful; and you've taught me lessons in life I would never have enjoyed without you. You were all success-full the moment you took your first breath; and each of you carry *within* what it takes to landscape this world with contagious and unfailing love. You're already doing it- and I can't wait to see where it goes from here!

My beautiful grandchildren. Zion, Tessa, Marlee, Daphne, Eleanor, Avery Jane, Will, and Oakland. You are icing on the cake of life for me! Each of you carry a unique divine design fingerprint that can never be matched by any other; that you may reach out and touch this world in special ways that make it more beautiful than it's ever been before!

My dear friend and manager, Tonya Brown, who's been by my side for many years; and a staff who cares for each person who enters our door with genuine love, care, and concern. What a joy to do LIFE with you!

My talented friend and brother, Matt McClay - **mcclaydesign.com.** Thanks for enduring my nitpickiness and giving me the *perfect* cover. I'll always be grateful; for I could have never done this without you.

Our LionsGate Fellowship group, whom I am so blessed to be part of, and thankful for all the things we've seen together over the years.

Mo Thomas. What life-changing things we've discovered and explored together! Your friendship, wisdom, and love are absolutely priceless!

Francois and Lydia du Toit. You continually reveal the Father's beauty in ways that awaken people's hearts and minds to a Love that cannot be bound or restricted. I love you both very much! Thank you for the Mirror Bible, Stella's Secret, all the videos, and passionately BEing <u>you</u>!

Kay Fairchild. Thank you for always being so generous with your time. I am honored to know you as a friend, teacher, and a sounding board of wisdom and life experience whom I trust and admire greatly.

Kyle Butler. River walks, late night talks, contemplating the 'what ifs' of things *almost* too good to be true. There's no one like you to me.

Michael Coller- **michaelcollerart.com/** Thanks so much for sharing your amazing gift with us. You made our swan even more beautiful!!

Those who read my entire draft and offered feedback to make it better. Kay Carringer, Paul & Kim Huffman, Al & Becki Carden, Douglas & Brenda Thompson, Kyle Butler, Mo Thomas, Billy 'Boo' Clark, Carol McGrath. You're a big part of this. I truly love and appreciate you all.

Paul Huffman. When I would wonder if writing this book would even matter, or if people were ready to search things out on their own, your timely, encouraging messages helped me see people *really were* ready.

My amazing family around the globe! You guys rock; and your voices of Love are changing the landscape of this planet through your actions, blogs, videos, books and posts. There are far too many of you to name, but I treasure each one of you from every country and background imaginable. You ARE loved... and you ARE making a difference!

Spin Master Ltd. for the creative fun and ingenuity of Etch A Sketch.

Biblehub.com / HELPS ™ Word-Studies for great reference material.

CONTENTS

The Journey Begins

This book *could* be seen as my ideas and opinions about God, and I don't have a problem with that. It's been formed from an interesting journey of life... *my journey*. There isn't one single thing ever written about God that hasn't come from someone else's ideas and opinions. We may not particularly like that thought, but liking it or not doesn't change its validity. Maybe you've never thought about it? We just want someone to tell us what we should believe about God- you know, the *absolute* stuff. Write it down, make it sound authoritative... and we're good to go. Many people wish God would just give them a detailed list of what they *need to do*- something they can look at and follow. Wouldn't that simplify things? Yet, what we have been taught as the absolutes of God, are really just ideas and opinions formed along other people's journeys, and then passed down to others. Once we're willing to open our mind up to accept that fact, we can then begin to embrace reality, and be led into actually knowing the truth *for ourselves*.

Contrary to popular belief, *to do* lists and absolutes are not how the Father of creation saw this whole life-thing playing out. The Source of all life, love, imagination, and humor didn't set all this into motion to be run by a bunch of robotic command followers building forms and filling them with concrete. We may have turned it into that, but that doesn't mean it was God's idea. We've used *our* ideas about God to create our own absolute boxes... and we're masters at it. Effectively, men have created god(s) in their own image-i-nation. Some of these gods have been quite distorted, and others are downright *scary*.

Finding out you're not actually required to believe what everyone (or anyone) around you believes, might just usher you into a more powerful and liberating life filled with love and joy than you've ever dreamed was possible. How do I know? *It happened to me.* My life is no longer restricted or confined by other men's ideas about God. I live by what I know about God, and what I know about me. While we can certainly be encouraged (or not) by thoughts and ideas of others, the only way we can truly *know* the divine Source of all life in a tangible, unshakable way, is through tangible, personal experiences as we learn how to participate with, and in that Source along the way.

Your ideas and opinions may be different, and you know what? That's ok. Also contrary to popular belief, is that this life isn't about getting a high mark on some pass or fail test at the end. There are however, a few things I've learned to ponder on along the way which have truly enhanced my life and made it more enjoyable. Am I present in the *moments* of the day? Am I grateful? Am I seeing through eyes of love? Am I partaking in, enjoying, and surrendering to all that's been provided and set in motion around me? I AM; at least to the extent that I see it *today.* I'm learning to enjoy the *now* of heaven all around me. This is what my journey has taught me, and I learn more every day.

Some of what you're about to read may resonate deeply and help you enjoy a greater magnitude of awareness, freedom, and personal peace. Some of it may be totally new to your thinking and cause you to go back and revisit specific things you once thought you were certain of. If you've spent many years around western Christianity as I have, some of what you'll read might even make you angry. While I hope awareness, freedom, and peace will describe your overall experience in this book, I understand that feelings of anger may also surface as well. My journey has produced many waves of emotions along the way; but today, I overflow with joyful gratitude and appreciation for all those who first offended what *I thought I knew* about God.

Jesus didn't go around giving people *to do* lists they'd first need to fulfill to become One with the Father. Instead, he revealed what the heavenly Father had done to forever be One with them. He told them that one day, they would wake up and know it for themselves. He taught continually with open ended parables having the possibility of various answers, all designed to *stimulate* their own thinking.

As the Son of Man revealed the Father's love, putting the Christ-life and consciousness on visible display, he asked his disciples,

"Who do men say that I, the Son of Man, am?"

As they began regurgitating the opinions of others, Jesus shifted the question's focus to catapult them into an entirely new realm of personal discovery. This journey they were now on, would not only reveal their own lives as mirrored in this Son of Man; but walking in this experience *with him* would open their eyes to an even deeper truth- that *all* other sons of men upon this earth were the offspring of God as well. This life-changing journey didn't start out because *they* were pursuing Jesus, or by *them* asking if they could come along with him. It started with Jesus invading their personal space in life, saying,

"There's so much I want to show you; Come on... follow me!"

All creation had been longing with tip-toed anticipation for the authentic sons and daughters of God to wake up to who they truly were, and leave the generational grave-clothes of orphaned, *alien*ated thinking behind. A vital question which actually initiates knowing the Father and *ourselves* is found in what Jesus asked his disciples,

"But who do YOU say that I AM?"

Was Jesus a divine scapegoat? Was he made a flesh *son of man* upon whom a distant record-keeping judge could then pour out all the stored-up anger and wrath he'd accumulated toward mankind? Was Jesus the only narrow gate passcode to an 'or else' fire insurance plan giving men an alternate destination of a distant and delayed heaven, rather than the eternal flames of hell the judge said they deserved?

I know what we've always been taught. I know what we've always
been told the Bible *clearly* says. All my life I've heard what other men
said about who Jesus (and God) is. I also know how my life changed
when the Spirit within stimulated my own thinking, by asking,

"But who do YOU say that I AM?"

What if Jesus really was the *perfect expression* of the Father? What
if Jesus really meant it when he said:

*"I have no judgment or condemnation toward men; and I only do
what I see my Father do."*

What if he really meant it when he said:

"No man has seen (grasped the literal reality of) *the Father,"* and, *"If
you see me, you can see* (grasp the literal reality of) *the Father."*

I actually (and literally) believe these reflective statements, and the
life Jesus revealed as the true nature of the Father. In order to do that,
it meant (at least for me) that those who had written their ideas and
opinions of a *God* they believed was a distant and disgruntled judge,
didn't, as Jesus plainly said, actually know the truth about him at all.

What if Jesus didn't come as a scapegoat to take upon himself the
punishment and violent wrath some distant and angry judge said all
mankind was deserving of? What if this beautiful Son of Man (who
knew the truth of a Father others hadn't) merely provided a *mirror*
reflecting this Father's love, so other men could finally *see* that just as
the Father had loved Jesus... so also, had this heavenly Father loved
them? What if *all this time-* through generations past, the belief of a
distant judge men needed to appease in order to avoid his anger and
punishment, only existed in man's *self*-inflicted alienated mindset?
What if this condemning and fearful judge, was actually a distortion of
men's own imagination? What if the reality of *heaven*, was the truth of
a loving Father who had nothing to pour out on mankind except the
fullness of his love? And what if this Son of Man, who never doubted
his Oneness with God, was simply trying to show other sons of men
that his Father had always *seen them* as extended offspring too?

I'm about to share some glimpses of my life's journey, and how I've come to *know* my paternal Source. It isn't based on what men have said in the past, but on Jesus' revealing the Father's nature- and what I now experientially know for myself. I'd be delighted if you'd join me.

In 1996 I pulled over on a little gravel road in southeast Tennessee, looked up in the sky, and spoke some short and simple words to God: *"I want to know you. Show me who you really are... and I'll do whatever you ask."*

That was 24 years ago at the time of this writing. I was 38 years old, and my life had been like a train-wreck of headline proportions up to that point. Not just one train-wreck either. It was pretty much a daily occurrence repeating itself over and over. From the age of 13 I had been surrounded by a life of drugs, violence, and danger. My father bootlegged beer, moonshine, and drugs from our house in a dry county. He was a gambler that traveled around with a circuit of other men who did the same. I ended up being his chauffeur when he was too out of his mind to drive- which was most of the time.

My mother was the most precious, loving person I've ever known. She loved me even at the pinnacles of my unlovableness, but the summer before I started high school, she moved out. She had tried the best way she knew how to provide a safe home environment for me, but it had come to a place where she now feared for her own life. My dad's drinking, drug use, and aggression was no longer bearable for her. I fully understood. She pleaded with me to leave with her, but the excitement of drugs, guns, money, and women already had its grip on me. When I was 15, my dad shot me as we fought over drugs. I wasn't the only one. Others also found the end of his gun; and some, were much less fortunate than myself. By the time 1996 rolled around I had been doing drugs on a regular basis for over 25 years. Meth, cocaine, opioids, hypnotics, tranquilizers, and other drugs were just part of my everyday life. But 1996 was different for me. *Very different.*

My daughter Lea, was 8 years old, and was from an unplanned pregnancy. Well, *unplanned* from my end anyway. No words could ever describe my heart's gratitude as I now realize there was a much bigger destiny awaiting me- far beyond the scope of anything I could dream or imagine back then. This little blonde-haired bundle of joy was strategically dropped into my train-wreck existence as the catalyst to unleash that destiny. Out of nowhere she came roaring in, wasting no time taking her place as a heavenly picture window of what real life was all about. It's easy to look back now and see she had come into my life of darkness to reveal daybreak glimpses of things *heaven* held in store for me. I didn't realize it as we chose her name, in fact, I didn't know it until I started writing this book, but the name, Leandra Dawn, means *lioness of first light*. Yeah, you can't make that stuff up.

I'd been approached over the years with a turn or burn message, saying if I didn't change my ways, I'd end up in *hell*. Quite honestly, that type of fear-based message doesn't have much effect on someone who's lived in hell most of their life; and it sure never had any effect on me. Up till then, my motto had been "If you're not living on the edge, you're taking up too much space." But my perspective was changing. I was getting tired of hanging over the edge; and I'd been introduced to glimpses of a life and love I'd never before personally known. I had experienced my first light and a sweet taste of heaven, and if there was more where this came from... *I wanted it.* So here I was pulled over in the grass beside a little country gravel road. Something was burning inside my heart, and my head wanted, and desperately needed, to know it was real. *"Are you real, God? Show me, and I'm yours."*

I can't fully describe what happened to me- but I do remember it was like everything melted around me. All I could feel or be aware of was what was burning inside me. I remember feeling like I wasn't alone. I didn't want to leave this *presence* I was experiencing, but at some point, I started my car and drove the rest of the way home. When I got there, it became blatantly obvious that what was burning intensely within me on that little gravel road, was still there, and it *wasn't* going away. I spent several hours digging out hidden stashes of pills and powders, and flushing them down the toilet. I cut syringes in pieces with scissors till my hands hurt, and burned them in a garbage can out back. On November 17, 1996, I walked away from the life of anger, violence, and drug addiction that had held me in a life-sucking downward spiral since I was 13 years old... *and I never went back.*

I went to a small country church nearby, filled with loving people who had come by the house the summer before and asked to take Lea to vacation Bible school. I'd never been in a building with that much love. I didn't feel like they looked at my long hair, earrings, or tattoos, but they looked at me like I was one of their own. When I told them what had happened to me, they explained my experience was known as being *born again*. I was told that this experience could happen to anyone who would repent of their sins, believe in Jesus' death and resurrection, and ask him to come live in their heart. Even though I hadn't done any of those things, I took their word for it. After all, I really did feel like a new person; and who was I to question proper Christian protocol- *something I knew nothing about.*

Many people would later ask if my instantaneous departure from all those years of heavy drug use had left me in withdrawals. I knew what that looked like up close and personal. Too many times I'd spoon fed my dad as he sweated, tremored, and vomited. Too many times I'd laid in bed with my legs drawing up, feeling like my feet were turning inside out as week-long binges of shooting morphine, Dilaudid, or Demerol worked their way out of my body. But there were none. Not once. It was like someone flipped a switch and it was gone. My desire for drugs had totally disappeared; but that burning urge I'd felt within to know who God really was, kept drawing me in toward it. In fact, the desire I felt burning within me on that little gravel road only became more intense with each passing day.

I found an old King James Bible my mom had given me many years before. Though my craving for drugs was gone; I'd found a new object of affection. This book, *so I was told*, contained everything about God

I could ever want or need to know. I couldn't wait to get home from work each day, dive straight into my recliner and soak in all I could, until finally falling asleep in the wee hours of morning. Then I found out there were other translations of these scriptures. Not long after, I was introduced to special dictionaries and concordances meant to help me explore things others wouldn't find in casual reading. I bought them as well. I'd stay up late at night studying. I'd spend my weekends researching and making notes. This had moved beyond consuming my interest; it was consuming me. I was addicted with a hunger I'd never known; and no matter what I saw or learned, *I wanted more.* Before long, I had questions that people around me didn't have answers for. It was then I began to realize *certain* questions made certain people uncomfortable... especially regarding topics that weekly sermons and Sunday School hadn't *prepared* them to answer.

About six months after my gravel road experience I was asked to come to a local jail and share my story. *It was all on then.* I didn't have any problem telling others what I had been rescued from, and no problem at all talking about this God I'd been discovering. I was about to explode from everything I'd already realized of just how good this God-life was, so being with a bunch of people who'd been down some of the same roads I had, was the perfect place to release it. The week after my first 'testimony' at the jail, I received a call from the ministry coordinator asking if I would consider coming back. She told me: *"These guys haven't stopped talking about God since you left."*

I was a little bit stunned- and a whole lot excited... so of course I went back. What people called *preaching* wasn't really something that appealed to me. I just loved sharing my story, reading scriptures about how Jesus went around doing good to all, treated everyone the same, and taught them about their "Father in heaven." I couldn't get enough of talking about this new life I was enjoying, a life I didn't have to go anywhere to find or do anything to get. I simply loved telling people how this new and amazing life had actually *come and found me.*

Well, that's how it all started. People would just stand up while I was talking, walk up where I was and say, *"I want to know this God you know."* Often, when one got up and moved, others would stand up and I'd begin to hear *"me too"* coming from all around the room. There was nothing I loved more. These were my people. They easily related to my past pain, anger, violence, and addictions, and I couldn't have been more comfortable than being right there in the middle of them.

That jail led to another jail. Then to several jails in several counties. In 2000, I was invited to the men's prison in Bledsoe county. Then the state women's prison in Nashville. That all led to a regular circuit of jails and prisons I would travel to, sharing the Good News and helping the staff with counseling programs and events within the prisons. The services overflowed. The jail officials expanded my visits, as people would show up to chapels with no remaining seats. At one point I was doing 3 services on Sunday afternoons after I left my church. When there was no more room in the chapel, I'd apologize to the guards for all the work they had to do to keep things organized. One of the guards told me, *"Don't apologize to us; we're glad to see you coming. These guys are different after you come, and that makes our job easier."* They finally began putting us in the gym where everyone could get in at the same time. That meant the guards also had to come because of the size of the crowd. Often, I'd see guards weeping right beside the inmates, as love filled the atmosphere like a warm heavenly blanket.

At times, I'd ask to go in solitary confinement rooms that even the guards wouldn't go in. Some of these inmates were convicted of violent crimes and multiple murders, and they survived by keeping a hard and heavy reputation behind the bars. I remember guards asking me: *"Are you sure about this? You don't know how crazy this guy is."* Thirty minutes later a scarred and tattooed murderer would be sobbing like a little boy in my arms, as the guards stared through the vision panel in the steel door. *"How do you do that??"* would be the usual response when I tapped on the door to be let out. *"I just told him how much God loves him"* I would say, wiping the tears from my own eyes.

Eventually, I was invited to churches that were interested in prison ministry, as well other churches who simply wanted to hear me teach. The response was usually quite receptive, and at times, overwhelming. I'd just talk about the Father's love and amazing gift of life given to us, and people would come to the altar weeping. I didn't talk about sin, as I figured people already knew it if they were doing harmful things and their life was a wreck, and they didn't really need me to come point that out to them. If I had an altar call, it didn't revolve around scaring people with judgment, hell, or giving them a list of hoops they'd need to jump through to know God. I didn't have them confess sins of the past, ask forgiveness, or ask Jesus to come live in their heart. I didn't have them promise to do anything special in the future. I'd just share the Father's love the same way it had come to me and had changed my life in such drastic measures. Then I'd usually say something like:

"If you've seen the Father's love today and all Jesus did to show us that love, and you want to know it in your own life, stand up."

When people would stand up or walk to the front, we'd say a very simple prayer. Sometimes I'd have them to repeat the date, only so it would be etched in their memory of a specific day they'd felt their hearts burning to know and embrace this gift of the Father's love.

Our prayer would usually be something like:

"Father, today I've seen your gift of love for me. Thank you. I receive your love with open arms. Show me the truth of who you are, and teach me how to walk enjoying this gift of life and love. Amen."

That was it, nothing complicated. It wasn't unusual for people to erupt with tears, shouts, or wanting to openly testify of something they knew changed for them that day, or of a certain weight they'd felt lifted off of them. Since my gravel road experience, I've stood face to face with thousands of people offering this simple prayer of recognition and gratitude. I've joyfully watched as many of them were released from prison, becoming reconciled with loved ones and turning out to be loving, influential assets to their families and communities.

At times, certain ministers have strongly implied my altar prayer was not enough. Really? *Who said we even needed a prayer?* I was no stranger to being approached by leaders concerned about my teaching style and altar call. They wanted to know *why* I didn't preach about judgment, hell, or confessing sins to be *saved*. I was told I should take people down the 'Roman Road' to make sure their salvation was legit. I've heard it many different ways; yet no one was ever able to show me anywhere in scripture where Jesus or the apostles did anything that resembled what we require of people in our western altar protocol.

There were still plenty of people that wanted to hear what I had to say though, so I just kept doing what I saw Jesus do in the scriptures. I'd hit the streets at nights and on weekends, where teenagers would be hanging out drinking and doing drugs. I'd listen as they vented about their problems, and then tell them how much they were loved and all that was meant for them to enjoy. I'd go into bars and drug dens and sit with hurting people just trying to cope with the world and make it through another day. I'd patiently sit and listen till I had a chance to tell them how much they were loved, and that there was *another way* that could fill their days with light and love.

I often traveled doing commercial construction of nursing homes, so at night, I would visit with elderly people who had no families. I'd simply read their favorite scriptures to them or just let them share their memories of the past. I'd never leave without holding their hands and telling them how loved and precious they were in the Father's eyes. It was sad to me how many people in their 80's and 90's never knew just how loved and valuable they were- until a stranger came in their room to tell them. I remember how beautiful it was to feel them squeeze my hands as emotional tears of joy, and sometimes *relief*, streamed down their cheeks. Finally, they would hear the truth about who they were and who they belonged to. They could now know their life truly mattered, and that their heavenly Father had made sure they would enjoy knowing that for the rest of their days.

Not satisfying the preaching requirements of certain churches didn't keep me from being an active part of one myself. I passionately served, finding great joy in doing behind the scenes work, construction projects, singing on the praise team, ministering when asked, and supporting the pastor and other members of the staff any way I could. I didn't see it as serving; I saw it as doing something I loved with my whole heart. Through it all, the fire and hunger that consumed me on that gravel road never let up. I devoured the scriptures and parables of Jesus. I studied many various Bible translations along with words and phrases in the original language. I saw things in overwhelmingly better ways than I'd been taught. I'd often smile as I uncovered these hidden treasures, being reminded from within of those few words I'd uttered upward through my windshield, *"Show me who you really are."*

I was falling more in love every day with this Father I'd asked to know. The more I learned to recognize this voice within, the more I realized it was saying some of the same things I'd heard whispered in my darkness long ago. It was becoming obvious that this *voice* wasn't something new that just started speaking to me because I pulled over that day. It had actually been there *drawing me from within* all along. *I just hadn't been ready to listen.*

At some point I began to realize how much focus was placed on one certain aspect of scriptures. It didn't seem like a bad thing at first, but I soon realized people weren't too happy if I saw something could be read one way *literally*, yet look entirely different from a *metaphorical* view. Especially if *that way* didn't fit snugly in a specific doctrinal box. I was told *God's Word* was meant to be seen one way- *literally*. The more time I spent in concordances and teacher's commentaries, the more I noticed binding themes that certain scriptures had been woven around from one *idea*. These commonly embraced viewpoints held by commentators, often portrayed quite a different image of the Father I knew who'd dove into hell with me and refused to leave till I did. Things I read and heard taught that God *literally* and *intentionally* did to certain people in the Bible, didn't sound like Jesus to me *at all*.

I then started becoming acutely aware of my surrounding Christian culture. I saw how we'd been raised to 'teach the Bible'- a book that's helped to inspire much goodness and life, yet has also been used as the anchor point for horrific wars and destruction through the ages. What determines its use? The reader's *perspective*. The lens through which *they interpret* what's inside. Things of great beauty have been inspired and then carried out in the same intentional flow of love from which they came. Those same things however, when seen through a *skewed perspective*, can be interpreted, written down, and then carried out in a manner ending up *worlds apart* from anything that looks like love.

Something was happening that drew me into places of intimacy and love I'd never known. This wasn't just between me and *heaven*, it affected how I saw others right in front of me. Sure, I could see the evidence of outer scars and pain in people's lives- but I began to see deeper things of the amazing treasure of heaven hidden beneath those scars. Yeah, I had loved people before; but this was a whole new depth where I began seeing myself as *one* with them. I was also enjoying a deeper peace and rest within myself that didn't come and go, but was always right there within me whenever *I chose* to bask in it.

Sermons I heard preached about *God* sounded much different than the Father who rescued me. Even words to *worship* songs and prayers began sounding strange- opposite of what I knew in my heart. I was hearing much more about living in sin, doing warfare with the *devil*, what to do, and what not to do, than I heard about living from the fullness of peace, joy, and love. Sure, we were told we could *attain* peace, joy, and love; but we would have to press through, work hard, stay on course, and battle enemies from all sides to get it. I heard more *laborious* ideas from doctrinal perspectives than about the Father of restoration, provision, and healing I now had personal knowledge of.

I began to realize what this world needs
isn't more Bible teachers.
It needs more carriers of the Father's heart.

I kept noticing underlying tones of separation, distance, and delay, which continually permeated our corporate gatherings. Of course, we didn't realize it, because of what we were always taught to do; but it didn't change this tone and unspoken implication that we were *here*, and God... *was somewhere else*. We'd pray to bind the devil so the word could come forth. We'd put oil on people while speaking to this same villainous satan, commanding him to GET OUT of their bodies. We would open up our services with prayers and songs crying out for Holy Spirit to come down where we were and let us *feel* the presence. We'd ask for just a *touch* of heavenly glory to refresh and renew our strength. All from the same Father and Spirit that Jesus said we were complete in, and One with, who would *never* leave us or forsake us.

Please don't take this as me judging or making light of people who do these things. I'm not, as I was right in the middle of it and did them myself for many years. Yet the time came when I had to question what I was doing, and *why* I was doing it. How could I believe I was One with God, just like Jesus, and still feel the need to engage in such prayers, pleadings, rituals, and warfare with a defeated foe? At their core, they implied I wasn't *really One* with my divine Source of life at all. But these were just a *few* things pricking my awareness that were opposite of the love and peace I was being consumed with from within.

It didn't stop there. I found myself being adamantly warned not to stray outside the *camp* to teachings or information not supported or endorsed by our doctrinal beliefs. Yet after what I had seen and been through, I wasn't afraid of some spiritual boogie man overpowering me and stealing what I'd been given. I started studying the historical timetables of other cultures and civilizations, *what* they believed, and *why* they believed it. During my research of the documented history of many different people groups and the timeframes in which they lived, my eyes were opened to huge new discoveries. I uncovered a plethora of things I had never heard in any of the evangelical or charismatic word of faith camps I'd spent so much time in. What I did begin to see, was an exclusive culture all its own constructed by the ideas of men, and wrapped up tightly within specific doctrines existing only *inside* the walls of the church. Searching these credible resources began to reveal that much of what we were taught as God's unshakable truth, didn't actually line up with historical or factual evidence at all. Not only that, but much of what I'd been taught, stood in direct opposition to the Father's inclusive love which Jesus so clearly displayed.

I didn't set out looking for this journey. *It came looking for me.* I'll admit there were plenty of things that could have offended me if I had listened to others and stubbornly defended the camp perspectives I'd been trained in all those years. I would often lie in bed struggling with what was taught as the *only* way- versus this intense pulling in my soul toward something that felt so much better, made much more sense, and actually looked like the Father's heart of love Jesus revealed. I'm not talking about little surface aggravations or minor things every now and then. This was stuff that was rocking the foundational core of what I'd been taught Christian life was all about. *Literally.*

It started like a single light switch illuminating one room so I could see things I hadn't seen or been taught before. Even though they had always been right there, *I hadn't been able to see them.* As I would explore this room and all it contained, I'd become deeply and utterly convinced of its amazingly beautiful truths now clearly revealed in the light. This was forcing me to put what I had been taught in the past, up on the table for re-examination. Here, as I re-evaluated what I'd been taught alongside what was now being revealed in the light, it became blatantly obvious to me that one was truth... and the other *was not.* It started a domino effect of everything I'd been taught to embrace as *pure* theology. As this enlightening truth began *un*veiling my vision in one room, the new light shining *from* it now directly affected how I saw the things in other rooms around it as well.

What I was seeing in this *new light,* was far more beautiful than anything I'd seen in the past. A couple times I paused briefly to look back, realizing how far I was moving away from what many had warned me was the only safe ground. But deep inside I knew it was already too late. Where I was now was real. It was full of light and life, right out in the open. Here, questions weren't just allowed, they were encouraged, and I began finding answers that actually *made sense*. There was freedom to move in fresh, new, wide-open places, where love was *always* the backdrop of what I felt and saw. This wasn't just some story in a book I was reading, it was my own vibrantly tangible experience. I found myself no longer *reaching up* to grasp the divine, only to graze it now and then with my fingertips. Now, everything in my midst became holy to me. It wasn't something just briefly seen or felt during a worship song or service. It gushed in divine connection with everything around me as One. This was beautifully more exciting and life-giving than anything I had ever before known.

I had clearly crossed a point of no return, where that which I had searched diligently to grasp back *there-* had nothing to compare with all that now came from every side to encounter and engulf me *here*. The further I moved away from traditions I had been told I must take part in, the more I began to realize what a deep groove of fear-based tunnel-vision I'd been entrenched in. I never meant to offend anyone by enjoying this new and amazing life of truth and reality that had consumed me; yet some were clearly offended that I would even dare consider venturing away from the pack. I soon began to realize I was learning more about the kingdom of love from some of the very ones that I'd been warned to stay away from, than I had from those who had issued the warnings.

Today, I now know that I could never go back, nor would I want to. I couldn't see it from the cultured moat of fear I'd been surrounded by so long, but once I got out, *everything* became much clearer. I now see that fear is not only the darkest blindfold man can ever wear; it's also the most effective tool in herding alienated minds to keep them under religious control. Where tones of fear present themselves in the form of ultimatums, conditions, or ideas of torment, it *can't* be rooted in love. There is absolutely no fear in the message of love... *even* if it comes dressed in a suit with scriptures and theological degrees.

I'm grateful for everything and *everyone* that provoked me to take another look. I'm thankful for ideas and experiences outside the walls I had been camped inside for so long. I'm thankful I ignored warnings to *not go* looking *out there.* I can look back now and see some of my greatest growth and maturity has come from refusing to stay huddled within the fears of an exclusive mindset that things *outside* the walls... were my *enemy.* There's no part of my life today that isn't richer for it. Fear of what's *out there,* is gone. I love others around me like never before. I do it because I finally know what Jesus knew. We're all *One.* There isn't any part of my life or any expression of it that could be separate from my divine Source even for a moment. And what I now know about my life, I also know about the lives of others as well.

A great lesson I've learned during this transformation, is never be afraid to venture off from the pack mentality. Just because it runs in a herd doesn't make it truth. When the blindfold falls away (and it will) you'll be able to see this amazing journey is worth it all. You'll never stop being thankful for those first baby steps you took. They lead to much enlightening truth along heavenly paths, moving you forward into the freedom and love you were meant to be enjoying *all along.*

This book contains a few topics regarding beliefs I was taught in western Christianity which I *now* see through a much different light. **It is not meant as judgmental toward others or what you believe.** If my words come across that way- then what I hoped to convey hasn't come through as intended from my heart. This is merely the story of my journey. It's about things I experienced in my life, and how my perceptions have *changed* along the way. I know there are those who have no interest in doing or believing anything different than what they've always believed. I'm ok with that, and if that's you... I love you. I also know those who are of the persuasion I should just quietly enjoy these areas of enlightened awareness and peace, keeping my thoughts to myself (and mouth shut), and leave others to find it on their own. I also understand that aspect of thinking, and I love you dearly as well.

I'm not set on bringing some great awakening to others. I, nor any other man carries that power or ability. Only the Spirit within, flowing as our divine Source, can remove our veils. Still, I'm personally very thankful for a love that was willing to invade my space. Not in some intrusive pushy way, but in a way that provoked me to think, ask some questions, and help me *see* a life I now wouldn't trade for anything.

I believe that from time to time, certain paths are meant to cross where one's journey can be enjoyed alongside another. It may be for a season, or merely just a few moments, but special gifts designed to be enjoyed from deep within, can come seemingly out of nowhere. Quiet whispers can become like the roar of a lion. The tiniest glimpse of first light can come and invade our space like the morning sunrise beaming off the ocean waves. These are things I *know* from my experience, and nothing, or no one, can ever take them from me.

I know there are many who are questioning things they've been searching for answers to. I'm convinced there are pews and prayer rooms full of hungry people whose hearts have been crying out *"Show me who you really are."* I already know the streets, bars, and prisons are full of this same yearning to know what life is really all about. I sure don't claim to have all the answers. In fact, I have more questions now than I've ever had. I truly believe we can learn from each other's journeys. What to do, what not to do, and *new ways* to see. Perhaps there's a few of you who will relate to my journey. The part before my gravel road experience, or the part that came afterward. If that's you, then you're who this book is for. One thing we all eventually realize, is this life is *one big journey*, the parts in the darkness, and the parts in the light. And whether or not we realize it at the moment, we are all, each and every one of us... on this journey of life *together*. My true desire is that as you explore this book, you might possibly find the courage to ask some questions you've been holding inside a long time. Often, the questions we're *afraid* of asking, hold the keys to set us free.

I'm just an ordinary guy on an extraordinary journey I've grown to love in more ways than I can express. I'm not trying to start any new doctrines or pour concrete around my views. I'm not asking you to believe anything because I do. We've tried that for too long, and I can't see we've changed much because of it. We desire absolutes written in black and white *today* that we can be absolutely certain of *tomorrow*. One thing I'm convinced of at this point in life... *there aren't any.*

I hope you'll read this book like an old friend is in your living room sharing from a heart of love, for that's how I've written it. You'll find errors in my punctuation, and I'll go ahead and ask for up-front grace with the grammar patrol. But even in my admitted lack of professional writing etiquette, I hope you'll be able to hear and feel a heart of love.

TODAY is THE day you've been given to enjoy all the fullness *heaven* holds. Sometimes life gets turned into a mechanical, mundane process we find ourselves trudging through, jumping through hoops with lists we *think* are necessary to attain a distant end. *That's* when we should take time to ask some questions we should have asked a long time ago.

This life of ours wasn't designed to feel like we're heading out to yet another day of work, waiting on a paycheck somewhere in the distant future. Our life is meant to contain the wonder and awe of a child just given a free pass to the most amazingly fun and exciting amusement park the universe holds! May we all find ourselves waking up with the wide-eyed wonder of a child on the greatest *adventure* of all time. May this child-like passion be kindled fresh and new every morning, *and may we never lose the wonder of it all!*

This is your *now* Journey.
Partake. Participate.
Be present.

Enjoy

CHAPTER ONE

Nick at Night
Drawn to Light in the Darkness

"YOU MUST BE BORN AGAIN!" The crux of Christianity as we know it. The one and only possible way a man or woman born with a sinful nature can be changed, deemed worthy, and allowed to enter the Kingdom of God. After all, Jesus said so in his nighttime conversation with Nicodemus- a Pharisee and respected member of the Sanhedrin. We Christians have settled in on a belief that is commonly adhered to week after week, year after year, everywhere from churches, to mission fields, jails, streets, and office Bible studies. Anywhere that Christ is preached in hopes of people being *saved*.

While there may be certain variances between individual churches that aren't poured in concrete, the basic understanding of the process remains pretty much the same. One must first realize and admit they are an unworthy sinner, guilty of having been born into a life which is displeasing and offensive to God. Due to having being born *dead* in our sins, we are destined to receive the inescapable wages of our sin debt, which is a paycheck of death. Upon our open admittance of said failures and displeasure to God, we then proceed to ask forgiveness for those sins. We ask Jesus to come inside our heart and be our personal Lord and Savior, and make a commitment to adhere to the scriptures and follow Jesus to the best of our ability from that point on.

It's at this point, all the other believers around us now stand to their feet and applaud as they behold a new creation! This once dirty sinner, worthy only of God's fiery wrath, is now an instantly changed, born-again child of God. They are no longer headed for God's wrath and the eternal fires of hell. In a miraculous experience compressed into a single moment of time, they are instantly transformed from an *enemy* of God- to a *friend* of a loving Father. They're now assured of a home waiting *one day* in heaven. Because of one short prayer at an altar of their choice, heaven no longer sees an evil sinner deserving death. It sees a beloved son or daughter who is now included in the death, burial, and resurrection of Jesus that happened 2000 years ago.

In commonplace conversations among believers, it isn't unusual to be asked questions by others like: "How long have you been saved?" "When did you confess Jesus as Lord?" "When were you born again?" Our statements of faith imply *we made a decision when* we would be born again, *when* we would enter God's kingdom, and *when* we would become God's child. It's like we walked right into the 'high court of heaven' and not only had our death sentence overturned, but got an immediate application of a divine inheritance. All from the *same God* we believed only moments before, had every *right* and was perfectly *willing* to execute his holy judgment and plunge us into everlasting conscious torment for *not choosing to choose* to love him.

Have you ever wondered why nothing else recorded in the Bible remotely indicates anyone asking the questions we so commonly ask others about being *saved*, born *again*, or on their way to *heaven*? There isn't one single recorded incident resembling our traditional born-again protocol involved in any who came to Jesus or the apostles in the New Testament. If being born *again* was truly the required pathway into the kingdom of God, why is it never mentioned before, or *again*, after John 3? If it really is the key to everything relating to the kingdom and the only possible way one can truly *know* God, wouldn't that have been something Jesus might have talked about in places other than a covert nighttime conversation with a Pharisee??

We're told being born *again* is the *only* way to become acceptable to God, allow him to see us as his child, OR, for us to know the experience of heaven. If this was really *why* Jesus came, don't you think the Son of Man missed some really good chances to let the cat out of the bag, so to speak? How about the multitudes gathered for the beatitudes teaching? Jesus goes up to a natural hillside amphitheater and is being listened to by people of every ethnic culture from all the surrounding cities of the entire region. Wouldn't that have been a great place to have at least dropped a hint that they were born with an *evil* nature, and must first be born *again* to ever have a chance of knowing God?

Let's go one step further. If Jesus *knew* they were born with an evil nature and destined for 'eternal torment' *unless* they were born again, wasn't it somewhat misleading (even irresponsible) for him to refer to God as *your Father in heaven* at least 15 times during this hillside discourse, without ever once indicating they must first be born *again*? There's not one time recorded of Jesus mentioning a spiritual *rebirth* to another single human. Neither is there any indication (not one) by any New Testament author instructing others that this must occur.

The gospel of John, the one and only time anything like this is mentioned, wasn't written for *at least* 50 years after Jesus' lived. How were early believers to know it was THE determining prerequisite that must take place *before* they could be recognized by God as his children? And if they weren't properly taught how to be born again, how then could they have possibly seen *or done* all the miraculous *kingdom works* recorded throughout the New Testament?

Are we to believe Jesus wouldn't have taught this life-changing precedent upon which the future of all humanity depended, to all his disciples to then go preach (using specific *born-again* language) to the whole world? Should we also believe Matthew (the detail-oriented tax collector who doesn't miss a thing in describing Jesus' entire earthly lineage), just skips right over mentioning Jesus now being able to offer this new *Spirit* lineage to all mankind? What about Mark? We see this gospel coming at Jesus' life from a perspective of describing his works and miracles of divine magnitude. Doesn't it seem a little odd that in all these stories, Mark decides not to include the greatest work and miracle of all? That men could *decide* to have the defective spirit they were born with, miraculously born all over *again* to (instantly) receive a *new* one, along with a divine nature that was pleasing to God?

Is it not strange that Luke (trained in thoroughness and dedication to proper procedures as a physician) neglects to mention in his gospel (or the book of Acts) this unprecedented spirit/heart transplant now on the market, which can cure all humanity of this inherited terminal plague? Paul, or letters using his name, end up with a third of the entire New Testament describing mysteries of heaven revealed to man. They speak of 'Christ in you, the hope of Glory,' and 'setting your minds on things above, where your *real life* is hidden with Christ in God.' They declare the 'surname calling of God' from the womb, and say that men were seen by God as 'holy and blameless in love' before the foundation of the world. This ex-Pharisee unashamedly proclaims nothing (nothing) can separate men from the love of God in Christ. Where do Paul's letters describe being born again as a prerequisite for these amazing declarations to become true? *Nowhere.* Our imperative doctrine of men having to be born again doesn't get as much as an honorable mention in any of these writings. It's at this point, if we're honest, we should now be asking ourselves- could it possibly be that Jesus might have actually been talking about *something else*??

Let's look a little deeper into Nick's covert meeting.

We see in John 3, a story about a man named Nicodemus (we'll call him Nick) who came to Jesus at night. The popular assumption is that Nick came by night because he was a Pharisee and member of the Sanhedrin who feared being publicly associated with Jesus. In this particular story however, this *night*-time reference seems to carry a much deeper metaphorical significance than merely the time of day, or a setting of *physical* darkness.

The story takes off at this point where Nick is within a close enough proximity for them to have a fairly lengthy conversation. Scripture records at least 21 verses here for our reading, and we don't know what all transpired in other words, thoughts, and new revelational awareness that came to Nick through this nighttime encounter.

Nick's first comment, and Jesus' reply, are paramount to help us understand what actually happens here. Hearing this message from most pulpits today will all but *skip over* what Nick says, handing the mic straight to Jesus. According to our traditions, Jesus then immediately begins teaching Nick (and all of us) how we're going to need to be born *again* to even be able to see, understand, *or get into* the kingdom of God/heaven. Nick approaches Jesus with a loaded question in a comment form. This respected member of the Sanhedrin is a little more than curious about this laid-back miracle worker, and his covert efforts to get alone with Jesus prove it. Nick has questions; and Jesus has more of an answer than this educated Pharisee knew how to handle at the moment. We see Nicodemus make his opening comment in v.2, and then v.3 says, "Jesus *answered him.*"

2 This man came to Jesus by night and said to Him, "Rabbi, we know that You are a teacher come from God; for no one can do these signs that You do unless God is with him." 3 Jesus answered and said to him, "Most assuredly, I say to you, unless one is born again, he cannot see the kingdom of God."

Let's dig a little deeper and actually listen to the conversation that transpires between them.

v.2 "Rabbi, *we know* (the word *know,* means perceive/be aware) that you are a teacher who comes from God; for no one can do these signs that you do *unless* God is with him." Using the word, *we*, Nick indicates this awareness is not privileged information that he alone enjoys, but everyone who witnesses the things Jesus does also looks on in amazement. They are amazed because of their understanding that Jesus, and all he does, *is from God*. And they (all of them) saw and now perceived that no one (no one) could do them, unless the very kingdom presence of God was with them.

v.3 Jesus answered Nick and said to him: "Most assuredly, I say to you, unless one is 'born again' (this term in the original language is actually *generated*, or *born from above*) he cannot see (the word *see* means perceive or be aware of) the kingdom of God. Now in the NKJV, the term 'most assuredly' is used as Jesus begins his answer to Nick. Other translations say 'verily, verily.' In the original language, the term is actually *amen, amen*. This term is a transliteration of the Hebrew for *Truth, Truth*, and was used over 20 times by Jesus in John's gospel alone. Jesus used it like a gate going from one field to another. In doing so, he was verbally gesturing or lovingly implying for them to *"Pay attention now to where we're going,"* and he would then usher them forward into an area of greater revelation they'd not previously seen, *until Jesus walked them through that gate.*

It's vital at this point to focus on what they're actually *saying to each other,* and not just what we've heard preached all these years. It helps to realize there is a fairly lengthy dialog between two individuals going on, and not the one-sided *prerequisite Jesus decree* it too often gets turned into. Taking it in reverse order helps us grasp it a little clearer. Jesus tells Nick no one (no one) could see (perceive/be aware of) the kingdom of God or the works thereof- *unless...* they were born (birthed, sired, begotten, generated) from above. As we saw earlier, the term Jesus uses in the original language is *generated from above*. Scripture says this was Jesus' *answer* to Nick's comment, which was what? "Rabbi, we all know (already [presently] see, perceive, realize, understand) that you and your works are from God (God's kingdom), and we know (it's clearly obvious in our sight and perception) that no man could do these things *unless* God was with him."

Looking at it in this light reveals that when Jesus answered him, he wasn't telling Nick what he would have to *first* do *to begin* seeing the kingdom works in, and of God himself. He was explaining to Nick *why* he was *presently* able to recognize what he (and all the others) had already perceived and defined as the undeniable works of heaven.

In retrospect, it becomes clear that Jesus first listens to Nick's statement of recognizing the kingdom works of God in Jesus, and then Jesus simply says "amen, truth, truth," agreeing with it. But Jesus doesn't stop with merely agreeing with Nick. He then pushes the gate open to awaken Nick's awareness of truth *even further*. That truth is, that he, as well as all the others, must be the down-generated offspring of God, or they couldn't have recognized who Jesus was and what he was doing to begin with! John later records Jesus as saying:

"No one could even come to (recognize) me without the Father drawing him."

Essentially, Jesus was saying to Nick:

"The Father's Spirit residing in me, is recognizable only by the same Spirit of the Father residing in you."

I have to chuckle as I imagine the "Huh??" look on this educated ruler's face as he finds himself struggling to wrap his mind around what Jesus *sounded like* he was actually implying.

Francois du Toit's Mirror Bible is a beautiful paraphrase resource which Francois says "Is not meant to replace any translation. It is a study tool that will assist both the casual reader as well as the student of scripture to gain highlighted insight into the promise and Person revealed in the Bible as being the mirror image of the invisible God redeemed in human form." Let's look at the next portion of Jesus' and Nick's exchange, as recorded in John 3:4-7 of the Mirror.

v4: Nicodemus did not understand this answer at all and said to him, "How can a person be born if they're already grown-up? Surely one cannot re-enter your mother's womb and be born a second time?" (Nicodemus looks at the subject merely from the physical side. His 'second time' is not the same as Jesus' 'from above.' As Godet remarks, "he does not understand the difference between a second beginning and a different beginning.")

v5: Jesus answered, "you have to get this, unless someone is born out of the water (the womb) and Spirit, there would be no possible connection with the realm of God!"

v6: Whatever originates out of the flesh is flesh; but what is sourced in Spirit is spirit! (The Message says, when you see a baby, it's just that: a body you can look at and touch. But the person who takes shape within is formed by something you can't see and touch- the Spirit).

v7: Don't be so surprised when I say to you[manity-plural!] You couldn't get here in the flesh unless you got here from above! (See John 1:13: These are those who discover their genesis in God beyond our natural conception! This isn't about our blood lineage or whether we were a wanted or unwanted child- This is about our God-begotteness; we are His dream come true! We are not the invention of our parents! (You are the greatest idea God ever had!)

Now if you're like me, you won't believe something like this just because some guy you don't know wrote a book about it. Honestly, I would be disappointed if you did. I also understand what a challenge it is to your thinking if you've been in church most of your life and had it historically taught and ingrained in your mind. If you're willing to look further and have some things revealed by the Spirit within, you might begin seeing *new* things. In order to see them however, you'll have to be open to set aside pre-conceived training, traditional commentaries, notes from sermons, and getting alone with an accurate Greek New Testament, Greek Interlinear Bible, Strong's concordance (or other reliable study products), and allow the Spirit to guide you into truth, just as Jesus said would happen. Remember- the Spirit within is the teacher *bypassing* the errors of man with divine truth. (1 John 2:27)

The term 'born-again' in our bibles comes from the Greek words *gennao anóthen. Gennao* (Strong's #1080) means to beget, to be born, birthed, generated, conceived. *Anóthen* (Strong's #509) means from above, from the beginning, or anew. The term 'born' isn't where the overall question arises. It's the *when, where,* and *how* that should cause the question. For many years I heard my fundamental Bible teachers consistently saying, "Always let scripture interpret scripture." So, let's apply that here and see what we emerge with.

The word anóthen is used 13 times in the New Testament. Of those 13 occurrences, the *only* time the translators chose to insert the idea of 'again' (as a new or subsequent beginning) was in Jesus' conversation with Nicodemus. Let's look at it all the other times it's used, and then compare it to the translator's choice of wording in John 3.

#1) **Matthew 27:51 (NKJV)**
Then, behold, the veil of the temple was torn in two (anóthen) **from top** to bottom; and the earth quaked, and the rocks were split,

#2) **Mark 15:38 (NKJV)**
Then the veil of the temple was torn in two (anóthen) **from top** to bottom.

#3) **John 3:31 (NKJV)**
He who comes (anóthen) **from above** is above all; he who is of the earth is earthly and speaks of the earth. He who comes from heaven is above all.

#4) **John 19:23 (NKJV)**
Then the soldiers, when they had crucified Jesus, took His garments and made four parts, to each soldier a part, and also the tunic. Now the tunic was without seam, woven (anóthen) **from the top** in one piece.

5) John 19:11 (NKJV)

Jesus answered, "You could have no power at all against Me unless it had been given you (anóthen) **from above.**"

The verses we've just seen show an obvious action occurring from the top downward- '**from above.**'

The following verses refer to something existing from the very first, '**from the beginning.**'

#6) Luke 1:3 (NKJV)

It seemed good to me also, having had perfect understanding of all things (anóthen) **from the very first**, to write to you an orderly account, most excellent Theophilus,

#7) Acts 26:5 (NKJV)

They knew me (anóthen) **from the first**, if they were willing to testify, that according to the strictest sect of our religion I lived as a Pharisee.

Then we have this verse written to the Galatians:

#8) Galatians 4:9 (NASB)

But now that you have come to know God, or known by God, how is it that you turn back again to the weak and worthless elemental things to which you desire to be enslaved (anóthen) **all over again?**

Here, the word anóthen is seen denoting 'anew'; but *only* in the context of *returning back* to a former position. For the Galatians, this was merely a different flavor of bondage. They had already been in bondage, by '*serving those who by nature were not gods*' (v.8). Now, they're seen *returning* to yet another form of bondage by serving the law, which never applied to them to begin with. The Galatians were now taking on *even more* bondage in powerless observation of rules, regulations, and Jewish calendars. It's important to realize Paul wasn't describing them entering some fresh, new, unknown territory. He was describing them as going *back* somewhere they'd once already been. *Returning to* a state of bondage they'd *previously* existed in before.

An important side note on this verse: Paul told the Galatians he had come (through un-scaled vision) to the awareness of being called with the *kaléō* surname of God from his mother's womb. It's the same language used in Isaiah 49:1-6. It was spoken over Israel and every descendant of Abraham from the farthest ends of the earth (41:8-10), to let them know they *also* belonged to God from their mother's womb. We see Isaiah use this *womb calling* language in 49:1, and 5:

"The Lord has called me from the womb; from the innermost matrix of my mother he called my name."

In 49:6, Isaiah declares the Jewish nation was meant to be a light to the gentiles so *they too* could see they'd been called and chosen by God as well! This surname calling was exactly what the inner CHRIST had revealed to Paul, and was exactly what Paul now declared to the gentiles! In Galatians 1:15-16, Paul makes his 'IN' me *from the womb* calling quite clear. He was now declaring this same womb calling of God IN the gentiles. The wording 'among' the gentiles in our Bibles is a blatant mistranslation. In the original language, the same word used for 'IN' me, is also used for 'IN' the Gentiles. Paul wasn't saying he was going into their midst with an offer for them to *make a decision* or receive something *new*. He spent those years going into their midst to passionately AWAKEN THEM to something that was already theirs!

Seeing it in context reveals that Paul's wording in Galatians 4:9, wasn't suggesting that God had recently *started* knowing them (anew) because of something they'd done (being born *again*), but that God had known them all along! The Greek implies something like this: *"Now that you've come to know the real God, and the realization that he's always known you, how in the world could you return to the kind of worthless false identity to which you were enslaved before?"*

You are known.

Again, these last 3 anóthen verses in the New Testament reveal an obvious action occurring from the top downward- '**from above**.'

#9) **James 1:17 (NKJV)**

Every good gift and every perfect gift is (anóthen) **from above**, and comes down from the Father of lights, with whom there is no variation or shadow of turning.

#10) **James 3:15 (NKJV)**

This wisdom does not descend (anóthen) **from above** but is earthly, sensual, demonic.

#11) **James 3:17 (NKJV)**

But the wisdom that is (anóthen) **from above** is first pure, then peaceable, gentle, willing to yield, full of mercy and good fruits without partiality and without hypocrisy.

Well, there we have it. Every instance (11) in the New Testament we see the term *anóthen* used apart from the 2 times with Jesus and Nick- it signifies *from above, from the beginning*, or *anew*, as in the context of *returning again* to something which once already existed.

Now Nick didn't actually present his words to Jesus in the form of a question; yet we're told Jesus 'answered' him, beginning with the words 'verily, verily,' which means *amen, amen*. It was a term we saw often used by Jesus as a transition point through which he would usher someone into a whole new dimensional field of awareness.

Let's look again at Jesus' reply to Nick, inserting the word *anóthen* the same way it's used everywhere else in scripture, and see how it changes the entire picture.

Nick comes to Jesus and says, "We (all) see these signs you do, and we (all) realize you are from God, because we (all) know that no one could do this apart from God being in them!" Jesus answers, saying:

"Amen, Nick! Amen! And I say to you, unless (any) one is born *from above, from the beginning*, or *anew* (as in returning to a previously held existence) he couldn't see (perceive, be aware of, or recognize) the kingdom of God, or the workings thereof!"

Jesus wasn't speaking imperative command language to Nick of something he (or any others) would be required to do to begin seeing the kingdom of God. He was presenting a confirmative explanation of why Nick and (all) the others were already able to recognize it! Jesus was now ushering Nick into the discovery of his own presiding genesis set forth by God in the beginning. "Each according to its own kind," and "Let Us 'make' (the Hebrew implies BEcome) man in our image." Jesus was simply saying to Nick: "The Spirit of God IN you, is what enables you to see/perceive the Spirit of God IN me."

Can you see it? I know the translators haven't done the best job of making it obvious, even as educated as they may have been. When people see themselves as *alien*ated from God, and trying to work their way back, the truth of the Father's intimate heart is veiled to them. Their own distorted vision window now carries through in all their translating. Even so, if we back up and pay attention to what *actually* transpires during this night-time visit, the truth comes out of the shadows as clear as day. Nick tells Jesus: "We all know you're from God by the works we see you doing." Jesus simply agrees with Nick by saying "Amen, Amen, you're right Nick!" He then goes on to tell Nick *how* they themselves, were [presently] able to see and know these things by telling him, *"Unless one is born from above, they wouldn't be able to see and know where my works come from."*

DOCTRINAL COMPLICATIONS

One day I was having a conversation with a longtime friend who's been in the ministry many years. As I shared my views with him, he said, *"Dave, understanding the kingdom is complicated."* I honestly can't think of any statement I would disagree with more.

Friends, the kingdom is not complicated in any way. We've made it complicated by trying to twist truth around our doctrinal *ideas*, rather than wrapping our doctrines around what Jesus actually said. Jesus never made things complicated. In fact, he said that until one could see it through the eyes and simplistic thoughts of a child, they wouldn't really be able to see it at all. In the church setting many of us were/are involved in, our beliefs, sermons, and training classes are predominately focused on a kingdom we were taught was a distant location called heaven. Our existence here and now, was merely *to get ready* for something future which is to yet come. We've been taught that we must *attain* an entrance pass into this distant kingdom by first doing, believing, or confessing certain things to please the king of this heavenly domain. Friends, this is not at all (ever) what Jesus meant when he spoke of the *kingdom,* or, of *heaven.*

The future attainment of a delayed and distant kingdom is *worldly* imagery produced from worldly thinking. It's fruit always reflects an offspring relationship to the original *satanâs* seed lie of separation which Jesus called *the father of all lies.* Jesus told his followers the kingdom he came to reveal was not of this world-ly imagery at all. The Son of Man never talked about men going anywhere; but taught often about *seeing the kingdom,* which he described in earthly terms and situations such as gardening, baking bread, and fishing. He talked about the kingdom that was within people in the present-tense, and people entering into the kingdom in the present tense. He actually warned those around him not to listen to anyone who indicated the kingdom would come from somewhere *out there.*

Jesus never implied the idea of men leaving this earth at all; in fact, he taught just the opposite. In John 17, his prayer of agreement with the Father sounded something like this:

"Father, I do not pray you take them out of the world, but keep them from believing the accusatory voice of evil (worthlessness), that they may become One in their understanding just as you and I are, so that the whole world may know you love them... even as you love me."

This *heavenly* kingdom that Jesus talked about was of the same metaphorical imagery as the garden of Eden paradise, the promised land, and the land flowing with milk and honey. They were beautiful pictures of an *inner secret place*. A place where those who learned to *abide* would be totally insulated by *participating with, and in* the God-kind of life. A place where nothing of this world could steal their peace or joy. It was the *aiónios quality* of divine life designed for man (having total dominion) to flourish and enjoy perpetual fruitfulness. All to be enjoyed while loving, serving, and living as One with others.

When Jesus talked about men 'seeing,' he used a word that meant just that, to *perceive* or *be aware* of. When he used the word 'within,' he meant just that, something *already inside*, as in the present tense. This kingdom within man was the Father's righteousness (equity), joy, and peace; which Paul said wasn't something like meat or drink we place within ourselves. It came preinstalled within us as part of our authentic design, just as Jesus taught. When Jesus spoke about people *entering* the kingdom, he was talking about *going in* to this inner place of abiding in the Father's intimacy and rest. He told the chief priests and elders that the tax collectors and harlots were *entering in* to the kingdom (present tense) *right in front of them.*

The narrow gate Jesus spoke of entering, wasn't about a literal tiny gate to some puffy cloud paradise in the sky. It was about pushing past narrow-minded thinking and powerless religious rituals the Pharisees adhered to right down to the nth degree of spices and mint, yet while totally disregarding God's true love and justice for their fellow man. Jesus loved showing men the unrestricted gate of the Father's love; yet the original Greek wording says this gate was 'cramped,' having now been restricted and made difficult to find the way through. Why? Jesus said the Pharisees were the ones *cramping the gate*. He said they themselves had *refused* to enter in. Now, he said, through their teachings and religious requirements, were making it harder for others who *listened to their restrictive teachings* to find their way in as well.

The Pharisees concentrated on things like scrubbing their hands, keeping the outside of their cups clean, and wearing flawlessly adorned robes. Yet Jesus said that what was on the outside was not the determining factor of equity or fruit in people's lives, but rather that which was on the inside. He told them their perfect clothes, sanitized hands, and spotless cups could never change their distorted orphaned mindset. It was a mindset which manifested fruit according to its own kind, resembling whitewashed tombs full of dead men's bones.

Paul, once a Pharisee himself, declared the *Christ* had revealed the kingdom within him so powerfully that it shook the foundation of his life to the core. In fact, he said what he *thought* he knew about God and the kingdom, was worthy of only one place- *the skubala pile.* Now we can pretend Paul was talking about rubbish, or even bull manure. But that's not what this former Pharisee was talking about at all, and if you've spent much time around religion, you know it. His inference to *skubala* (used only one time in scripture) was *quite bluntly* implying that after seeing things through un-scaled eyes of truth, he realized the things he *thought* he'd known about God up to that point, all ended up being nothing more than a heaped-up pile of manmade *sh-t.*

This Christ revelation, as we will get into later on, revealed 3 things to Paul about his life. This REVELATION OF THE CHRIST so drastically changed his view to the point he spent the rest of his life unashamedly proclaiming it to all who would listen. What were these things?

 1) The Father's kaléō *surname* calling is upon a man or woman even from their mother's womb.

2) All men are carriers of the divine Light treasure of God within their earthen vessels.

And knowing these things, meant that...

3) He could never again regard any man merely by their outer flesh, their culture, or their natural *earthly* existence.

Paul wrote to the Corinthians in regard to certain people who were continuing in the *deception* of trying to wrap their lives around illicit lovers, idolatry, taking, or coveting things which did not belong to them, and extorting others. Paul said these people would not *enter*, or inherit the kingdom of God. Where did Jesus say the kingdom was? He said it was within. Paul wasn't talking about these people one day going through some future distant gate. Nor was he in any way saying these people did not have a rightful inheritance. He was merely saying they were too *distracted* by the deceptions of a worthless outer realm, to *enter in* and enjoy the life of their true design which was hidden within! Paul was simply saying that these who continued to look for their source of life from a darkened world, wouldn't find it. Why? Because they were looking for it outwardly, rather than within. The Concordant Literal New Testament words it this way: *"They shall not be enjoying the allotment of God's kingdom."*

Paul wasn't saying *they* didn't possess the kingdom within *because* of their actions. He was saying that because of their dependence on outward things to bring meaning or worth to their life, they wouldn't be actively *participating in,* or *enjoying* the true fruit of heaven's allotted treasure hidden within them. In fact, during Paul's lengthy pointed rebuke of their *less than admirable* traits, he stops midstream on at least five different occasions during 1 Corinthians chapters 3 thru 6, to remind and encourage them of things like this:

(3:16) *"Do you not know you are the temple of God and the Spirit of God dwells in you?"*
(3:23) *"And you are Christ's, and Christ is God's."*
(4:14) *"I do not write these things to shame you, but as my beloved children I warn you."*

 (6:15) *"Do you not know that your bodies are members of Christ?"*
(6:19) *"Or do you not know your body is the temple of the Holy Spirit whom you have from God, and you are not your own?"*

Because of our misunderstandings, Jesus' and Nick's conversation about the kingdom within has been mistakenly perceived and taught as men *doing* or *becoming* something different, to *then* be able to see the kingdom. It's portrayed as a prerequisite formality to enter into a distant *members-only* pearly gated community with golden streets called 'heaven.' Friends, this was in no way what Jesus was describing to Nick in their nighttime chat. In fact, it was never about what anyone then, *or in the future*, would have to do or become at all! It was simply a conversation between Jesus and a curious religious leader who Jesus was trying to wake up from orphan separation mode, into the present realm of *authentic life* here and now. That's why it's *never* mentioned again by anyone in the scriptures, other than John always referring to Nick, when he is mentioned, as first coming to Jesus *by night*. Oh, but when we follow Nick's life after this covert meeting, we see the obvious evidence of him waking up to something so beautiful *within*, that he was never again afraid to come boldly right out into the light.

When Jesus said *"I go to prepare a place for you,"* it was right before the cross. Perhaps Jesus was setting up in their Jewish cultural thinking what he was about to do. He would soon be crucified on the cross, on *sabbath preparation* day. Jesus' desire was to bring them *out of* the prophetic shadows they'd lived in for so long, and introduce them to the authentic *present tense* life of perpetual *sabbath rest* that needed redeemed and rebooted in their awareness. It would be a place where they'd no longer be stuck in mere shadows of distant days to come. They would see themselves *resurged* in the total fulfillment *of enChristed* Sabbath rest and fruitfulness, in ways they'd never again forget. To-day is the day of salvation! They wouldn't understand many things at the moment, yet the Son of Man knew they would *one day* soon begin hearing his words echoing from deep within their spirit:

"You don't understand what I do for you now- but one day you will."

"I won't leave you as orphans- I will never leave you or forsake you."

"In that day you will know, I am in my Father, and you are in me, and I AM in you... as One."

As our Nick-at-night setting unfolds in John 3, Jesus was gently (and possibly with a little sarcastic humor), trying to stimulate Nick's memory back to the required studies of all Jewish males from their youth, and the even more intense studies to become a Pharisee and ruler of the high court. I can imagine Jesus leaning over face to face with Nick and a prodding grin that says *"Hello? Is anybody in there?"* *"You're a teacher of Israel- and yet you don't know these things??"*

I believe Jesus' comments were toned in love and encouragement, while coaching Nick along at the same time, *"Come on Nick, you can do this."* Jesus tries to resurrect Nicodemus' memory of his extensive studies of the Torah, Nevi'im, and Ketuvim: the teachings, prophets, and writings forming the foundational documents of Israel's culture. During this covert nighttime conversation, Jesus tries to re-generate, or *wake up* Nicodemus' remembrance of these ancient writings:

Isaiah 51:1 (NASB)
"Listen to me, you who pursue righteousness, you who seek the LORD: look to the rock from which you were hewn, and to the quarry from which you were dug.

Or how about this one?

Deuteronomy 32:18 (NKJV)
Of the Rock who begot you, you are unmindful, and have forgotten the God who fathered you.

Or a reminder that the Father's workmanship is perfect from its origin with no flaws or defects:

Deuteronomy 32:4 (NKJV)
He is the Rock, His work is perfect; For all His ways are justice, A God of truth and without injustice; Righteous and upright is He.

What Jesus was trying to do here for Nick, is exactly what 1 Peter 1:3 says he also did for his other Jewish brethren to *resurrect* them from the *dead.* Keep in mind Jesus' prodding Nick to *remember,* as we look at the wording of John 3:3 in contrast to what Peter says. Again, the subject of all this is man's ORIGIN. **Jesus was speaking to Nick personally about man's original genesis (gennaō) generated downward (anóthen) from above. Peter, would then later speak of a re-generating (anagennaō) upward to** (*resurrection* means to *arise,* or *resurge*) **other men and women as well!**

Here, we see Nick as an example of man's forgetfulness. Nick had forgotten the foundational passages reminding the Jews to 'look back to the Rock of their beginning- the quarry from which they were dug.'

In a larger scale *of epidemic amnesia,* men and women as a whole had forgotten their genesis as God's selfie BEings. These orphaned ones needed not only to be re-minded, but re-connected and re-booted in their awareness! The Son of Man said he, like a physician, came to heal those with this distorted mental dis-ease. A *resurrecting* of man's enChristed mind would be the redeeming mile-marker needed, that man could never again forget. A literal *re-booting* that would cause men to always remember, from that moment forward *who they were.* No longer operating *as* orphaned aliens from a darkened mindset, but standing *upright* in God's own light, holy and blameless in his love!

1 Peter 1:3 (NKJV)

Blessed be the God and Father of our Lord Jesus Christ, who according to His abundant mercy has begotten (anagennaō) us again to a living hope through the resurrection of Jesus Christ from the dead.

Let's look at this verse and the commentary from The Mirror Bible:
1:3 So let us boast about it and bless the God and Father of our Lord Jesus Christ with articulate acclaim! He has re-connected us with our original genesis through the resurrection of Jesus from the dead! This new birth endorses and celebrates the hope of the ages;

God's eternal love dream concludes in life! (The word eulogetos, means to brag, bless, or speak well of. Jesus <u>reminds Nicodemus</u> that we are born <u>anóthen, from above [John 3:3,13] and now through our joint resurrection, we are re-connected again to our original identity as sons.</u> The word anagennaō, from ana, upward, or can also mean by implication, repetition- and gennao, which together means, to regenerate or give birth. As much as Jesus' death brought dramatic closure to futile and failed attempts to justify and define ourselves, our co-resurrection with Christ revived the original blueprint of our Maker's image and likeness in us!)

Peter goes into further detail in the rest of this 1st chapter, to clarify what this regenerating resurrection was meant to take men *away from...* and what it was meant to *awaken them to*! Let's work our way through this passage in context to see what Peter was pointing out. Peter follows his explosive *'begotten again to a living hope'* comment in v.3 by explaining what that hope is.

1 Peter 1:4-5 (NKJV)
to an inheritance incorruptible and undefiled and that does not fade away, reserved in heaven for you, who are kept by the power of God through faith for salvation ready to be revealed in the last time.

Peter says this *resurrection* was to awaken them *all* to the reality of an inheritance that couldn't be corrupted, defiled, or ever fade away. It had been kept (guarded) in *heavenly* places, and would now be fully revealed through this *resurging of the Christ*. This is what Peter refers to as *'in the last time,'* which he saw as the fulfilling of every Messianic prophecy foretold, leading up to this cataclysmic event. Peter explains that those for whom this inheritance was preserved and guarded, were safely kept by *God's faith and power* until this salvific truth could be *unveiled* within the Christ. It proved this was *in no way whatsoever* dependent upon the faith of man, but was all God's doing *all along*.

It's true the agreement of man (as a partaker and active participant) in the divine nature, helps nurture tangible manifestations of all the inheritance holds. It is *not* true that man's faith had anything to do with producing it, guarding it, or delivering it to them in the mother's womb with the *surname* of God embedded in it.

This was all done with humanity being sealed unimpeachably holy and blameless in his love, before the *foundation* of the world, *or the disruption*. It could actually be described as happening before man *lost* his right mind. This was the truth about men from before the first moment the Breath of God filled them with life *from above*. Yet, because men had forgotten who they were, their true identity couldn't be realized or enjoyed *until* they could see themselves standing up and rebooted as *One* with this *Risen Christ*. It was the only thing that would allow them to come to their right 'I AM' mind, in an awakened realization of a life more abundant. This wasn't some *new* life which never before existed that men had to be born *again* to enjoy. It was the inheritance of an already existing life guarded in the Father's heart, that was waiting for men to wake up and come back home to all along!

I'm simply saying that what we have been taught all our lives about being 'born again' with a new *spirit,* is not what Jesus was talking to Nick about in *his darkness*. This night-time talk wasn't describing an event we supposedly choose the timing of by believing, confessing, or praying. Nor does it make God see us differently or have a mind change about how we will now be treated. No more than we were able to choose the timing of our natural *earthly* birth, do we have an ability to *make a decision* to receive a new spirit, or *heavenly* re-birth.

Jesus wasn't telling Nick he needed a new spirit to *begin* seeing the kingdom. He was helping him understand that once his eyes were opened to his authentic genesis- his, and all mankind's ability to see the kingdom of heaven within (and all around them) would never stop expanding in greater inner awareness *and* in outward manifestation!

I can't think of anything more emotionally and/or psychologically detrimental to the life of a child (or any other human) than telling them they were born *through no fault of their own*, with a spirit that was displeasing or evil to the 'God' who gave them their breath. Not only that, but until they *choose* to come and say they are sorry for this life (which again, is through no fault of their own) and are born *again*, they are destined to spend an eternity in tormenting punishment.

You won't find a single instance in scripture where Jesus or the apostles talked to people in the context of being *saved* or enjoying the *salvation* of God, which implied they must first be *born again*. But that hasn't stopped us from filling our kids (and adults) with fear by preaching a doctrine weaved together from *one* single line of *one* covert conversation that we didn't understand. An *idea* and *opinion* of a 'requirement' *never again mentioned* in the entire early church age.

This distorted idea doesn't stop here though. Because of how it was programmed in our minds by people we trusted (who'd had it taught to them), we end up going through our life concerned, wondering, and worrying IF we've done it *right*, or with our *whole heart*. People go to bed afraid they might have done something earlier in the day that would cancel out their 'going to heaven' if they died in their sleep. Put that together with well known 'preachers' saying no one is guaranteed to get into heaven no matter how hard they may have tried- and you have just described the *hell on earth* countless numbers of beautiful people have endured in *fear and torment* their whole lives.

God's mind *never* changed about man. The Son of Man's focus was to change man's mind about the Father *and* themselves. His passion was to crucify and bury man's orphaned, alienated mindset, *resurrecting* their conscious-ness to the original blueprint life intended. Jesus came to wake men up to their authentic genesis, *and to their right mind*.

CHAPTER TWO

Coming to Our Right Mind

The Prodigal Son story is an emotional metaphor of man's journey. Jesus tells a story of a man born as the son of a loving father. One day, the son's thinking changes about the life that is rightfully his; and he decides to go off to do things on his own. He moves away from all that had been provided, with the life of all he had known with his father now slipping from existence in his mind. This new mindset introduces him to labor, toil, and hardships he had never known at home with his father. Even though he tried laboring endlessly among strangers in a foreign land- his strength to survive this way dwindles to nothing. All the positive, consistent things that were originally his to enjoy, now rapidly began disappearing and *perishing* in, and around his life. In the midst of hunger and despair, the young man awakens to the reality of his present state of pig-pen-living and the self-created emptiness all around him. This tired and defeated son now starts to *remember* a place called *home*... and the Father who had given him everything.

Luke 15:17 (NKJV)
When he came to himself, he said, "How many of my father's hired servants have bread enough and to spare, and I perish with hunger!"

Other translations word it *'When he finally came to his senses.'* Here we see a man, who at an earlier point in time had a change of mind about *who* and *where* he wanted to be. He leaves the home of his father's complete provision with his new *do-it-myself* mindset. As time goes by, he begins realizing that everything he was accustomed to enjoying with his father had little by little vanished from his existence. Even to the point the *pigs* around him were eating better than he was. Because he was convinced his father could no longer honor him as *son*, he was willing to forsake being recognized as *family*. This son decides he would even settle for the meager role of *servant*. Willing to give up the title of *son* (and the rightful allotment that comes with it), the man turns back to face the home he had earlier chosen to leave.

As he approaches a home even more beautiful than he remembered, he hesitates momentarily while looking toward his father's house.

"Will he remember me?"

"Does he hate me?"

"Will he have me beaten?"

"Is anything left for me here?"

"Why did I even leave?"

"WHAT... was I thinking??"

As a plethora of fearful and confusing thoughts flood the son's mind, in the distance he notices a shadow. A blurry image was now moving toward him from the father's house with intentional speed. Suddenly the son realizes this running image... *was his father!* But wait, as the patriarch of the family, no one had seen the father run before. Yet here he came! The father's robe is blowing out in the wind behind him, tears streaming down his face in a full-run pursuit which only ends... *when he engulfs his SON in his arms!* In this embrace, the son finds himself being kissed on and laughed on and cried on all at the same time, and all he can hear is, *"MY SON IS HOME!!!"*

The servants, now out of breath, finally catch up with the father, still trying to figure out what could possibly make the family patriarch run. They arrive on the scene to behold a joy on the father's face that glowed like the sun, shining through the river of tears streaming down his cheeks. The son, overwhelmed by this unexpected gesture of love, now strains to remember the words of a *rehearsed speech* he thought would be necessary to set foot back on his father's land. A stumbling fragment of *"fath......"* is all he has time to get out of his mouth.

The son hears his father yelling passionately at the hired servants while motioning back toward the family homeplace:

"What are you waiting on??"

"Can't you see my son is home??"

"Get my ring, my robe, and the best sandals I have!"

"Kill the fatted calf and let us celebrate with joy!!"

"My son was dead... but he's alive and back home!!!"

"WHAT... are you waiting on???" "GO!!!!"

It's here we begin to realize this story was never centered around a son leaving home to partake in unholy things and wayward living. It's always been about a passionate, loving Father, waiting to lavishly pour out the same provision of everything the son had known and enjoyed *before* he journeyed off on his own *to a distant and foreign land.*

There's no discussion of *conditional* approval of the son's return. No chance to recite the *rehearsed speech* he thought would be needed to soften the father's heart. No talk of an inheritance already spent. **This man didn't come home to something new. He didn't have to reinstate, reapply, or be *reborn* as a son to his father. He came home to a sonship that had never faded from its original reality.**

Even though the son may have journeyed off with some money, servants, or goods on a wagon, it had absolutely no effect on what was waiting on him *at home* in the love and devotion of the father's heart.

The son's inheritance wasn't perishable, nor could it be defiled by anything he took part in. Nothing he did, or *didn't do*, could change how his father saw him. When he turned toward *home-* he found his inheritance right where it had been all along, kept and guarded, in the father's heart! This *resurrected life* story sounds a lot like what Peter later declared in the opening lines of his first letter. It echoes the voice of the Father's lavishing love and provision, as he's seen running with great joy and shouting, *"My SON who was dead IS ALIVE AGAIN!!!"*

1 Peter 1:3-4 (NKJV)

Blessed *be* the God and Father of our Lord Jesus Christ, who according to His abundant mercy has *begotten us again* to a living hope through the resurrection of Jesus Christ from the dead, to an *inheritance incorruptible and undefiled and that does not fade away,* reserved in heaven for you.

Jesus tells two more parables in this same setting. The scribes and Pharisee's grumbled at the fact that Jesus not only welcomed those the Pharisee's called *sinners* into his presence; he actually ate and drank with them in public. *Choosing* to break bread with someone in that day was seen as more than just eating together. It was like calling someone a friend, or even *family.* As the religious leaders voiced their displeasure of Jesus acting like best buds with those they saw as top scum on the sinners list, Jesus tells a parable of a shepherd with a sheep that wasn't with the rest of the flock. The shepherd leaves the main group and pursues the lost sheep until he finds it and carries it home on his shoulders. Then Jesus tells the parable of a woman who lost a coin. She lights up the whole house, searching with intentional care until the coin, which is *valuable to her,* is found. We don't find any mention of the coin needing to be resurfaced or requiring a new inscription. Its value remained the same *to the owner* no matter how long it was lost or how dirty it got. Each of the stories Jesus tells are seen ending in the same way, *with a jubilant celebration!*

1 Peter 1:18-20 (NKJV)

Knowing that you were not redeemed with corruptible things, *like* silver or gold, from your aimless conduct *received by tradition from your fathers,* but with the precious blood of Christ, as a lamb without blemish and without spot. He indeed was foreordained before the foundation of the world, but was manifest in these last times for you-

- NOT -

Peter clarifies man's redemption was from an aimless (perishable) conduct. *Not from an inherited sin nature because of Adam,* but from the *passed down traditions* of their fathers! Peter echoes Stephen's words to the religious leaders in Acts 7:41-51 just before they stoned him. Stephen says the Holy Spirit was *always* there with their fathers, BUT they *always* resisted God's desire to dwell IN THEM, by building gaudy external temples to which they would bring offerings to *idol*ized works of their own hands, *no different than the golden calf.* But this redemption would not be based on things valuable to man that can be corrupted, defiled, or pass away. In verse 23, Peter says this:

1 Peter 1:23 (NKJV)

having been born again, not of corruptible seed but incorruptible, through the word of God which lives and abides forever.

As we saw in the first chapter, Jesus tells Nick of man's original genesis (gennaō) *down-ward* (anóthen) from the Father of Lights, where every good and perfect gift comes from. Peter later uses a word describing a re-generation *up-ward* (ana-gennaō), re-conciling man to what was originally his *from the beginning*! The term re-surrection literally means to *re*-surge or stand up *again*. Peter is saying men were now *re*-deemed and *re*-booted to their authentic origin *from above,* which Jesus revealed to Nick during their nighttime talk. Men needed this visual *re-surrection* mile-marker to illuminate their awareness, and show them a divine *re*-deeming and *re*-connecting *up-ward* to the very God that man *thought* was angry and he needed to hide from.

re-surrection

regeneration from beginning
resurrection = to stand again

nothing in 1st Adam

Jesus takes man's distorted thinking of separation (Colossians 1:21 says 'enemies in *your own minds*'), their orphan mentality (*sin*), and anything remotely associated to *first Adam* thoughts of nakedness to the cross, crucifying it once for all. This would be the precursor for a resurrected consciousness where they could see themselves just as the Father always had! This enChristed *re*-conciliation would effectively *re*-deem, *re*-store, and *re*-boot men in their awareness as ONE with heaven! Through this *re*-newed Christ mindset, man could forever remember his authentic genesis as *coming down* from the One true Father of lights! It would be completed (finished) by this *Last Adam*, that it might never again be altered, changed, or reversed in any way!

As our eyes are opened to this truth, we begin to *see* that all this happened on man's behalf long before he could ask for it or agree with it. Does this knowledge and understanding diminish the power and testimony of what we've always thought of as our personal *born again* encounter with God? Not at all. Does it lessen the miraculous change and lasting fruit which then followed that encounter? In no way! *Wherever* and *however* your first awakening encounter occurred- it is seen as precious, holy, and is joyously celebrated by your heavenly Father! We now begin to realize *we finally stopped resisting* the Holy Spirit. Our encounter was merely us reaching out to *embrace* the One who'd been drawing us from within. And this *Source of all life* had seen us as living, extended *selfie* offspring, from our first breath!

I never grow tired of celebrating those places I began to see that the Father's spirit had been leading me, guiding me, and protecting me right up to that moment. I'll never stop being thankful for my gravel road experience, when I turned to face my divine Source and began to receive, enjoy, and rest in *the greatest love gift ever known to man!*

While Nick's beginnings with Jesus may have started in a covert nighttime meeting, it didn't stay that way long. Something happened to Nick that night that caused him to come out of the *dark* and into the *light.* Our Bibles say 'Nicodemus came to Jesus *by* night.' In the Greek it says 'Nicodemus came toward Jesus *of* night.' The word used for *night* here is *vux*, Strongs #3571. This word *night* is metaphorically used for '*the period of man's alienation from God.*' The word *toward* is *prós*, #4314, which means to face; to move with desire or intent in the direction of something to have access or nearness of it. It's actually used as a component of the word *proporeuomai*, #4313, which means *proceed* (as a guide, herald, or an usher), or to *go before.*

If Nick was coming *from*, or *of night*, as in the period of man's alienation from God (which Paul said was all in man's mind), then *what was Nick presently seeing in Jesus* that he was moving toward, wanting to be face to face with? What did John feel was so crucially important for his readers to see, that he came right out and kicked the doors of his gospel open with it? Let's take a look:

Nico. came face to face w Jesus in His alienated mind.

John 1:1-5 (NKJV)

In the beginning was the Word, and the Word was with God, and the Word was God. He was in the beginning with God. All things were made through Him, and without Him nothing was made that was made. In Him was life, and the life was the light of men. And the light shines in the darkness, and the darkness did not comprehend it.

Now, if you're anything like me, these are scriptures you've heard so many times over and over that they have become like *autoplay* in our heads. We hear them, and can quote them *without even thinking.* Read those last three words again- *without even thinking.* This is unfortunately, where our common familiarity with scriptures has brought us to. Being familiar with something isn't necessarily a bad thing; but becoming *so* familiar that we actually lose sight of what it was originally intended to be, can put us in the state of *autopilot.* It's like when we drive to work on the same path for so long, that we can't really tell anyone specific *details* of that day's journey. Sometimes we can't even remember making it at all. I'm reminded of something I heard Bill Johnson say many years ago that really stuck with me: *"We have become far too familiar with a God we hardly know."*

Let's go back and explore the words that so filled John's heart with excitement, that he couldn't wait to jump up on stage and blurt it out. This was the dynamic crux of everything else John would then follow up with in his gospel, and he hoped to captivate the hearts of all his readers with the same power-full *God-in-the-flesh-of-man* revelation that had captivated his! John now has his megaphone up in the air and with everything in him, boldly proclaims:

"In the Origin-al was the logos; the blueprint Source reflecting itself into all it faced. All came through this expressed reflection, and not even one came into BEing apart from it! It is the incarnate expression of Life and Light in all men! This Light came ripping through the veil of man's darkness; and even though darkness wasn't sure what to do with this Light, it became brilliantly clear that the Light... wasn't going away." *(John 1:1-5 my paraphrase)*

[handwritten margin note: All Humanity]

We've been taught John's prologue in a tone of thinking all *things*, like a Bible creation story with God speaking all *things* into existence. Yet the word *things* is not in the original text, and was later *added* by translators. Why is this important? Because John wasn't referring to *things* in his opening words! John was pointing to the Life and Light of ALL humanity! He was shouting out "NOT EVEN ONE WHO EXISTS COULD EVER EXIST APART FROM THIS FACE TO FACE BLUEPRINT ORIGIN!"

Our word *logo* represents a symbol or mark used for identification and recognition. The Logos that became flesh, is the divine prototype from which all others imprinted with it are associated. The Logo of our life (mine, yours, and all humanity) is the eternal UNIVERSAL CHRIST in whom Paul said ALL CONSIST and have their being. This Christ is not a single person, but a Source of life. The words 'he/him' John uses in this passage are pronoun types that can be used for he, she, her, it, they or them. The translator's word 'beginning' can also be misleading. The Source of Light and Life didn't *begin* at some point, but was the ever-existing Origin from which all others find *their* beginning!

[handwritten note: Beginning = ever existing!]

This enChristed Light and Life of all men was what Jesus desired so passionately to wake men up to! Jesus put this enChristed Life on display for all to see in tangibly resurrected power. He said that one day, all men would *know for themselves*, that they were One with the Father as their paternal Source, just (exactly) as Jesus was!

Colossians 1:16-17

For (by) **in** (Him) **αὐτός all** (things) **were created** (that are) **in heaven and** (that are) **on earth, visible and invisible, whether thrones or dominions or principalities or powers. All** (things) **were created through** (Him) **αὐτός and** (for) **into** (Him) **αὐτός.** (He) **αὐτός is before all** (things), **and in** (Him) **αὐτός all** (things) **consist.**

The above words in parentheses were added by translators. Bold words are actual Greek text. 'Him' is *αὐτός*; a type of pronoun used throughout scripture as he, she, her, it, they or them; and here refers to THE CHRIST. The Concordant Literal New Testament reads this way:

For in Him is all created, that in the heavens and that on the earth, the visible and the invisible, whether thrones, or lordships, or sovereignties, or authorities, all is created through Him and for Him, and He is before all, and all has its cohesion in Him.

Christ—blueprint of ALL men ...

As we gain deeper insight to Jesus' teachings, what Paul wrote, and what John was trying to describe, we realize that no one single *person* is 'the' Christ. All men were created and consist IN the CHRIST ORIGIN, which is the BLUEPRINT OF ALL MEN. I know it's hard to grasp after years of thought patterns programmed in our minds. *Christ* was not Jesus' last name. Neither is he the *only* person who has ever displayed this *anointing* (simply means divinely qualified/authorized) of *the Christ*. Jesus was the first person the Jews and others of that day had seen walking unashamedly in the knowledge and outward practice of sonship. He *mirrored* the extension of *God*. He never backed up on declaring he was ONE with the Paternal Source of all Light and Life.

Christ = origin = blueprint of all men

Jesus was called *the Christ* for the anointed character/attributes of *divine quality* he visibly put on display. 'Christ' wasn't attached to the common name *Jesus*; it was attached to the *uncommon attributes* the people saw him continually practice. When something is engrained in our thinking it's often difficult to embrace something else; yet others were *called* by their attributes and their continual practices as well.

Was Simon *the* zealot the *only* zealot? (Acts 1:13)

Was Matthew *the* tax collector the *only* tax collector? (Matt. 10:3)

Is this Jesus *the Christ* not Joseph *the carpenter's* son? (Matt.13:55)

Friends, this is NOT taking away from the *anointed life* of Jesus OR the CHRIST he so powerfully put on display! It merely recognizes the cultural practices and terminology scriptures have held all along, that are now being revealed in our awareness. We haven't seen it this way because we've been trained to see Jesus as heaven's *Goalpost* that we all need to *strive* to become like, *so God will be pleased with us.* **We haven't realized so many things the Son of Man did, were actually him holding heaven's mirror up for men to see who they *already* were, and how pleased the Father had been with them all along!**

Paul said in *him* [αὐτός /CHRIST] the fullness of deity is in human form. John said of *his* [αὐτός /CHRIST] same fullness we have ALL received. Paul said men's *real life* is hidden (consisting) within CHRIST in God. John said the anointing men received from *him* [αὐτός /CHRIST] abides in them, and they don't *need* any man to *teach* them. Paul said the One who divinely established, qualified, and anointed men IN Christ, and sealed them with the [same CHRIST] Spirit, is *God.* Jesus said if men 'knew' *him*, they'd 'know' the Father. And one day, they'd 'know' they were [ONE IN CHRIST] just like Jesus and the Father. Peter said "if any man speaks, let him do it as the [enCHRISTED] oracle of God." The word oracle is *lógion*- directly from *lógos*. It is a divine declaration; as a statement originating and flowing from GOD HIMSELF.

At some point in our journey we begin to realize the Good News was never about what *we must do* to become One with God; but what our loving paternal Source *has done* to be inseparably One with us. We just need to wake up to our true genesis... *to see it*.

This is where Nick's story begins. He's seen *coming from* the night *(vux)*, which we saw is metaphorical for man's alienation from God, which Paul says *existed only in man's mind*. This Sanhedrin teacher is being drawn toward something he doesn't know how to wrap his mind around. Yet, whatever it is, it's powerful enough to draw him like a moth to a flame. This flame attracting him, was the Light of God that Nick carried in his own origin. This *phós*, Strongs #5457, is as Vine's Expository Dictionary describes: expressing light as seen by the eye, and is metaphorically, *capable of reaching the mind*.

Nick had already expressed that he (and all the others) were able to see the works of God in Jesus *with their eyes*. Yet, even though this Light had penetrated their natural vision, their thinking remained in a state of *night*, a *vux mindset* of alienation from God that had been passed down through the traditions of their fathers. They desperately needed something to pierce *the darkness of that mindset*. To restore man's default thinking *back* to the face to face blueprint of authentic genesis, and the enChristed mindset man was originally born with!

Some very popular bible verses we know and quote are nestled right here in this nighttime conversation. Yet even though we've seen them with our eyes all along- what was actually being said between Jesus and Nick hasn't been truly rooted in our *comprehension* because we're still thinking (and seeing) from an *alien*-ated mindset. We have seen ourselves as *separate* from our Origin, needing to somehow work our way back. Any thinking that entertains distance, delay, broken fellowship, or having to *do* things (i.e. prayer, worship, bible study, fasting, etc.) to draw closer to God, or get God to draw closer to us, is still, whether we like it or not, a form of an *alienated (vux) mindset*.

When we see John 3:16-21 from a mind that envisions a separation from our origin, or that God has condemned man *until* we do certain things to appease his angered judgment- we'll see it backward from John's intention. Yes, I said we've seen it *backward*. First off, Jesus lived, spoke, and displayed a life that showed us he wasn't here to judge or condemn, and that he only said and did what he knew the Father did. Jesus said, as John records his words in chapter 12:

John 12:46-50 (NKJV)

"I have come as a light into the world, that whoever believes in Me should not *abide in darkness*. And if anyone hears My words and does not believe, I do not judge him; for I did not come to judge the world but to save the world. He who rejects Me, and does not receive My words, has that which judges him- the word that I have spoken will judge him in the last day. For I have not spoken on My own authority; but the Father who sent Me gave Me a command, what I should say and what I should speak. And I know His command is *everlasting life*. Therefore whatever I speak, just as the Father has told Me, so I speak."

For I have not spoken on My own authority; but the Father who sent Me gave Me a command, what I should say and what I should speak. And I know that His command is everlasting (aiónios) life.

Can you hear Jesus' heart expressing what he so often made sure everyone was aware of? He and the Father only knew the position of ONE! This was the face to face expressed reflection in the Origin of all origins! He said he and the Father never operated independently (or did anything opposite) of each other. Here, Jesus says whether people believe him *or not*, he does *no judging, nor does his Father*, for that is NOT why he came! He said his Father sent him with one command, one precept, one mission. His mission, in agreement with the Father's heart, was proclaiming this confirmed and final decree upon every man, woman, and child. And that decree was **aiónios quality life!**

Jesus come from ONE—light to show way to light—to show oneness.

John 3:16-21 (NKJV)

"For God so loved the world that He gave His only begotten Son, that whoever believes in Him should not perish but have everlasting life. For God did not send His Son into the world to condemn the world, but that the world through Him might be saved. He who believes in Him is not condemned; but he who does not believe is condemned already, because he has not believed in the name of the only begotten Son of God. And this is the condemnation, that the light has come into the world, and men loved darkness rather than light, because their deeds were evil. For everyone practicing evil hates the light and does not come to the light, lest his deeds should be exposed. But he who does the truth comes to the light, that his deeds may be clearly seen, that they have been done in God."

[handwritten: self condemn]*

Had we been able to actually *hear* Jesus words, we would have known the condemnation he spoke of with Nick, didn't come from the Father of our genesis! It was a *self-condemnation* that occurred in man's mind from thinking he was un-covered. It was an idea that made man *think* God was angry with him, and that he needed to hide because God wanted to punish him. It caused man to move out of his esteemed family title of rightful *sonship*, only to settle for a meager hired hand role of being a *servant*. None of those things were ever true! God asked Adam,

"WHO said you were naked?"

Adam's Father right away began to supply and cover them with things to make them feel better about themselves in the midst of their shame. The animal skins weren't supplied to make God feel better; they were to make Adam and Eve feel better. We've been taught God *required* blood to forgive, then *killing* an animal for that appeasement. Yet this kind of thinking falls right through truth's colander as we see the writer of Hebrews reiterating David, and the prophetic voice of the anointed One: "Sacrifice and sin offerings were not your will, nor did you require them or receive pleasure from them."

[handwritten margin: NO SACRIFICE]

Once this is firmly settled in our minds, these scriptures in John 3 take on a whole *new light* of understanding. They begin to make more sense as we see Paul's declaration that man's *alien*-ated identity status of distortion (which then led them into a lifetime of further distortions and wicked acts) only existed in man's mind, and *not* God's! Every evil thing man has ever done, came about *not because* God's design somehow became flawed and genetically passed down through Adam. It was because of the same distorted thinking that pushed Adam away from God in his inner garden paradise. It kept pushing others away as well through the ideas, traditions, and mindsets passed down from those earthly fathers through the ongoing generations *to all men.*

"For God so loved the world that He gave." Loved. Established in Love. Paul says mankind was chosen, holy, and blameless in this same *established* love of God, *before* the foundation of the world (or the fall of man's mind). There is no fear in love, for fear involves torment. *Torment* comes when one thinks he is condemned; for when one lives in the fear of condemnation, *that fear* brings torment. This continual torment detrimentally affects everything else around this person's life, producing a fruitless *perish mode.* The evangelical traditions I was raised in, taught me that being saved from *perishing,* meant saved <u>from</u> the fires of a future, distant place called hell... and saved <u>to</u> the beauty and tranquility of a future, distant paradise called heaven.

As I said earlier, we've been quick to jerk the mic away from this nighttime conversation without hearing what was actually being said. It's easy to look back now and see we were merely grabbing snippets here and there that sounded like they agreed with, and confirmed our traditional doctrines. There are no actual references to someone being *saved* or receiving *salvation* in scripture, where there was even the slightest hint that what was taking place was being saved *from* hell, or being saved *to* heaven. Salvation, in true context, meant taking on a belief that so radically and powerfully changed one's former way of thinking, that it consequently began changing the landscape of their current life, and even the lives of others all around them!

Please don't take my word for it! Go back and find every Bible story where someone is actually being referred to as *receiving salvation*. You will see for yourself that talk of distance or delay, heaven or hell, was never on the radar. There was no talk of something in a future day to come, but rather a present-tense manifestation of much different fruit now being produced from someone moving out of one way of thinking and believing, *and into another.*

We have constructed doctrines by pulling snippets and lines from various scriptures to form something which didn't actually exist in the surrounding original context. In fact, the *majority* of our doctrines don't accurately reflect the nature and character of the Father's heart the scriptures were intended to point to. I can honestly say from the bottom of my heart that I'm beyond thankful for things that *offended* my doctrinal beliefs to the degree that it provoked me to go back and prove truth for myself. It's a win-win situation. I had to slide all my doctrinal notes to the side, and go back to view things all over again. As I trusted the Spirit within to guide me into truth, I found I would either emerge having solidified my beliefs even more, OR realizing that I'd been seeing these things through the pre-scripted lens of man. As that veiled lens was removed, it opened my eyes to something much different than I had been able to see before. Consequently, the vast majority of what I'd been taught to believe was drastically altered, or removed altogether. And those scales and veils just keep falling away.

There are a couple popular stories about being 'saved' or receiving salvation. One is in regard to Zacchaeus in Luke 19, as Jesus visits a chief tax collector's home. Now a tax collector was considered by the religious community as the poster child for sinners, meaning, there existed no greater level of *sin*ning among *sin*ners. The religious elite made sure to scoff out loud with their disapproval of Jesus going to this chief sinner's home for a meal. Oh, and not *just* a mere meal. When Jesus said "I must stay at your house," the word he used, *stay* (menó) actually means remain, settle down, abide in, or dwell. Many biblical scholars agree that the use of this word implies Jesus quite possibly spent the night at Zacchaeus' house. It is the same word Jesus used when he said 'If we abide (menó) in Him as He abides (menó) in us, we would bear much fruit in life.' So, what happened here? Well, what we do know is *Jesus came to abide* at Zacchaeus' home.

At some point during this 'abiding' story, Zacchaeus *stands up* and boldly declares that he's decided to give half of everything he owns to the poor; and anything taken from individuals through manipulation along the way, he is now paying them back four times multiplied! I can just see Jesus placing his hands around Zach's shoulders, and with the biggest smile imaginable, saying: *"Today (in this present moment), salvation has come to this home!"*

There was no talk of a distant delayed place called heaven or hell, nor some escape clause from eternal torment because of a prayer that changed God's mind about Zach in any way. Why? Because salvation never had anything to do with changing God's mind about man. It changed man's mind about God, and... changed man's mind *about himself.* **Jesus followed up by saying that the entire reason the Son of Man (ánthrōpos) came, was to save 'that' which had been lost. THAT** which was lost. The word 'lost' *(apóllymi)* that Jesus uses here, is the same exact word he used in John 3:16. He said that anyone who believed the truth he brought from the Father, would not perish *(apóllymi)*, but would begin to enjoy the *everlasting* (a quality fullness of *aiónios*) life the Father had sent him to declare over mankind.

Here, Zacchaeus recognizes the backdrop of Good News that Jesus continually promoted as being *One* with the Father. Now he decides he wants to start participating in it too! Something drastic happened to Zach's thinking *this day* to make the entire landscape of his life take off in a different direction. And not only beginning to manifest in his own life, but in other's lives around him as well! Jesus said *"Today (present tense), salvation has come to this home!"* We've been taught it is *first* repenting for one's actions and inviting Jesus to come live in one's heart that is the *only way* to obtain *salvation*.

Did Zach invite Jesus to come abide in his home? Nope. In fact, we see right the opposite take place. Jesus told Zach to hurry down from the perch he'd climbed to so he could see Jesus go by. Jesus already knew that he was coming to *abide* IN Zach's house. Why? To show him what salvation really looked like up close and personal! Zach didn't ask Jesus; *Jesus TOLD Zach*! And even within Zach's home, do we see any indication of Zach first repenting for how he had wronged all those people before salvation came? I mean, if it was a preliminary requirement of being 'saved,' surely it would have been shown. Yet we're given no indication at all this happened. What we see instead, is salvation first coming to *abide*, and then, the fruit of true repentance (a changed mind) moves into action. The result? People's lives start being blessed right where they are at the moment!

Romans 2:4 doesn't say repentance brings the goodness (salvation) of God. It says the opposite; that salvation (the goodness of God) leads men to true repentance. Oh, by the way- the name *Zacchaeus* actually means *untainted, clean,* and *pure.* The Son of Man passionately desired to bring salvation (wholeness) to men's alienated minds which had led them into all kinds of distorted, vile, evil acts of manipulation. This story reveals a glimpse into Zach's *former* orphaned thinking. Yet here, abiding at home with Jesus, Zach becomes a living epistle of true salvation, un-veiled with a re-deemed and re-booted mindset *back* to the authentic blueprint, which *is* the mind of Christ!

Zach's new awareness propelled him into a fruit-full life that was untainted, clean, and pure; which was the nature and character of his *true* name! And not only was it Zach's true name, it's the same name all men are called (kaléō) by- holy and blameless, the very way the divine nature is expressed in *all* born from above. This is the beautiful picture of enChristed resurrection. Standing men up out of the tombs and old grave-clothes of dead thinking, and begotten again IN Christ! This re-booting *upward* to the Father's truth now unveiled the fullness of the intended authentic origin from which all men had come!

Another popular story of being saved is of the jailer in Acts 16. The jailer asks Paul and Silas, *"What must I do to be saved?"* To which Paul and Silas answered all he needed to do was believe; and that not just he, but his whole family would be saved. For almost 20 years, I was a preaching, teaching, evangelistic machine. If it moved and had a pulse, I saw it as my job to make sure it was saved! If our eyes met somewhere and there was a minute to talk- I was gonna find out if you were saved or not. If you weren't, we were gonna fix that before I left. That may sound intense to you, but I was intense in my beliefs about God. I have prayed with thousands of people as (I thought) they were receiving the gift of salvation and got saved. But I always had questions about this line *"You and your whole family will be saved."* How could that be? I mean, I believed God was good. I believed God was SO good that I've never preached about hell or talked about it in an altar call even once in all those years. *But doesn't each person have to believe for themselves to be saved?* How could one's whole family be saved simply by the head of the house believing?

I'm honestly much more thankful for divine life today than I ever was back then. I've seen some things that I used to believe, become much clearer in my understanding and actually begin to make sense like they never did before. One day, I began to realize that if I could be that intensely passionate about people enjoying *salvation*, how much more then, would God be? I began to see certain things I had been taught, believed, and had in turn taught others, in a new and different light than ever before. It wasn't like one big bomb dropped all at once, but more like a light coming on so I could see something differently than before. Then I realized seeing that one particular thing, stirred up new questions about other things that couldn't possibly remain the same, *after* seeing the first *in new light*. It was like dominos falling. One light switch would illuminate a new room, and as I explored that room, I'd see another light switch at the end of it. It was a progressive *enlightening*, which, before I knew it, had shined a whole new light on almost everything I had ever been taught or believed.

Today, many questions I once had have been answered. I still have LOTS of questions, but I've seen certain things along my journey that have so dramatically changed my thinking and perspective on life and the Father, that I could *never* go back to how I believed before.

So, back to the jailer and a little surrounding context of what was going on before he popped the question *"What must I do to be saved?"* Paul and Silas had caused quite a stir in town earlier, where they were dragged to off the marketplace and beaten with rods for many blows. After being severely beaten, they were thrown in the prison. The jailer had been commanded to keep a *special watch* on them himself. Our apostle friends had stepped on the toes of some very influential people while they were in town; and these folks wanted Paul and Silas to understand they didn't appreciate it at all. The jailer's assignment was a little stronger than just a simple *"here... keep an eye on these guys."*

Luke narrates the scene as an *earthquake shakes the foundation* of the prison so violently that the doors fly open, with the bindings and chains *falling off* the prisoners. AWAKENED *from his sleep,* the jailer sees the doors wide open and chains all gone, and pulls out his sword to kill himself. If he dies by his own hand, it will at least be quicker and more merciful than at the hands of those who had commissioned him to guard Paul and Silas. Paul sees the guard in the shadows with his sword drawn and cries out:

"DO YOURSELF NO HARM! WE ARE ALL HERE!"

The jailer *calls for a light,* runs in and falls before them asking, *"WHAT MUST I DO TO BE SAVED??"*

Scripture has become *funny* to me in a sense, making me chuckle as I see how it's one big *set-up* after another in shadows, allegories, metaphors, name meanings, etc. They've always been there; but our *literal* Bible training has kept us skimming right over them. The Greek thought for 'calls for a light' says that *he is requesting illumination.* Remember Vine's description of the word 'light'? It expresses light as seen by the eye, and, metaphorically- capable of *reaching the mind.* Paul called it *comprehending the fullness* of God. (Eph.3:18-19)

Light = capable of reaching the mind —
Comprehending fullness

Let's go back earlier in the day. These prisoners had been beaten probably worse than anything we can imagine. Paul and Silas were then dragged through the streets further ripping their wounds, and delivered to this jailer. Now they were in *his house*. Now it's *his turn* to continue making them aware of just how unwelcome and unwanted they were. The jailer had received a personal command to make sure they didn't escape. Suddenly, he's *awakened in the night* by a shaking to the foundational core within his own house. Seeing the doors wide open, he thinks he's failed his assignment, and starts to kill himself. Yet he hears Paul's voice of assurance that they are *with him-* and not to harm himself. It's then, he *calls out for light*, and falls at their feet.

It's important to realize these apostles hadn't been sitting around a cell with this jailer having a Bible study. They hadn't been handing out tracts telling him of a future place called hell, or a distant paradise called heaven if he would only say the sinner's prayer. Here he is, on the ground before our two injured apostles. They had every imaginable right to enjoy the idea of this jailer being punished and beaten (perhaps by the same floggers who'd beaten them) for failing his job, right before he died a slow and painful death. Paul and Silas could have been long gone from the jail (and his darkness), *but they weren't*.

Not only did they save his life from his employers by not running; they saved his life from his own hands, just seconds before he would have taken it himself. The jailer then falls at their feet asking, *"What must I do to be saved?"* He didn't ask for a get-out-of-hell-free card; he was asking for illumination that could help his mind wrap around what he was visibly seeing here. He was asking how he could have *what they had*. He wanted to know *how* he could enjoy this life of bold, yet gentle wholeness he'd seen in them. A life that not only refused to take offense, but would actually reach out and save the life of another who deserved to die, *rather than saving themselves.*

This overwhelming gesture of selfless love the jailer had *seen* in them, was the undeniable fruit of salvation's work in men who simply *believed* Jesus' message of their authentic identity he had unveiled.

Their answer to the jailer about how he could be *saved*, was *"Just believe* (like they had) *and you and your entire family can begin to enjoy this same life and love you've seen in us, and now desire for yourself!"* The *prison* doors hadn't been opened this night so Paul and Silas could escape; they were opened so the jailer could come toward the light he had seen in their life! And what time were they opened? *At midnight.* Just a coincidence? I think not. The term 'midnight' is yet another metaphorical light switch hidden to illuminate the inner workings of this *salvation* the Son of Man revealed to all around him.

Mid-night is formed from the word *mesos*, #3319, which means in the middle of, or in the midst. Think of all the scriptures we see that refer to 'Jesus being in the *midst* of them.' It comes from *meta*, which is a component of the word metamorphoō, the word that Paul used in Romans 12:2 for *trans-form*. The word is used like this: metá #3326, (a preposition)- properly, with ('after with'). As an active 'with' (metá) looks towards the after-effect of change, or result, as defined by the context. The other half of the word midnight (yep, you guessed it) is *vux*, #3571; the word *night*, which is used metaphorically as the period of man's *mental* alienation from God.

Friends, THIS is the picture of salvation! It is *not* Jesus standing alone as some distant theological goalpost for men to push toward, striving to attain to *become* holy and righteous. It is *not* trading in a default destination of eternal torment for a distant gated paradise with streets of gold. This was the hands-on work of a Great Physician coming into the *midst of man's darkness*, plunging himself into the deepest tombs of man's dis-eased and infirmed (perishing) state. It was the Son of Man revealing the Father's divine nature in the same flesh we woke up with this morning. The same exact skin suit Adam ran from God and hid in. It's meant to show us the picture of our own *enChristed* origin, and that there was *no reason* for any sons of men to hide from God to begin with! It was Jesus coming unashamedly into man's state of orphaned existence, declaring the Father's passionate message: **"I refuse to leave you *thinking* you are orphans!"**

The incarnation Jesus revealed (divine nature in the flesh of man), was needed to remove their *alien* mindset of guilt and condemnation, along with the distorted consciousness of *sin*, evil and death that came from it. Jesus, displaying the Father's heart, *effectively* took that dark and distorted thinking to the cross, crucifying it with him. Only then could other sons and daughters of God (who Jesus called brethren), finally emerge from their tombs of mental captivity and bondage to death. This *up-right re-surgence* of their authentic God-life would be the reboot that men would need to see themselves *begotten again* in new-man awareness with the *mind of Christ*. It would clearly renew and reflect the logos blueprint they were originally expressed from!

We are his workmanship, created IN CHRIST for good works, which God prepared beforehand that we should walk in them; just as he chose us in him before the foundation of the world, that we should be holy and without blame, before him in love.

For too long we've been taught a message where man's beginning was more focused on Adam's fall than what God had eternally finished on man's behalf long before whatever Adam did that made him run and hide in fear. Adam's outward actions didn't take God by surprise *or* change his thoughts about man at any point along the way. Why? Because God had made an eternal inward determination about man long before this garden scene and fig-leaf *cover-up* ever took place! This loving Father declared the truth and equity of man's authentic genesis long before the fall of man's thinking. That *truth* is that man's divine logos design *in tabernacles of flesh* can never be changed!

Friends, this is the love from which all men are created and consist. It's man's enChristed *born from above* origin; the *expressed extension* of divine DNA that can never pass away. This love Source is so deep and providing, that John the Baptist and the earliest followers of Jesus believed he would take away the *sin* of their world. It was meant to wake them up, stand them up, and bring them back home, to finally participate in the life more abundant they were always meant to enjoy!

When the jailer asked Paul and Silas what he must do to be saved, he was asking how he could possess this fearless life of conviction and kindness they had boldly displayed. He was asking them about this life and love that was humble and gentle enough to stay with him in his darkness, while serving him a life-saving dose of forgiveness. This jailer didn't have the luxury of reading Paul's letters, for they had not yet been written. He didn't yet have a clue of the amazing fullness of this salvation he was stepping into; but he'd seen something in Paul and Silas that he wanted. He saw something so beautiful and real that he cried out for *enlightening* to help him wrap his mind around it! Well, he got it; and not just for him... *but for his whole family!*

We later see this family welcoming Paul and Silas into their home, washing their wounds, feeding them, and were *baptized* in their own awareness of Oneness in Christ. This joy of love and salvation (peace and wholeness) is highly contagious! We see Zach choose to reimburse others 4 times over without them even asking for it. This jailor's life and his *entire family* would be forever affected by the life-changing wholeness which opened up the doors of *his own prison*, destroying its inner chains, and *setting him free from his own bondage.*

When Paul cried out to the jailer *"Do yourself no harm!"*, he was actually saying, as the Greek reveals: **"You should be committing nothing evil unto yourself!"** This takes us back to Jesus telling Nick why he had come; that whoever believed in him would not *perish*.

The word *perish* means a whole lot more than the narrow scope of destruction that we've been taught. As we saw earlier in Zach's story, when the Son of Man said he came to save <u>that</u> which was lost, the word 'lost' (apóllymi) is the same exact word as 'perish' (apóllymi). Yes, it is certainly used at times for utter destruction, but is also *often* used not as an actual *destruction* of life, but to **describe the current state and *quality* of life in the present tense, and, how the *quality* of that existence plays out in the days ahead.**

lost /perish = actual destruction of current quality of life

This word we have been taught was pointing to eternal torment or destruction, is also used for the *lost* (apóllymi) sheep the shepherd carried home on his shoulders. It was used for the *lost* (apóllymi) coin which the owner refused to stop searching for until it was found. It's used of the *lost* (apóllymi) son who found himself *perishing* (apóllymi) with hunger. The son didn't actually starve or die but comes *to* himself or, *to his right mind.* Now awakened to truthful reality, he moves out of this foreign land of *pig-pen existence* to find the Father's same love and inheritance he thought he'd *lost* (apóllymi) still belonged to him!

The stories of Nick, Zach, and the jailer are all meant to be pointers to the life men were meant to enjoy, *entwined as One* in Christ-Life. They are stories that *set men free* from the fear and condemnation of man. They don't *promote* it. They are stories of what salvation truly looks like; wholeness, peace, love, joy, no offense, and laying down a life of love for one another. None of them are *do-it-yourself* stories, but are *you-have-all-you-need* salvation stories of love and provision from a greater Source of God's *before* plan and intended design! Paul cried out to the jailer **"You should be committing nothing evil unto yourself!"** Evil, #2556, means *intrinsically worthless.* To do, or think evil toward one's *self* means one sees their *self* (in their consciousness) worthless to the core. Paul was actually saying, *"We're in agreement here, and we release you!! Don't condemn yourself to death!"*

Now let's take a minute to think. Did the Son of Man tell his Jewish brethren no one had seen the Father or known him except the Son and those to whom the Son would reveal him? Yes, he did. What about when religious minds quoted Moses and the laws he'd written that said the woman caught in adultery must be stoned? Did Moses imply he had heard this from God? Yes, he did. Did Jesus agree with Moses? No, he didn't. Why? Because Moses didn't know the Father OR carry the Father's heart the way Jesus did. We hear lots of ideas about what Jesus said to these well-dressed stone holders, but the truth is, no one knows for sure. What we do know, is that whatever Jesus said to them as he scribbled on the ground, made them realize *none of them* had a

Moses - Jesus did not agree

right to condemn this woman the way they thought they did. Oh, and they didn't stick around to argue with Jesus about whether Moses was right or not. When the woman raised her head *to face* Jesus, he said:

"Woman, where are your accusers?" "Who now condemns you?"

She looked around and said:

"No one Lord; condemnation disappeared when you showed up."

Jesus' love and authority became very clear that day as he did what he came to do, by revealing the Father's heart. He showed the rulers that they, nor the law of Moses, had any right to condemn this woman. When Jesus told her *"go and sin no more,"* he wasn't just releasing her from a life of bondage to *sin* (which simply means missing the mark of intended identity), but was actually telling her:

"Neither do I condemn you. Now go *in peace* and stop living your life like an orphan child who doesn't know who she is."

John 3:16-21 (NKJV)

[handwritten: lost in context of life]

"For God so loved the world that He gave His only begotten Son, that whoever believes in Him should not perish but have everlasting life. For God did not send His Son into the world to condemn the world, but that the world through Him might be saved. "He who *[handwritten: awake]* believes in Him is not condemned; but he who does not believe is condemned already, because he has not believed in the name of the only begotten Son of God. And this is the condemnation, that the light *[handwritten: see]* has come into the world, and men loved darkness rather than light, because their deeds were evil. For everyone practicing evil hates the light and does not come to the light, lest his deeds should be exposed. But he who does the truth comes to the light, that his deeds may be clearly seen, that they have been done in God."

Jesus explains to Nick this condemnation was *never* from God to begin with. It was a *self*-imposed condemnation from a worthless toil and labor mindset of fear, which was then passed on to others through men's *alienated traditions* not originating in the Tree of Life.

Men had been introduced to the same *perishing* existence of toil and hardships Adam had taken on, by choosing his own *do-it-yourself* perception over the *been-done-for-you* blueprint of true life. As we saw earlier, Peter said this aimless (cul-de-sac) conduct was then passed down through the doctrines and *programmed* traditions of their earthly fathers before them. It wasn't because of some genetic death gene passed down from Adam. As Solomon wrote prior to Peter's life: There are ways that *seem right* to man; but **true life** will never be found waiting at the end of these dead-end roads."

Jesus is simply telling Nick that anyone who believes in him and the intimacy with the Father he came to reveal, would *stop groping around* in a darkened, perishing state of *vux* night-time existence. They would no longer see themselves *alien*ated as enemies of God in their own mind. They would know Jesus didn't come to condemn them; but to save them from seeing themselves as condemned and hiding in fear when God wasn't even mad at them. Jesus was telling Nick that man was *already* living in THAT condemnation. Not one that came from God- but from man's own distorted, *orphaned* perception.

Remember the definition of evil? **It means intrinsically worthless, which in man's case, was seeing their 'self' as worthless to the core in their own consciousness. Jesus was simply saying if someone didn't believe what he revealed, they would *continue* to remain in <u>that</u> condemnation they'd been mentally entrenched in for so long.**

When man sees the light of truth drawing him toward *his reality* (as the treasure of God in an earthen vessel), it pulls him out of this orphaned, alienated state where he once viewed himself intrinsically worthless, or *evil*. Turning toward Christ-truth within and believing what Jesus came to reveal, removes the veils and scales of distortion so man can see that his inner works of origin (workmanship) were done in the blueprint of Christ, *which is the light and life of all men.*

Could it be that Jesus explaining all this to Nick, made him see for the *first time* that his works of origin were done in God and not man? Could it be that Jesus' humorous, sarcastic prodding now triggered something that echoed from deep within Nick, causing him to see himself like never before? Whatever happened, Nick was far from shy in the next accounts we see of him. John 7 records a much different picture of Nick, with him taking a bold position that even put him at odds with his constituents! John records how the Pharisees and chief priests were hearing of the uproar this rebel rabbi was causing among the people. When they learned how many others were now starting to believe his words of freedom, they sent the temple police to take Jesus captive. Later (v.45-47), when the officers return empty handed, the frustrated Pharisees began grilling them, saying,

"Where is he??... Why have you not brought him??"

The Passion Translation (tPt) records the officers reply:

"But you don't understand!" "He speaks amazing things like no one has ever spoken!"

At this, the elite leaders began mocking their own officers, saying:

"So now you also have been led astray by him?? This ignorant rabble swarms around him because none of them know anything about the Law! They're all cursed!"

Now picture this scenario unfolding: The Pharisees and rulers of the high court are angrily facing their own officers who have blatantly disobeyed direct orders to take Jesus captive and bring him to them. And as if there isn't already enough tension in their holy courtroom, our one-time covert night-flyer, Nicodemus, now stands up among his own elite brotherhood (v.51) and boldly asks them this question:

"Does our law judge a man before we've even heard what he is saying and knows what he's doing??"

I can just imagine a symphonic gasp among them, followed by a moment of such silence you could hear the temple gnats breathing! What the Nick was going on here??

who is Jesus?

Remember the sarcastic jab Jesus delivered to Nick that first night?

"You call yourself a teacher of Israel, and yet you don't know these things?"

Sure, it was delivered with prodding love meant to awaken Nick to his true place in life, but there was also a residual sting in the tone of this punch as it landed! Our one-time night-flyer now stands up in broad daylight to deliver a similar punch to the Pharisees, while using the same tone Jesus that used on him. Can you hear it?

"You guys call yourself righteous judges over the people, and yet you've already declared this man guilty without even hearing what he has to say??"

The days of tip-toeing around in the shadows for Nicodemus were over! Nick's tone and visual stance that day were obviously enough to offend and infuriate those he once took sides with, even to the point they began to see him as having transferred the allegiance of his heart! Verse 52 in the tPt records it like this- They argued, saying:

"Oh, so now you're an advocate for this Galilean!?! Search the scriptures Nicodemus, and you'll see there's no mention of a prophet coming out of Galilee!"

This meeting had now moved beyond any point of return. This well-dressed judgment team was having a royal melt-down as their own police force unapologetically disobeyed their retrieval orders.

The next time scripture reveals Nicodemus is in John 19.

John 19:38-42 (NKJV)

After this, Joseph of Arimathea, being a disciple of Jesus, *but secretly*, for fear of the Jews, asked Pilate that he might take away the body of Jesus; and Pilate gave him permission. So, he came and took the body of Jesus. And Nicodemus, who at first came to Jesus by night, also came, bringing a mixture of myrrh and aloes, about a hundred pounds. Then they took the body of Jesus and bound it in strips of linen with the spices, as the custom of the Jews is to bury.

Now in the place where He was crucified there was a garden, and in the garden a new tomb in which no one had yet been laid. So there they laid Jesus, because of the Jews' Preparation Day, for the tomb was nearby.

Can you see what John, *not so subtly* includes to pop out to his reader's in the first line of this passage? Joseph of Arimathea came... *but he did it in secret.* Here we see a man (Joseph) who is referred to as a disciple/follower of Jesus. Yet he remains in the secret shadows of darkness where *he feels comfortable.* By now, Nicodemus had come out in broad daylight in respect to his association with Jesus, even to the point of being identified and *accused* by his Pharisee constituents as an advocate for this rebel rabbi. At one time, Nick *himself* chose to remain in secret shadows of darkness, where it was more comfortable for him *at the time* than coming out and being seen in the light. Could it possibly be that Nick's story was a type, or a shadow of the rest of the Jews? Those needing to see the *true function* of divine Light, so *they too* could emerge from their own shadows of fear and darkness?

My thoughts go to the first recorded shadows of fear that occurred when Adam's mind changed about God in the garden. They hide from their loving Source in a place of darkened understanding. They had *imagined* God was angry with them, causing them to see themselves in danger, condemned, and deserving of punishment. Something had switched in man's mind, and he no longer saw his Source as nourisher, provider, and friend, *but as a judge.* What did God do? He confronted this change by pursuing and asking Adam, *"Where are you?"* Clearly, God's sense of locating Adam wasn't lacking and needing assistance. God knew exactly where Adam was and was trying to stir his own awareness to it by asking, *"Can YOU see where you are, Adam?"*

Genesis 3:9-10 (NKJV) 9 Then the Lord God called to Adam and said to him, "Where are you?" So he said, "I heard Your voice in the garden, and I was afraid because I was naked; and I hid myself."

Listen carefully to the words Adam (the proper name for humanity) says: "I (my-self) was afraid (my-self) because I was (saw my-self) naked, and I hid my-self." Adam had now become so consumed with *earthly-self* awareness that it completely VEILED his awareness to the truth of his enChristed *spirit-self.* Yet God never stopped seeing Adam as anything other than his (God's) own self-image BEing. We see the Father pursuing his divine BEing, trying to jar his *consciousness* from this dis-eased contradiction back to the truth by asking one question: **"<u>WHO</u> TOLD YOU THAT YOU WERE NAKED??"**

Allow me to paraphrase John 3:19-21 to describe what I believe Jesus was really trying to get across to Nick as they sat together in the shadows of Nick's darkness:

Herein lies the great dilemma: The light came into the world, but men chose to remain in the darkness, fearing the light had come to expose their evil. For when man has settled for living in the distorted lies of worthlessness and separation, his fear of *exposure* will keep him hiding in the shadows of darkness. But those who *see* the truth shining beyond the distortion, realize the light came *not to expose* them, but to *reveal* something much deeper than worthless acts of the flesh. The light pierces through to the very core, revealing man's true origin as beginning and existing in God! The fear of worthlessness no longer has anywhere to hide in the light of truth. The light didn't come to expose something evil; it came to UN-VEIL the masterpiece of the ages! This light reveals humanity as authentic workmanship of heavenly design; not merely flesh sons of men, but as the legitimate sons and daughters (offspring BEings) of God!

This covert *in-the-dark* meeting revealed that Nicodemus' life was an example of the distorted, lingering shadow effect of the state of mankind's awareness. Just like Adam, they had forgotten and become totally unaware *of who they really were.*

We see Nick eventually leaving his shadowy state of darkness in bold outgoing moves. It proved he was no longer afraid of what would be seen by all, as he began stepping out into the light. John later wrote (1ˢᵗ John 1:7) that if other *night dwellers* would step into the light they were once afraid of, they too, would clearly see the light revealing their Oneness with the Father. This light would display the truth that Jesus had removed every stain of their *sin*, along with all the tormenting consciousness of fear and death that came with it! Oh, I guess I should mention the name *Nicodemus* properly means '*Victor of the People.*'

At this point I'll ask you to put aside everything you've been taught about original sin, inherited evil nature, along with a condemnation that originated with God and said you deserved death. I'll invite you to take a journey of *"What ifs"* with me back through the scriptures, to possibly see a picture quite different than we've been programmed to believe all our lives. Can you now look back over your life and see things that were done on your behalf that you had no clue were being done at the time? Can you, *in retrospect*, now see entire pictures that were once merely fragments and dots along the journey until the Spirit *showed you* how they all connected? Can you see that all these things have actually been working toward good in your life all along?

Most of us have been taught we were to have a passionate resolve to learn, memorize, and defend certain scriptures and traditions to *prove* what we *thought* we knew about God. We've studied, presented, and re-presented those scriptures with a dogmatic form so rigid, that we've actually passed right over many expansive possibilities and mysteries hidden within them. There are many scriptural shadows, nuances, and metaphors, much like passageways to vaults of treasure never seen *or even imagined* by those who stay on the well-worn path everyone else is familiar with. It's interesting these same scriptures tell us Jesus never spoke to the crowds without using parables. Parables aren't a list of rules; nor do they draw lines and narrow parameters of dualistic thinking of right or wrong, good or bad, light or dark.

parable

Parables are meant to open and expand awareness and stimulate our own thinking. One can't reasonably point to a single dimension of one of Jesus' parables and say "There! That's the whole reason Jesus told that story!" Quite the opposite is true. A parable is meant to open our eyes and doors to possibilities we may not have previously thought about or considered- *causing us to dig for buried treasure.*

**It's the renowned character of God to bury a treasure-
but the splendor of kings is reserved for those
willing to dig it out. (Proverbs 25:2 dcv)**

Mark said Jesus always spoke in parables. He then went on to say that when Jesus was alone with his disciples, he would explain these things in greater spiritual depths to them. Did Jesus get them alone and say *"Ok guys- here's the one thing I want you to get out of that whole story?"* I don't think so. Jesus' stories remained open ended for the most part; not meant to confine thinking to one specific area, but to expand the depths of what was hidden within his Spirit/Life words. It was to awaken men's eyes, ears, hearts, and every facet of life to the *un-bound* truth of the Spirit realm. May those with ears, *hear.*

Jesus had no interest in starting a new religion or giving a list of rules on how to act. In fact, he broke many of the laws men were so focused on following. In all the times Jesus publicly hung out with drunkards, tax collectors, prostitutes, and thieves, you won't find a single example of Jesus pointing a judgmental finger at specific (verb) acts of sin and telling them to *"Stop it!"* Why? Jesus came to make men think. He had no desire to put the focus on *how* they were living, *as if* they didn't already know. His desire was to open their eyes to the root cause of *why* they were living that way. His passion was to show them they didn't *have* to live like orphans, because they had a loving Father who would never leave them or forsake them. Jesus knew once they comprehended this truth, it would change their vision, along with every fruit-full *heart issue* of life flowing from within them!

I think Paul was trying to convey this treasure-hunting truth as he quotes Isaiah in the first letter to the Corinthians. It's one of those passages that gets ripped out of context, creating whole teachings and theologies about God's ways and thoughts being beyond man's reach, without reading the next line, which immediately changes *everything!*

1 Corinthians 2:9 (NKJV)

But as it is written: "Eye has not seen, nor ear heard, Nor have entered into the heart of man the things which God has prepared for those who love Him."

Paul seems to agree with Isaiah's statement that it's impossible for man to grasp the depths of God through what we see or hear in our *natural flesh* eyes and ears. Then, Paul gives the spiritual masterkey which unlocks every door to uncover all the deep things our Father always meant for us to know and enjoy!

1 Corinthians 2:10 (NKJV)

But God has revealed them to us through His Spirit. For the Spirit searches all things, yes, even the deep things of God.

Here, Paul confirms Jesus' words of man's personal tour guide, the Spirit *within*, helping us to dig out the hidden treasures of God, while at the same time being guided into more truth. Why? That we may comprehend all those deep things that are impossible to know in the natural senses of our eyes and ears alone. Here, Paul points out the possibility of listening to the same parable everyone else is currently listening to; yet utilizing an *inner Spirit ability* to hear a much deeper truth that other's might not be perceiving at the moment.

Keeping these things in mind- I'm going to throw a few scripturally verifiable dots out there to see if a *coming to our right mind* picture possibly starts to take form in our awareness:

What if- 'Nick' represented the forgetfulness of all men? What if he was meant to be a picture of first fruit, like an usher going before the Jews to bring the awareness of their original genesis, straight from the Son of Man who came to seek and save *that* (mindset) which was lost?

What if- Nicodemus' name, *Victor of the People*, wasn't just some coincidental name; but was a title describing a revelational, spiritual illumination which other men *would then be brought into?*

What if- Jesus' words to Nick describing the condemnation that was in the world, and men choosing to stay in that darkness rather than coming to the light- was describing a contradictive *lost* mindset of fear in man, which never originated with God to begin with?

What if- **John 3:21 "But he who does the truth** (the Greek implies one being *aware and participating in* truth) **comes to the light, that his deeds** (érgon; works) **may be <u>seen</u>, that they** (his *érgon* works) **have been done** (achieved/accomplished) **in God"**- was actually Jesus describing what would happen when men discovered their true origin (and their inner BEing workings) were all generated from above, and in God's eyes *had never changed at all?*

What if- all men could come boldly out in the light with no fear whatsoever, only to see that all their (inner érgon) works were done (achieved/accomplished) IN God from the beginning, even before the foundation [mental fall] of the world? *For we are his workmanship, created IN Christ for good (érgon) works, which God has prepared (completed) beforehand that we should walk (participate) in them.*

What if- Jesus personally taught Nick, *Victor of the People*, all of this as a precursor or an *ushering in* kind of awareness, so other men might clearly understand things like Peter's resurrection description when he later wrote: **Who has begotten** (re-generated) **us again, to a** (re-surged original) **living hope through the resurrection of Jesus Christ from the dead... to an inheritance not able to be corrupted, not able to be defiled, and not able to ever fade away?**

What if- all this was to reveal an inheritance reserved in *heavenly* places (the Father's heart), kept *and guarded* by the power of God; having been preserved for this *re-*deeming, *re-*storing, and *re-*booting to the shalom wholeness of living-hope life, now revealed and having been RE-SURGED in that *Last Adam* time?

What if- Joseph coming out of the secret shadows with a burial tomb for this crucified Son of Man, was a picture of other sons of men coming out of their own darkened thinking to bury *once for all,* every distorted *I am not* thought passed on from Adam and the traditions of their earthly fathers, to also be crucified on that cross with Jesus?

What if- this contradictory sin and death consciousness (which didn't originate with God) that spread to all men in accusation (you're naked, you're un-covered, and you need to hide), was all caused by man *seeing himself* as an alienated enemy of God *in his own mind*?

What if- this contradictory mental disruption to God-thoughts and God-plans, then led those men into all kinds of other vile distortions and worth-less acts not originating with God; which also contradicted (always falling short/missing the true mark of) the authentic blueprint design of the Father's plan and purpose?

What if- all this happened, simply because man had missed the intended goal of true identity *in his mind*; and it was never about an *evil nature* passed down through Adam's bloodline at all?

What if- when the woman Jesus saved from stoning was told: "I don't condemn you, now go and *sin* no more," he was telling her, *"Now go enjoy the bulls-eye truth of the Father's love and who you really are- and stop missing the mark by living like an orphan!!"*

What if....

Jesus - in the Christ....
Anointing - mind -
Way not to salvation but unto
identity of man in God's
total inclusion...

CHAPTER THREE

Taking the Bible Out of the Box

Before we go any further, I should probably tell you a few things that will *hopefully* help you hear my heart and better understand some of the core reasoning behind this book. One day in 2012 as I was teaching in front of a group of people, I had a vision, or *visual image* of Jesus standing beside me, reaching toward me for something. As I looked to see what he wanted, I saw a child's Etch A Sketch was in my hands. 'Well that's weird,' I thought, but then I saw myself surrendering it over to him. Removing it from my hands, he turned it upside down and shook it thoroughly. He turned it back over, and after he'd made sure everything previously on it was completely erased, his face lit up with a huge grin, and he then *placed it back in my hands.*

In 2016, four years after my Etch A Sketch experience, I was sitting in a long-time friend's church where I had been invited to speak the following week. My pastor friend asked me to come up the week before and get familiar with their service style, and to let the people become familiar with my face. While sitting in the congregation, I was led into a vision, or visual scene, where Jesus was on a park bench beside a winding grass trail through some woods. The bench was across from a beautiful open grassy area. As I walked toward him, I noticed he had a rectangular box in *his* hands. When I sat down beside him, he smiled and placed the box in *my* hands. I was pretty much frozen in time at this point. I mean, Jesus just *personally* put something in my hands, and was sitting beside me on this bench. I can't fully describe what I felt in that moment. It may just be a story in a book to you; but it was very real and personal to me. As I sat there just staring at this box, I realized that Jesus was still sitting there *right beside me.*

When I finally managed to pry my eyes off the box, I looked back to my right side where he sat, *obviously* waiting for me to get over my initial shock. When my eyes met his, he tilted his head in the direction of the box as if to say, *"Well... do you want to know what's inside?"* When I lifted the lid, I saw a brand-new Bible. The cover was perfect, and the pages had unblemished gold around their edges- revealing to me that it had never even been opened. Again, as I had first done with the box, my eyes locked on the outside of this perfect Bible in a frozen stare. Wow. Jesus had just personally handed me a brand-new Bible, which clearly had never been taken out of the box, let alone been opened and explored. When I looked back at him (I guess I should say *"Thanks?"*), it became obvious that he was enjoying this moment in a much bigger way than I knew how to at the time. I can't describe his smile. It was the most peaceful, consuming, love embrace of affection wrapped up in a heavenly facial expression. I felt like he was hugging me as he gazed into my eyes. It was then I realized Jesus was looking at me *in the same way* I had been looking at this treasured gift I was holding in my hands. Just when I felt like I was about to melt through the slats on the bench, his loving smile slid into a sideways grin. It was kinda like a grin your best friend or brother would have as he playfully jabs you in the side, nudging you *toward* something he wants you to look at. This provoking grin left no doubt to what he was thinking: *"Well? Are you gonna open it up or what???"*

I looked back down, almost afraid to spread it open. I knew that once I touched those pages, the gold luster of their ornately trimmed edges would never be the same. With another nod of encouragement, it became clear Jesus wanted me to forget about the gold on the pages.

I placed my thumbs on the edge of the Bible and opened it up. Before I even noticed what book or chapter I had landed on, the letters and words came up off the page. They instantly turned into dancing music notes and began leaping away from the pages. In an animated way they hopped off the book, and during their descent toward the ground, they turned into little children. As soon as these *kids* hit the ground, they ran across the path toward the grassy field. Running along the way, several of them grew into adults before my eyes. They started interacting with one another, and I soon realized they were living out scenes depicted in the scriptures right before my eyes!

There was so much movement going on it was hard for me to focus on any one thing. As though he knew my attention was being pulled from every side, Jesus leans closer to me and begins pointing out things for me to look at. *Ok, let me get this straight.* I'm sitting on a park bench with Jesus. He hands me a brand-new Bible, which then comes vividly alive right before my eyes. Now, he's nudging me like an old friend and pointing out specific things for me to look at.

The Son of God is narrating a new Bible to me in person??

Yes. *Yes he is.*

I'm not sure how long all this lasted, or when Jesus and the park bench disappeared. I don't remember knowing what story or scripture I watched being lived out. I don't know how long I sat there in a state of being blissfully stunned. When I came to, or out of the vision (or whatever terminology works for you), I had no idea I was even in a church. My elbows were on my knees, my hands holding my head, and when I opened my eyes, the first thing I saw was a large wet spot on the floor below me. My eyes and face were drenched with tears. I heard noises around me and began to remember where I was at. I'm sure I probably looked about as wild as I felt in that moment, and you know what? *I didn't care.* I had just enjoyed a realm beyond anything I'd ever known or experienced in my life, and I still become emotional every time I stop to think about it and relive it.

In the years that have passed since my park bench experience with Jesus, I've come to understand many new things. I now know that envisioning my Etch A Sketch *turned upside down* and shaken clean, was symbolic for my mindset being cleared of old scribblings drawn in an immature past. I also know this visionary Jesus had no interest at all in giving me a new Bible with perfect pages. This spirit encounter was showing me my old worn Bible was about to come alive with vivid imagery right before my eyes; that is- once I learned how to take it out of the traditional box I'd been taught to read it from all my life.

We all have our own personal Etch A Sketch images of the *God we think we know* stored in our thinking. They're pieced together with disjointed lines and fragments of immature child-like scribblings that don't really form a clear picture at all. There are also blurry images not drawn by our own personal imagination; but were already *existing* images that were passed down from pastors, teachers, or parents who traditionally taught us to view things *just as they'd been taught.*

Many of these images come from the ideas and opinions of Old Testament writers who were doing the best they could to describe what they *thought* they were hearing at the time. We've been taught to place inerrant, infallible perfection on their words- a doctrinal idea of man that the Bible itself never claims. We've placed holy reverence on *literal* depictions of stories and actions that don't look or sound at all like the Living Word, Jesus; who stated that no man before him had seen the Father, nor could they know God *apart from* the eyes of the Son. We've all but ignored the story of Moses and Elijah disappearing on the mountain in Jesus' presence to validate that truth. They don't just move to the side or step *behind* Jesus. They completely DISAPPEAR at the sound of *heaven's voice* pinpointing WHO men should listen to.

You'll never hear me argue that anything *God* inspired wasn't perfect; but how that perfect word gets interpreted and then written down by the hearer, can become a completely different story. There are stark differences in many things expressed by the Old Testament writers, as *opposed* to what Jesus said and lived out-loud for everyone to see. If we can't clearly see and admit that, then we have a logistical reality problem and lack of understanding about what the Son of Man revealed. The book of Hebrews is coined as 'the book of better things.' *Much better things* revealed by Jesus than the law of Moses, or any of the prophets who *thought* they knew God's heart. In the opening of this groundbreaking letter, we see the author of Hebrews eluding to this very thing, and effectively shaking the traditional Etch A Sketch the people had held in their tribal imagery of God for so long. *Quantum brings had to ques. christ Jesus*

The first 4 verses of Hebrews could be stated like this:

In the past, our fathers were told various ways the prophets believed they'd heard God speak. But in these last days, God has bypassed any chance of error through a prophetical middleman and has spoken to us clearly by the Living Word, in the face to face person of his Son. This Son, came to reveal the I AM truth of the Christ-life, where all things consist by the same word and same power. He reveals the perfect image and reflection of the Father in every way; that we may know and behold him as One *for ourselves*. It's in this Christ-life alone where our ideas of sin, sacrifice, and separation are purged from our thinking once for all. For *in Christ alone,* is revealed an incorruptible inheritance of life much more excellent than any of the prophetical messengers beforehand knew how to show us.

Quantum shows NO Distinction!

It's vital that we understand the background, culture, language, and the current living situation of those who were writing these letters to *others* who also lived in the *same* timeframe, culture, and language. If we don't keep these contextual points in mind, there will no doubt be things described in those writings which will be misconstrued and viewed in the wrong light. It's up to us to study these things out on our own, and decide what is actually relevant to *our life today*. There are many historically documented facts to help us see the truth in *proper context*. Unfortunately, the actual timeline of these things didn't make the top 10 list of 'most important things' we heard in church.

To see things clearly in the Father's grace and truth, it is vital to keep the life, sayings, and actions of Jesus before us as we read any other scripture, and *especially* when listening to man's doctrines. If what we hear from them doesn't look like *what we see in Jesus*, then we need to ask ourselves if we actually believe what Jesus said and did. If so, we'll soon realize that all other ideas are immature Etch A Sketch distortions of men who Jesus said *didn't actually know* the Father.

Each of us are free to decide what we personally believe, and I don't have an agenda to make you believe what I do. I am, however, passionate about sharing what my journey has revealed to me in the past 10 years, and even more so in the last 4 or 5. Anyone who knows me, knows I was a 'word man' and needed a Bible verse for anything I was expected to believe. I didn't just read the Bible, I devoured it. Not just one Bible, but shelves full of them. I explored every detail I could find in words, phrases, and scriptures in various concordances and Hebrew and Greek dictionaries. I studied varying tones and wording between the Aramaic (which Jesus spoke) and the common (koine) Greek of the New Testament. I had to see things for myself, and I just loved to study. I *once* had a great desire to be a Bible teacher, which I did *(I thought)* for many years. I now see the power of perception and extent to which one's own personal philosophy becomes a *life-lens* through which we see and relate to everything (not just scripture) all around us. I look back and realize how, in the institutional church, we were fitted with philosophical and doctrinal lenses; a pre-scribed view through which to see everything, *without us even knowing it.*

Around 2008, I read 'Destined to Reign' by Joseph Prince. Then I read it again, four times. I'll have to credit Pastor Prince with opening the gate on the stall for me to come out. There were things in that book about freedom from sin and condemnation that were far better and made more sense than anything I'd heard in my little Bible-Belt town. Boy when that gate swung open... I never looked back. Today, I'm not shy about telling you I don't believe much of anything about *God* (or myself) that I did back then. Any desire I had to belong to a specific group was superseded by my desire to know the truth. I just wanted spiritual things to actually make sense to me. I grew tired of being expected to believe or say certain things just because everyone around me did. I haven't heard Pastor Prince in many years; but I'll always be grateful for the courage I received from reading his book, and the permission I felt from within to no longer have to climb on and ride the local belief bus just because all my friends were on it.

From there I began to see many new and vital components of a contextual nature; yet no church I attended felt they were important enough to teach on. These are all things you can *and should* easily search out on your own. Also, this is **not** an indictment against the pastors and teachers in the churches (whom I love dearly) that didn't teach me these things. They were merely teaching us what was taught to them in the seminaries or denominational trainings they took part in. I've had some wonderful pastors with hearts that truly desired to love and help people. One in particular who I will always be grateful for is Pastor Bob Malone. Pastors Bob and Sandra were (and still are) more like parents to me than pastors in a pulpit. He would always encourage me (and the entire congregation) to never take his word for something just because we heard him say it. He told me more than once, to always dig in for myself and let the Spirit teach me; and if I ever saw something that ran counter to what he was teaching, to bring it back and share it with him as well. I can't say enough good things about this humble father figure in my life, and if anyone has ever encouraged me to never stop searching for truth, it was him.

So many times in church I heard people say that Jesus taught more on hell than he did on heaven. **Then I discovered that Jesus never once** **talked about hell.** *Not once.* **No one told me the very word and idea of hell had been blended into Christian schools of thought from Greek (Plato) philosophy, and were mythical stories not depicting literal or real places at all. Even then they didn't show up until** *hundreds of years after* **the establishment of the early church.**

The eternal torment doctrine we hear preached today is largely influenced by Tertullian and Augustinian beliefs. We can look back and see that within the span of just a few hundred years, things regarding 'Christianity' underwent quite a change from what it looked like among the first followers of Jesus. This *focus change* was further influenced and empowered by the Emperor Constantine during his reign (AD306-337), who declared Christianity to be a *legally sanctioned* religion in the Edict of Milan in AD313.

The first 7 ecumenical councils of the 'church' (please look it up for yourself) were convoked and presided over by *governing emperors*. In case you didn't know, these 'councils' were the men and meetings which decided the wording and statements of faith the church would be formed by, and, to a great extent, which letters would (or would not) make it into the 'official canon' we know as the Bible. Emperors and other forms of *govern*-ment are typically more concerned with levels (ranks) of certain people, or *exclusive groups* retaining power and control, than they are with an inclusive unity among people where love, forgiveness, and serving others is promoted as the highlight. With that being said, it's important to realize that Jesus had no desire whatsoever to be a lord, ruler, or a king; nor did he have any desire to start some new religion with his name on it. His desires and actions were simply to put the Father's heart on display; which included all humanity as One in love, forgiveness, and serving each other with joy. It was the Father's heart of love *to all* that Jesus openly revealed; effectively setting men free from all forms of fear-full religion, rituals, and govern-mental control that had held them in bondage so long.

I'll disappoint you here if you're expecting an exhaustive referential exposition listing the *who's who* of early church writers and their stances for, or against hell. I don't depend a lot on who wrote what in the past as the foundation for my own beliefs, especially about God. That's something I need to know in my own experience. If I don't know it for myself, then what others may have thought in days long past contains no tangible power to help me navigate life *in the now*.

While I can certainly appreciate the views of others in the past, I also realize people of that day were not exempt from personal veils and their own blurred vision of reality. I know there were a few who wrote things which *seem* to agree with the church's pet hell doctrine, yet I still hold that they were merely writing from a blurred vision of scriptural texts; taking something literally that was really meant to be seen in symbolic imagery. Even then, few they were, *as in a handful*; and should never be misconstrued as a majority, or even common.

The English word we know as *hell* was derived from Old English *hel*, or *helle*. It all went back to the roots of the mythological Norse goddess figure, and the underworld abode (with the same *hel* name) she was overseer of. After researching some easily found documented evidence for ourselves, things like this are no longer too surprising. We begin to discover that many of the stories we've been taught as having *literally* happened to the Jewish people, were actually ancient *mythological* stories embraced and passed on by other cultures which existed *long before* the Bible was ever written. We'll talk about a few of those later on; but let's stick to this idea of *hell* for now.

The ancient Jews had lifelong familiarity with the concept of *Sheol*, one of *four* (4) different words our Bibles translate as *hell*. To the Jews, *Sheol* didn't have anything to do with suffering or torment at all, but was simply a dark, still place where the departed went. While I can share verifiable historic facts with you- if someone *chooses* to believe in the judgment of God as a form of punishment or eternal torment, then nothing I (or anyone else) can say or write will change their minds. Only seeing the *Father's heart* for themselves can do that.

Augustine (AD 354-430) was the driving force behind the idea that all children are born with no choice but to carry the penalty of another man's (Adam's) sin. From *his opinion* he taught the practice of infant baptism; teaching that even though they had no personal sin acts of their own, they had *inherited* the condemnation of sin at birth. This idea was later morphed into a term we know as 'total depravity.' This *un*-godly term is used to describe an unavoidable inherent corruption every human is supposedly born with. Beliefs such as this are clearly the offspring of the same alien-ated *seed thought* that made Adam think he was naked (un-covered). It's amazingly sad that even today this distorted thinking (and doctrine formed from it) is still gobbled up hook, line, and sinker by people who don't know the truth of who they *really* are. Terms such as 'penal substitution,' and 'separation between God and man,' were also spawned from Augustine's writings.

Athanasius was also actively involved with certain power councils who promoted the idea of eternal torment, keeping it up on the table. While I'm no expert historian, I have spent some time reading certain documents and writings of Athanasius. From what I have read, it *appears* he was in a place of conflicting tension even within himself regarding eternal torment. In one place he gives the idea that (1) if man doesn't fall into line with his created purpose, his existence will then revert back to a state of nothingness from which it had first come. In yet another place, he appears to say man's soul was immortal and (2) would continue to exist in the same state of death and destruction he had chosen over becoming a reflector of God on earth. These ideas can be found woven within the first chapter of ON THE INCARNATION, written in AD 318 by Athanasius [AD 296/298-373] when he was around 20 years old. The backdrop of most of his writings (from what I've seen) infer that (3) mankind was completely separate from God. The only way they could have part with their divine Source was to believe and confess faith in Jesus; at which point, man would then be *allowed* to partake in communion with God. For the record, the back cover of this book should make it abundantly clear I don't believe *any* of those things; nor do I see it as what Jesus revealed to men at all.

The Athanasian Creed came on the scene around the 5th century and was venerated by the Roman Catholic Church, and also by certain Protestant churches as well. Although it was later revealed Athanasius didn't actually pen the creed himself; no one has ever argued that the creed's existence was undoubtedly formed from his core beliefs and the things he taught and wrote about. The creed ends with the words

"They that have done good shall go into life everlasting, and they that have done evil into everlasting fire. This is the Catholic Faith, which except a man believe faithfully and firmly, he cannot be saved."

I'm well aware these guys have many fans; and as the famous deep thinkers of their day, I also realize they're credited with doing some genuinely good things. I'm not trying to take away from those good things at all. I'm merely stating that their influential positions and beliefs helped to establish a *platform* of fear *which still exists* around these ideas of depraved identity and eternal torment. None of these ideas previously existed in the ancient, common Jewish culture.

These deep-thinking heavy hitters provided the core inspiration for many of the doctrines still embraced by the church today. Yet while some of those ideas may be considered as having knocked the ball out of the park in grand-slam victories- these guys also struck-out hard at some really important times. The teachings of inherited sin nature, total depravity, and a place of eternal torment (hell) where a loving Father would send his own offspring... was a *huge swing and a miss* that the church is *still* trying to rally back from today.

It saddens my heart that the centerpiece of Christianity has been reduced to a heaven OR hell message; where hell is always the starting point- as in, men are *definitely* bound for hell. Why? Because you deserve it. Well, technically not because *you* deserve it; but because *you were born* carrying the judgment sentence of some guy long ago, whose *spiritual death gene* was passed to all who came after him. *They* say it's written somewhere in the really blurry fine print. Now you didn't ask to come out of the womb. You were pushed, squeezed, and pulled out; and if you were especially stubborn, the doctor cut your mother open and forcefully took you out. *So much for free-will.*

This is where you'll need a pre-scripted lens supplied by a doctrinal interpreter to help you through this *really blurry* fine print. Someone will need to *system*atically explain how you were born with free-will; which basically means everything regarding your eternity boils down to your choice alone. Well, everything *except* those first couple details of your choice to come into the world to begin with; *and* your choice to be the recipient of some terminal death gene passed on to you through no fault of your own. This *spiritual death gene* carries a judge's verdict of you having to pay for some other guy's free-will who you, or your parents never even knew. It seems like a good place to ask; does this sound like the perfect workmanship of an all-providing, pro-visionary Source of life, light, love, and harmonious universal creation to you?

So, here *all* of us are, *born* with hell as our default destination. HELP! *Can someone pleeease que up some 'good' news?* Ok, wait! This same all-knowing perfect Source of love has now provided an *option* to keep you from having to bear this eternal fiery torment due you (through no choice of your own) from a passed down death sentence of some guy you, your parents, *or their parents* never even knew.

An alternate destination is now put on the map of possibilities for your life. It's a distant place called heaven; and whatever *hell* is... *heaven* is the exact opposite. Rather than an inescapable underworld crock-pot boiling with eternal torment, we now have another *option* of a place high above the world. This location is a lush paradise with gold streets, fruit trees, crystal-clear water, beautiful mansions, and people just like us. Our fuzzy math says we were born with this predisposed death gene, not intentionally doing *anything* to receive it; but we must be *totally intentional* about wanting to go to heaven. Yet someone still has to die. *Someone* has to pay to get all this recorded sin debt taken off the books. And besides, gold streets and mansions aren't cheap.

Before you get too excited, you should know this so-called *good news* comes with a disclaiming reminder: that even if you *do* make it to heaven, it won't be because you did *anything* good to get there. You could *never* deserve that. Remember, you were born inherently evil because of *some other guy's deed*, and all your 'good' combined won't amount to a hill of beans in the eyes of Judge Gawd. But hey- it's still good news, right? At least now someone else *besides you* will pay for all these damages. What relief! You won't end up in the fires of hell, but on the golden streets of a lush exclusive paradise called heaven!

But don't start celebrating just yet. Any good fire-insurance plan comes with premiums and fees you are responsible for up front. The policy fine print says these benefits are revocable and subject to being cancelled at any time in the event of a relational breach with your agent, brought about by negligence or misuse on your end. Herein lies the crux of our good news message. You always get the bad news up front, because apparently there has to be bad news *first*, before good news means anything. The bad news is- *you're going to hell*. Yet with the right insurance plan, you can obtain a new map which leads to heaven. BUT you have to stay on the right path along the way, or you'll get lost again (policy language calls it backslidden) and find yourself right back on the route to your original default location of hell. Oh sure, there are other benefits that come along with our acceptance of this fire-insurance plan, but the bottom line of our 'good news' is still (and always) that you were saved from hell, and saved to heaven.

In the grace and truth of heavenly reality, there's a much better bottom line which existed in the beginning. A foundational blueprint that reveals everything about the Architect's plan *as Good News*. It starts as we realize there's no gavel of legalities, or some formal desk plaque that reads JUDGE GAWD. His real name is Abba Father. He won't be found in some rule-keeping court case ending in conditional parole. This divine Source is known by the Fatherly love Jesus came to reveal.

That's Good News in itself, right? Yep- but it gets wayyy better. We see the intentionality of an unwaveringly passionate Father who will *always* refer men back to their authentic blueprint design. This plan isn't affected or altered by Adam's or *anyone else's* fall. It's based on an inheritance set into motion with this loving Father seeing *all* of his creation holy and blameless in love. A love that no life or death, angels or demons, heights or depths, nothing past, present, nor any future thing can ever separate us from. In fact, through the Father's eyes, mankind is the self-image extended BEing of who this Father is and all he has! This loving paternal Source has never been caught in some disgruntled dilemma over what to do with an *un-rule-y* offspring.

Quantum

Authentic blueprint disyn!

Jesus was the express image revealing this Father who saw the love of his heart wandering off in an orphaned mentality. They totally miss the mark of their true identity; *and this Father comes after them.* He'll leave the 99 who know who they are, to come after the one who doesn't- searching every nook and cranny until they're pulled from an orphaned pigpen mire to fully participate in what's rightfully theirs.

Man's vain imagination has skewed the reality of what free-will actually is. *Yes,* we've been given much power in making individual (choose this day) choices; things we will *or won't* participate in on a *daily* basis. *Yes,* these choices can effectively create an environment around us which reflects certain aspects and imagery of heaven or *hell.* Yet our ability to make free daily choices never has, and *never will* include the power to change the Father's authentic and eternal design of how he sees us. God has never changed his mind about man. *Man changed his mind about God.* Man forgot who he was; and **when men don't know who they are... they'll live like who they're not.** Jesus lived to renew man's thinking to Christ-mind truth of who they really were; and how to live like the offspring BEings the Father had seen them as all along. THAT'S the unadulterated Good News.

Truth doesn't need bad news first to make it beautiful. This is the Good News of our authentic *born from above genesis.* It's where we finally begin to see that our hellacious eternal torment doctrine was never anything more than the twisted imaginations of man that were all built around fictitious places of ancient mythology and lore.

So, how did hell find its way into our Bibles? While early Latin Catholics weren't literally *forbidden* to own a Bible, they were *strongly persuaded* not to possess a Bible that wasn't properly authorized by Latin Catholic rulers. Furthermore, while they were not forbidden to read the Bible, they were *strongly influenced* to limit their reading to official papal mass only. There, priests could 'properly interpret' the details of scriptures they were told they couldn't understand on their own. God has never done *anything* that wasn't meant to be enjoyed by all men and women without others having to explain it to them.

Our actions create reality!

I don't personally own a Latin Vulgate Bible (AD 400), but most of the information I find agrees *hell* was translated into the scriptures within it over 100 times; and was then followed by the 1611 King James (English translation) Bible with around 54 times.

Hell isn't the only word or idea that was *engineered* into scripture by translators. The idea of repentance (in the tone we've been taught) didn't exist in Jesus' day or in early church thinking. The original word was *metánoia*; which simply meant changing one's mind- a shift, or a turning in one's thinking. In the Latin Vulgate however (and from there forward), the original *turning* idea of metanoia morphed into an entirely new *work* role. The Vulgate changed metánoia to *paenitentia*; which means penance or *acts* of penance which must be proven if one hopes to obtain grace. It also carries a tone of fear and retribution, as in a looming punishment. It's where the word *penitentiary* originates.

This distorted idea of re-penance, or re-turning regularly to bring confessions and offerings to obtain grace, continued right up to what is taught in most churches today. If something must first be done or believed to obtain grace, then what is given in return has nothing to do with grace at all. It is merely required religious *reciprocation*. It's no different than the Old Testament Jews bringing approach offerings to the priest to *then* obtain forgiveness. While we may find *metanoia* in our concordances, the tone though which it gets taught today usually carries the same fear and reciprocating requirements of *paenitentia*.

When we know a little bit of actual history, and aren't afraid to accept it honestly for what is really is, we begin to recognize certain workings of exclusive power and control put into place which hold people in the grip of *fear*. When fear is instilled *into* people with ideas of looming judgment, along with a physical place of eternal torment specifically prepared for those who don't 'get it right'- it establishes a fear-based platform to work from. It won't matter that such a place of torment doesn't *actually* exist. The people will create it in their own imaginations, *especially* if you borrow a few ideas and images from ancient Greek mythology and/or Renaissance art, while intentionally keeping them from understanding scripture on their own. From this fear-based platform, people were taught that in order to avoid this looming judgement, they needed to *regularly* do specific things. These things came in the form of re-turning, re-penance, paying tithes and offerings, along with other varying forms of *self-sacrifice*. Oh, and it never hurts (to help keep fear activated in their minds) to make sure they only possess a so-called *authorized* Bible version that says what you want it to say, just in case they do decide to read it for themselves.

That's pretty much the core workings of the institutional machine. Just keep fear-based ideas up on the table and in the people's minds; and the fear will systematically do everything else on its own. Innocent people will line up to voluntarily participate. Who wouldn't volunteer to do something to keep from going to eternal torment?? Not only does this platform help control the masses by keeping them bound to fear; it will also assure them bringing the financial fuel to keep this industrial machine of sin-consciousness in perpetual motion. This self-sustaining platform of fear worked well for Constantine and all the other emperors. It worked well for Latin Catholic power leaders. It worked well for King James. Unfortunately, it's still working among us to fearfully control people today.

Again, this is not an indictment or accusation toward those involved in ministry. I don't personally know anyone who purposely or maliciously tricks people into bondage. I do however, know many wonderful people who have passionately devoted their entire life to teaching certain doctrines because they (just like I was) have been taught to believe and teach them with their whole heart. Some of you know what I'm talking about. Not only did we have fear and bondage instilled in us from youth; we grew up unconsciously guarding and maintaining the very chains which held us in that bondage. We did it because we believed (because we were taught) *that it was good for us.*

As our eyes become open to actual facts and historical truth, we begin to see we were unknowingly domesticated into the mechanical workings of an institution of control. One that makes you *think* you're doing something that God wants or has required. For many years, I was in the boiler room of this mechanical mindset with a full steam ahead attitude. No one taught us that the very idea of *hell* came from an origin describing a *mythical* god and *fictional* place of domain; and would have never been uttered in the Aramaic thoughts or language which Jesus spoke. No one told me that the many times our trusted *authorized* King James translation referred to hell, describing four (4) completely different words, that the actual context and subject matter of those scriptures had *absolutely nothing* to do with what we've been taught was a place of eternal conscious torment. $\smile$hco$\int$

Let's look at these 4 words. (1) *Sheol*, used in the Old Testament, was merely the Hebrew word for the underworld or *unseen* realm of the dead where departed spirits went. **Remember the word *un-seen*; it will be beneficial just a little later on.** *Sheol* was understood to be a place of *stillness* and *darkness*- with no hint of punishment or torment whatsoever. Let's look at a few scriptures that use it:

Genesis 37:35 (NKJV)

And all his sons and all his daughters arose to comfort him; but he refused to be comforted, and he said, "For I shall go down into the grave *(Sheol)* to my son in mourning." Thus his father wept for him.

Was Jacob implying that Joseph was in hell, or eternal torment? Not at all. He was merely using *their* terminology describing cultural beliefs of *their* day regarding a place where departed spirits went after death. A place which had *no ties to punishment or reward* in any way.

Psalms 88:1-4 (NKJV)

O LORD, God of my salvation, I have cried out day and night before You. Let my prayer come before You; Incline Your ear to my cry. For my soul is full of troubles, and my life draws near to *(Sheol)* the grave. I am counted with those who go down to the pit; I am like a man who has no strength.

This is one of the songs of the sons of Korah, woven into various places in the Psalms. It's a *blues song* based on the cries of a man who feels *his perceived* God has deserted him- *even after* he has cried out day and night without receiving *any* help. Is he talking about going to *hell* or eternal torment? Not at all. His lyrics merely describe a worn and weary soul who sees himself as *having been in hell* on earth too long already. He's without hope, strength, or any forward vision. The whole song is a *woe is me* lament of a guy whose eyes are now on the grave; with death being the only relief he will find from a cruel world.

The word 'pit' simply means a hole bored or dug in the ground. Language of 'being swallowed up by the pit,' 'cast down into utter darkness,' or 'cut off from the land of the living,' merely described physical death and the grave or tomb in which the body was buried. It carried no tone of recompense *or* retribution other than physical death itself, *even when it was applied to those seen as God's enemies.*

Psalm 138 7-8 (NKJV)

Where can I go from Your Spirit? Or where can I flee from Your presence? If I ascend into heaven, You are there; If I make my bed in hell *(Sheol)*, behold, You are there.

How could David *make a bed* in a place of eternal torment where there was no rest and people suffered endlessly in flames that never ceased? It's not what David was saying because that's NOT what *Sheol* means. David wasn't singing a *blues brothers* tune. He was meditating on the goodness of *his perceived* God until it exploded from him in adoration! Even if David started a Psalm with a blues line- it would end up in joyful praise before it was over. Just a little *soul inspection (how could you even consider being downcast?)* would soon have him shouting about the God *he knew* who faithfully delivered him from darkness, lions, and facing life's giants. Here, David is simply stating that NOTHING from the starry skies to the depths of the sea, or even the darkened pit of the grave... *could ever separate him from his God!*

Have you ever wondered why God didn't make a point to tell Adam and Eve if they ate from the wrong tree, they would be punished with eternal torment? Does it seem just a little odd that even the law Moses gave the people, *never once* mentioned eternal punishment for those who didn't keep it? I mean if God *really* hated all those people the way Old Testament writers said he did, and he sent his 'armies' to brutally mutilate and murder them in cold blood... wouldn't they have been prime candidates to be made examples of with them being cast into this unquenchable fire of eternal torment? Yet there's no mention whatsoever of any such fate awaiting them. Why? Because a physical location of *hell* or a place of eternal torment wasn't something the Hebrew language described or the Jewish people believed.

HADES

The word (2) *Hades*, also translated in the KJV as hell, is a Greek counterpart of the Hebrew word Sheol. *Hades* however, had many additional attachments to Greek mythology and beliefs of imagined places, things, or beings, *which don't actually exist*. Let's take a few moments to explore the reality of this word apart from how it's been distortedly misused by our translators and from our pulpits.

Earlier I asked you to remember the word *un-seen*, as we looked at the word *Sheol*. The word hades, or *hádēs*, is made up of 2 parts. The 1st part *(ha)* is a negative participle which means *no/not;* with the next part being *idein/eidō*, which means *to see*. This is how our friends at Biblehub.com show it in their HELPS Word-studies section;

hádēs (from 1 /A 'not' and *idein/eidō*, 'see')- properly, the 'unseen place,' referring to the (invisible) realm in which all dead reside; the present dwelling place of all the departed (deceased); *Hades*.

Does it seem odd to you that there's absolutely no tone or mention of punishment/torment in the *actual meaning* of a word translators decided to *engineer* into describing eternal conscious torment or *hell*?

The word *hádēs* simply means *not* to see, or the *un*-seen.
Keeping this true definition in mind, allow me to re-highlight some things we've already looked at, as well as a few others which then fall into place to help us better understand how this word was actually intended and *originally* used.

Man, long ago forgot who he truly was. It wasn't God who forgot... *it was man.* Even though man stopped *seeing* the truth about himself, God never stopped *seeing* the authentic blueprint origin of man's life. Man began to see himself as *alienated* from his Source; an alienation which Paul said in Colossians 1:21, only existed in man's mind. Seeing himself now as an orphaned alien, man then begins to blame God as *well as others-* creating a stage production of false life in the distorted imagination of his mind. *Man was lost.* Veiled and scaled perceptions had him chasing ways that *seemed* right, which only led to dead-end results with no clear vision of his authentic *born from above* life.

Man's perishing mindset begins to bear *offspring* fruit of its own thinking. Evil (worthless) thoughts morphed into worthless, wicked deeds. This deceived state of orphaned thinking *re-seeded itself* over and over through many generations until Jeremiah said the following:

Jeremiah 17:9 NASB
The heart is more *deceitful* than all else and is desperately sick; Who can understand it?

The word *deceit* means **the act of accepting, or causing someone to *accept* as true or valid, what is false or invalid.** Man had accepted as true and valid *in his own mind*, that which was false and invalid in the mind and logic of God. This veiled distortion had spiraled so far out of control that man no longer even resembled the blueprint image he'd been patterned from. Man's heart was deceit-full and desperately sick. Jesus came to destroy the *satanâs* accusation that started it all in man's mind; not as a judge to condemn, *but as a physician to heal.*

The Son of Man came in the Jew's darkened state revealing the true Light and Life of every man coming into the world. Yet through veiled eyes they had no comprehension of (could not see) what he was trying to show them. He came to his own; not only as a Jew, but as One who was like his brethren *in all ways*- yet they received (recognized) him not. They had dwelt in their self-made condemnation and darkness for so long it had taken their affection and energy captive. That energy was now being used for worthless works of evil, rather than producing the good fruit their true inner workmanship was designed for.

One day, Jesus had asked his disciples, "Who do YOU say I AM?" Simon Peter recognized THE CHRIST in Jesus and *expressed* it out loud. The comments of Jesus to Peter following this revelation were among the most gratifying, exuberant words the Son of Man ever spoke while on earth! Jesus passionately tells Peter (imagine Jesus grabbing his shoulders with great excitement) that none of their earthly *flesh and blood* fathers could have revealed this enChristed truth to him, but only his true heavenly Source. No one was more excited about this epic moment than Jesus! Finally- *other sons of men* were beginning to see the Light of what Jesus so passionately desired to show them!

Peter discovers the Father that Jesus had been talking about all this time, was the SAME Father that gave HIM this understanding from above! Jesus, with an ear to ear smile and tears of joy, tells Peter this revelation which he'd heard from his true heavenly Father, was the foundational truth upon which the entire *ekklésia* would be supported.

What did Peter recognize in Jesus? THE CHRIST. What is the true *ekklésia*? Not the *church*, as in a man-made institution run by boards on a business model. *Ekklésia* is made of 2 parts. *Ek* is a preposition *always* denoting origin- as in, *coming out of, or expressed from*- and *klesia*, from *kaléō*, which means a *validated surname identity*.

Jesus then tells Peter that men finally being able *to see* they were ALL called with/from the same enChristed surname Jesus was, would ensure the restrictive gates of *hádēs* (their darkened inability to see) would never again be able to prevail over them or hold them back!

Ek
&

Ekklesia — Coming out of —
Identity —

Scriptures about death and *hádēs* being cast into the lake of fire (*pýr* #4442) have absolutely nothing to do with punishment; but are written in the REVELATION OF THE CHRIST describing every darkened *satanâs* accusation of man's separation from God, as being *purified* and cleansed from their consciousness. This isn't describing a future sci-fi event with a literal person called the 'anti-Christ' in some last day's epic battle. It is purely *symbolic imagery* depicting the cleansing of people's *anti*-Christ mentality and them *not being able to see who they were*. It resulted in them being released (once for all) from the fear of death which all their lifetime kept them *subjects* of bondage. We'll look closer at this pýr-i-fying, consuming fire in a later chapter.

Tartarus—

(3) *Tartarus* is the third word the King James translates as hell, appearing just one time in 2 Peter 2:4. In *Greek mythology*, Tartarus was a deep abyss used as a dungeon of torment and suffering for the wicked, and was a prison for the Titans. Tartarus is the *mythical* place where, according to Plato's Gorgias (c.380-400 BC), souls were judged after death and the wicked then received divine punishment. Tartarus, according to Homer, was a deep and sunless abyss, as far below Hades as the earth is below heaven, and was closed in by iron gates. We weren't taught that many of the things and ideas spoken of in scripture had been blended in from other cultures *and myths* along the way.

Our teachings didn't include the fact that every instance (12 times) our King James *inspired* translations have Jesus talking about a place called *hell*, he was actually talking about (4) *Gehenna*. He used the word Gehenna *because he was talking about a literal place*. Gehenna was in the Valley of Hinnom; a place which still exists to this very day, and is explored by thousands of tourists each year. Gehenna could be clearly seen from many of the sites where Jesus' recorded teachings took place. It was the former site where rebellious Israelites burned their own children as sacrifices to honor the Canaanite fire god, Molech. *Read that last sentence again*. The children of Israel had a way of life that revolved around killing, blood, sacrifices, and other forms of tribal rituals and fire. Those ideas didn't come from God either; they came from pagan ideas of many other cultures that had been absorbed and blended in with the Israelite's belief system along the way. We'll talk more about that later. It's also interesting to note Jeremiah (19:5) wrote regarding human sacrifices to Baal, that **God said burning humans was a despicable deed, and the thought or idea of doing such a thing would never enter his mind!**

Now, one can find certain articles telling us that Gehenna was a trash dump where flames burned continually day and night. According to these articles, dead bodies were regularly cast into this dump, and worms (maggots) fed upon the corpses. So, when Jesus talked about Gehenna, he was possibly gesturing toward the visible smoke with his hands while talking about the fake righteousness of the Pharisees. He could have been saying their equity, or *righteousness,* was like that of a smoldering trash heap- like fancy painted tombs full of dead men's bones. Jesus could have possibly been pointing toward this dump as he warned his listeners if they didn't flee Jerusalem to be saved from the coming destruction, they would perish and their bodies would be thrown into the fires of Gehenna. This has been said to have actually happened to those who didn't heed his warnings to flee. *Other* articles can also be found implying that there is no tangible evidence *today* (2000 years later) which can conclusively substantiate this supposed burning dump, or it being filled with mass amounts of bodies.

Throughout this book I will often remind you that my goal is not convincing you to believe the things that I do. My goal is to prompt you to think and search things out for yourself, so you will know *what* you believe, and more importantly, *why* you believe it. As I said in my introduction, everything that has ever been written about God, has come about from someone else's ideas and opinions *about* 'God'. You may not particularly like that thought, but that doesn't change its validity. Perhaps you have never considered it. The Source of all life has never written *anything* with pen and paper, nor is Jesus shown writing anything, other than *reportedly* with his finger on the ground.

What has been *written* by God, is in the DNA of humanity and the meticulously interwoven design of all creation around us. Paul said men were the living epistles of THE CHRIST, not written with ink, but with the Spirit of the living *God*. Not engraved on stone or parchment, but *embedded* in the deepest matrix of man's own heart and being.

I don't require tangible physical evidence (today) of a dump that existed in Jerusalem (2000 years ago) to form my beliefs about *hell*. I don't need substantiated burial evidence for the vast amount of people slaughtered when Jerusalem was destroyed, to decide what I believe (today) about hell. Depending on whose *opinion* you read, you will find estimates of anywhere from 100,000 people, to 600,000 people, all the way up to the 1.1 million people estimated by Josephus, who was a popular, respected historian who lived in that day. Whichever number you decide to go with, it's a LOT of corpses that were obviously *left behind somewhere* within the limited amount of acreage which comprised the area of Jerusalem back in those days.

Jeremiah wrote (7:31-33) that God told him the entire valley would become like a cemetery that would no longer be called Tophet, or the Valley of the Son of Hinnom; but would be called 'Valley of Slaughter.' He wrote that bodies would be buried *until there was no more room*; and the left-over corpses would be food for the beasts and the birds.

Again, I don't need that evidence to *not* believe in hell. There isn't anything in me that remotely believes the idea of some place of eternal conscious torment *or annihilation* coming from the passionate design of our heavenly Source. To believe in hell, or even the slightest idea such a fear-full tormenting place could be conceived by the Source of divine love, is intrinsically opposite of love itself. It is diametrically opposed to the Father's all-inclusive heart, and the expressed image life that Jesus lived and shared with every person around him.

We've taken words and phrases written in scriptures which Jesus spoke, that we didn't, *and still don't* understand, and used them to fear-fully warn people of what God was *going to do* to mankind one day in the future if they didn't live or *believe right*. We're so wrapped up in our judgement doctrines (consuming our thoughts and actions) that we cruise right past the actual evidence of what God in Christ *did do*, to, and for humanity while Jesus was on earth! We skip right over the places where Jesus plainly said *"I didn't come to judge the world"*; and *"I only do what I see my Father do."* We've basically ignored all the times that Jesus *could have* judged someone according to the law of Moses, but instead did something completely *opposite* of the law. Jesus revealed the Father's love; a perfect love of inclusion that the rule-keeping, blood-sacrificing, judgement-minded religious elite of *that age* didn't have a clue what to do with.

I don't think about hell at all, other than when I see the obvious torment in people's minds and the landscape of their current life even *today* as a result of the fear *taught by men*. I don't think about 'sin' anymore. *Ever.* I know the true meaning of sin isn't even close to what we've been taught. That doesn't mean I don't recognize that I have faults and failures like everyone else. It means I know there isn't some distant deity keeping track of them somewhere, *and there never was.* Nor does the Source of Life require something or someone to *first die* to justify what we've distortedly viewed as 'forgiveness.' *Sin*, in true form, is simply living from an orphaned mind, missing the authentic goal of extended *divine* offspring, and the *intimacy* it brings with it.

*Transfor*mation is an ability divinely instilled within us all. It has a life-changing, fruit-bearing effect that takes place as we learn to *morph* out of *flesh* awareness into higher *Spirit* consciousness in life. It isn't about *becoming* something else *or* another person at all. Paul wrote about it to the Romans (12:2). It's peeling away (un-con*form*ing) our association with ideas and imaginations confined in the traditions of men. These contain ways that *seem* right to man's mind... but never held any *real* life at all. It means that as I get all of man's traditions (*skubala* as Paul called it) out of my thinking (along with redundant rituals and practices), I will learn to live and thrive in the true equity and wholeness (righteousness and joyful peace) which was originally deposited as Light treasure in my earthen vessel to begin with!

I don't start my day (or end it) wondering if my life is *pleasing* to God. God was pleased at the first thought of expressing beautiful and unique attributes of the divine nature through me (and you) as One! Nothing can ever change that. I don't wonder if I'm doing enough to serve a kingdom yet to come. I'm no longer trying to get anyone *saved* or convince them to believe like I do. I *now* know the only thing we need saved from is our own *vain* imaginations and every distorted implication that we're not *already* carriers of divine treasure. It's sad that this alienated, orphaned mindset of separation, and teachings of broken fellowship, still run rampant in the church (of all places) today.

The very premise of this book, *Born from Above*, is that you, and I, and all mankind, were created in the original passionate pleasure of a paternal Source! It's where *real life* is eternally hidden IN enChristed glory; holy and irrevocably blameless, with every blessing heaven has, *already* within us. And I get to share this amazing goodness (and I do) with every single person that comes into the zone of my life! There's *no hell* in my life, because there's NO HELL in the life of my Father!

For many years, I didn't know there was such a thing as Young's Literal Translation, or the Concordant Literal New Testament, which never use the word hell a single time. I also didn't know that most all the other popular translations had followed in the footsteps of King James ideas. Even though they had different names, publishers, and a few word or phrase changes, they weren't actually *original* at all. Furthermore, I had no idea how many other (at least 28) translations existed, *some dating back to the 1700's*, that never once mention the word *hell*, or any of the ideas of eternal torment we associate with it.
These many misunderstandings, coupled with twisted views of the book of the Revelation of Christ (drastically skewed through already existing distortions), have us believing and teaching things *about God* that are as far from the truth of the Father's heart as one can get. Death and Hades being cast into the lake of fire (Revelation 20:14-15) was never about *people* being cast into fire- something God said was a despicable thought that would never even enter his mind. These same

distorted mindsets and man's vain, mythical imaginations have kept us in self-created tombs of darkness, wearing foreign grave-clothes that carry the stench of death, which never belonged to men to begin with! What's *metaphorically* burned up in this *pýr* (fire) sulphur lake, is the realm of the unknown (hádēs) in man's mind, which is *opposite* of the truth of God's original logos blueprint for men. This *purification* process is where people of *that* age began waking up, as unveiled eyes now saw the REVELATION OF THE CHRIST. The dross of their distortions of fear and death was *burned up* as they beheld the treasured equity and divine inner *érgon* works within every man, woman, and child!

This is why Jesus told Simon Peter his REVELATION of the Living Christ- **the truth that all sons of men could hear and enjoy intimate Oneness with the heavenly Father,** was a truth so power-full that the gates of hádēs (realm of the unknown and any association with death) would never again prevail against it! No longer could any boundary, gate, or resistance hold man in bondage to mythical imaginations or darkened realms of *unknown* truth! *NO illusion in Christ mind.*

As we turn to this Christ-life *as* our own inner Source, our veils of distortion are also consumed. Our personal 'revelation' of the Christ now reveals GOD IN US; the INCARNATE EXTENSION of the divine dwelling in temples not made with hands. The purified clarity of this REVEALING will always show us we are *recognized and known* as One. When will we see and know it? Every time we look in the mirror! No longer will the darkness of hádēs prevail in our lives. We'll never again walk away from the mirror *not seeing,* or forgetting what manner of men and women we are! Never again will we forget our authentic genesis! We will always know and partake of, actively participating in, the divine nature we're born of and carry within us. *"In that day you will know* I AM *in my Father,* you ARE *in me, and* I AM *in you. One."*

If we choose to research the actual origins of these mythical words and places for ourselves, the truth is plentiful. If we choose to believe in a *God* who created a place of eternal torment that his own creation (those who don't believe, say, and do things as we do) will be cast into, then that's an opinion we will have to live *out of* every single day. This particular belief however, always has and always will bear the fruit of an exclusionary *us and them* landscape. *Look around us.* This tribal mentality isn't a lot different than the ways of our ancient brothers and sisters; a distorted *philosophy* of life Jesus gave *his life* to lovingly rescue them from. It's also important to realize that no matter how we dress it up and sugar coat it with our *love glaze wording*, if such a place had truly been created for the purpose of tormenting humanity (or even *angels*), it would stand in complete opposition to the divine perfect love given to cast out all fear. Fear always involves torment; and *there is no torment whatsoever...* in love.

Jesus didn't say "Give your offender 490 chances and then cast 'em into the fire." He said, "Never stop forgiving your brother." Jesus knew his disciples would eventually realize that forgiveness was merely the precursor to taking no offense at all. I find it amusing I ever believed I could 'offend' *God*. David said (Psalm 139:13-16) that God formed each wonderful and marvelous detail of our inner workings. The Hebrew language actually implies that God BEcame man.

When James and John (Jesus called sons of thunder) asked if they could call down fire (like Elijah) on those who didn't look like them, Jesus replied "You don't realize what Spirit you're born of; if you did, you'd know I and the Father love giving life... not destroying it!" When Paul said 'Love keeps no record of wrong,' he wasn't describing a trait God was exempt from, as though we were told "Do as I say, not as I do." Our signs and tracts are sugar-coated with good-news images of Jesus; while the **fine print of our underlying message** says- if we don't do certain things to *prove* we believe this good news- Jesus' Father will torment us in hell *forever.* I weep at any thought that I ever remotely believed such distortion. I *know* better now. The idea there had to be bad news first (hell) so we might have an *option* to receive 'good news' to make a 'choice' to go to *heaven* instead, is just another big steaming pile of manmade skubala. The Father's love and goodness isn't reliant on bad news *first* to manifest or substantiate heavenly goodness to all.

Teaching a child or *anyone* that the Source of divine love which they are the very extension of, will cast them into eternal torment *unless* they adhere to a certain set of beliefs (along with ongoing hoops they must then jump through the rest of their life), is nothing short of *terror*-ism. In effect, we have subjected our children to life-sentences in a mental concentration camp, where this looming fear always lurks in the backdrop of their thoughts and activities. We've taken parables and scriptures which due to our own blindness we didn't understand; pointing toward them as supposed substantiation for our terroristic backdrop, *not having a clue what we were doing.*

When Jesus uttered *"Forgive them Father, they know not what they do"* hanging on the cross, he wasn't asking God to stop counting man's sins or wipe some divine accounting slate clean. He used the word (*aphíēmi* #863), which means 'send away,' or 'release,' as in pushing away or putting distance in between. Of course, we've used the word how we wanted to support our doctrines, but the original essence could be described like *releasing* ropes that were binding a ship in a *foreign* harbor of confinement so it could be pushed away or separated from the dock, and *set free to sail in its intended function.*

Jesus is placed on the cross between two criminals by the rulers of that day, who also saw *him* as a rebellious (criminal) threat to their institutional powerhouse. Here, in the midst of his own (voluntary) torture and murder, he agrees with the Father's heart to bring men out of their darkness and *set them free* to the enjoy their authentic life of enChristed design. It was this same fearful mindset of alienation and blame that originally spiraled Adam (man-kind) off into a laborious perishing existence; which now drove these power-hungry religious and government leaders to place Jesus in between two criminals to die along with them. It was here, as this alienated darkness now covered the *earth*, this Son of Man echoes the Father's love when he cries out; **"Set them free from their bondage to fear and death... for they don't have a clue what they're doing!"**

As 3rd John 4 says, I also say: "I have no greater joy than knowing my children walk in truth." It gives me great comfort in knowing I lived long enough to apologize to my first daughter, Lea, for ever teaching her *anything* resembling these ideas in any way or form. And I'll never apologize for being passionate about *all* my children knowing there's no such thing as *hell* or some God-created place of torment. **Man alone creates it; and then man lives in it-*from his own mind*.**

My heart leaps with gratitude knowing that our children's *children* won't to be need *untrained* as we have from these fear-based fables. They won't have to peel away all the layered grave-clothes *we wore* through some guilt-ridden system of scheduled returning, trying to draw near to God, and striving through futile attempts to attain a level of intimacy and Oneness *that was ours all along*. Generations to come won't have to weed through these religious cul-de-sac 'God theories' of man; nor will they be held captive listening to distorted *turn or burn* doctrines twisted in among the Good News of the Father's love.

But hell is only one among many other fear theories...

Jesus spent much time and effort warning people around Jerusalem of the impending destruction he knew was about to come *in their day*. Without understanding this *up front*, his words can be misconstrued to form an image of something which has no validity or truth in our present reality *or* our future. Along with Jesus' desire to redeem their mindset (to save *that* which was lost), he also often used words like *save, perish*, and *destruction*. He used them in his warnings for them to be aware and prepared- *in order to be saved* from the destruction he knew was coming. Because we weren't taught these vital time-line details (at least I wasn't), Jesus' warnings were twisted into futuristic sci-fi imagery. As a result, we've been filled with fear-full cataclysmic imagery of things supposedly coming in *our day* or the future; rather than the contextual reality of what Jesus said *would happen in theirs*.

These *last days* warnings spoken by Jesus, are seen in the apostle's letters that followed, right up to Jerusalem's destruction in AD 70. Jesus wasn't *just* warning people in an effort to *literally* save their lives. He was also declaring the last days of a worthless mechanical system that bound his people to repetitive rituals and blood sacrifices they'd been taught were necessary to appease a distant record-keeping deity. Jesus was announcing a new day where man's mental bondage of *sin-consciousness* would be eradicated from their thinking. When we read scriptures about the *last days*, it's vital we view them in the proper context of those immediate days leading up to this climactic event. These warnings were about *their* last days. They had absolutely nothing to do with our current days, or any days in the future. In our misplaced attempts to bring an ancient Jewish reality into our own, we've actually fed and nurtured a mindset and life of futile traditions, rituals, and *ideas* of sacrifice that Jesus desired to set them free from.

We continue to perpetuate immaturity and exclusion through our stiff-necked, non-sensical doctrines, like not allowing women to teach or hold offices of authority in the church. Why? Because we latched on to the ideas of an *ancient* culture having absolutely nothing to do with our own. These blatant misunderstandings and stubborn refusals to move away from powerless traditions, have caused much unnecessary fear about things *that aren't even real*. It's how we've ended up with fictional books and movies about people being left behind, and others about blood moons and divine judgments coming upon people in our day and time. We've taken symbolically coded language they wrote in, and because we didn't understand it, we've morphed it into all kinds of fictitious events, along with some sinister superpower bad-guy and his band of evil culprits that are supposedly always out to get us.

We were taught the idea of *one being taken and another left* was describing a future secret *rapture*. In historical reality, these warnings have absolutely nothing to do with some futuristic event of Christians being covertly *snatched away* from the earth; but clearly describe a past-tense event having already occurred during *the great tribulation*.

Jesus said there would be certain *signs* providing a last-days alarm for the inhabitants of Judea to flee for the surrounding mountains and not look back. This is when the armies of Titus would seize Jerusalem and destroy it. Jesus warned people it wouldn't matter if they were *sleeping* in bed, *working* the field, *grinding* grain or *nursing* the baby; the destruction *was coming-* and would be swift and sure. When that time came, there would be *some* immediately killed with their bodies **left** on the scene; while *others* would be **taken** into captivity and made slaves of by the armies of Titus... *which is exactly what happened.*

The idea of a secret rapture also turns out to be another of man's more recent 'dreamed-up' imaginations; constructed from quilt-work snippets of misconstrued scriptures woven together in our immature doctrinal scribblings. Neither the Jews nor the early church believed or taught such a thing; and only during the 19th century (mid 1800's) did it surface in man's thinking. This idea of a covert *snatching away* was then picked up by C.I. Scofield, the former attorney/politician turned minister, theologian, and writer. Scofield is famous for his annotated Bible and commentaries which popularized the ideas of *futurism* and *dispensationalism* among fundamentalist Christians.

Later on, ideas such as this were embraced and inflated by a few other energetic preachers and authors who wrote books about blood moons and other pending judgments of gloom and doom. Not one of these so-called 'prophecies' of divine judgment has *ever* occurred as predicted. That, however, didn't deter further fear-based books and C-grade movies depicting empty clothes, vacant crashing cars, and co-worker scenes where one person disappears, while another is left behind during a dramatic *snatching away* to club Christian paradise.

Jesus never taught men about leaving the *world* for some distant location called heaven. In John 17:15 he actually prayed the opposite (more on this in the next chapter). Jesus taught the disciples to pray for the earth to be *heavenly*. He taught of an inner provision already within them, which was like an entire kingdom of *light treasure* they could actively release as days of *heaven* upon the earth.

We were taught that passages about the sky rolling up, mountains being removed, the sun being darkened, and stars falling from their place, described some science fiction scene of the world coming to an end. These were merely symbolic imageries depicting the downfall and overthrow of governments and religious powers. Within this downfall, would also be the end of an institutional machine fabricated by human hands; a profiting cover-up system that kept common people in fear and bondage. It had become a lucrative business manipulating people and *conveniently* supplying them with *fee-based* approach offerings every time they returned and were told they needed to appease God.

We learned the term *weeping and gnashing of teeth* had to do with those thrown into hell and eternal torment. I later saw it had nothing to do with those things, and was a term often applied to rebellious physical responses of stiff-necked religious types. They had *no desire* to hear the truth, and would become angry when confronted with it. The term reflects actions of a vicious animal about to attack because it feels threatened. There are at least five times recorded in scripture where the religious leaders were so threatened by Jesus, that they openly sought to destroy him (Matthew 12:14), throw him off a cliff (Luke 4:29), or stone him (John 10:31).

The Pharisees were known for deep-rooted anger toward Jesus; yet common people saw he taught with a genuine love and authority much different than the institutional elite. But nothing made the religious leaders angrier than when Jesus claimed he was *One* with God. Jesus said (John 14:20) this was a heavenly truth that all men would one day wake up to realize and *know within*; that they were also *One* with God, the *same way* the Son of Man was. It's a truth that still causes some teeth gnashing anger among certain groups of people even today.

A clear example of this (please read it for yourself) is in Acts 7:1-60. Stephen is about to be stoned by the holier than thou power-players. But before they kill him, he releases a string of truth bombs about their culture all the way back to Abraham, *not holding anything back*! Stephen reminds them of the tribal views of their fathers, intent on keeping holiness confined to a tabernacle, when God actually dwelled in *human* temples alone. Stephen said everything these stone holders did was in *opposition* to the Spirit of God- the same way their fathers had before them. Verse 54 says 'they were cut to the heart, becoming so furious at him that they began *gnashing at him with their teeth.*'

These exclusive system leaders were threatened by the Christ-mind truth which set people free from religious rules, regulations, yokes, and bondages, rather than keeping them oppressed by them. In the seven times this *weeping and gnashing* term is used, it reveals certain ones who thought they 'looked the part' and had worked their way into special celebratory events such as feasts or weddings. Yet each time, they're exposed (even thrown out) as being far from the love-core and heart needed to *genuinely participate* and take part in the festivities. They are described as hissing and growling with anger *outside,* while others lovingly shared in the festivities of an inclusive joy-full event.

The older brother in the prodigal son story is a good example of such record-keeping finger pointing. They're focused on themselves so much they'll choose to stay outside alone grumbling in anger, rather than enjoying a heart of unity and celebration with others. Jesus told the Pharisee's the very people they called sinners, ill-reputed hookers, outcasts, and drunkards, were entering this kingdom celebration *like* sons and daughters coming home, right before their eyes. He said these religious finger-pointers chose not to enter in themselves; even cramping the gate and making it *narrow,* hindering others who longed to move past their hypocritical self-righteous teachings.

Amidst Jesus' warnings of Jerusalem's last days and terrible times was a continual message of Good News; the grace-full reality of truth that all men and women were One with *God,* who Jesus referred to as, *"your Father in heaven."* It was their state of orphaned thinking Jesus sought to destroy in the mindset of all who heard him, even when they tried to kill him for it. He refused to leave people thinking they were orphans; and he publicly and privately ate and drank with the very ones the religious power players referred to as outcasts and sinners.

Narrow is way to truth- hindered by religion!

As we saw in chapter 1, we have greatly misconstrued the concept of man having a spirit that is *evil*; which, through no fault of his own, now needs to be born *again* with a new one that's pleasing to God. We don't need a *different* spirit which would supposedly allow us to begin to *see* divine things, communicate with God, or actually *become* God's children from that point forward. You *won't* find any scripture that says that. What you *will* find are small snippets of various scriptures men have removed from their original context, to then form their own quilt-work project. The results? So-called *foundational* doctrines such as this one, which are no small thing. In fact, this core doctrine of the church (having to be born again) has led to several other doctrines being built *around* it. Upon closer evaluation of the scriptures, these can be seen to have also been misunderstood and mistaught as well.

I'm no stranger to these doctrines. In fact, for a third of my life I was one of the most passionately driven, soul-winning, evangelistic machines you could imagine. I honestly believed (because it was what I was taught) that I had a mandate from God. I believed I was part of a divine commission to get everyone on this planet *saved*; and as far as I was concerned, I was definitely going to do my part!

I went to all the local jails, and traveled a regular circuit of state prisons; volunteering, serving, and preaching to inmates and staff every month for almost 20 years of my life. Why? Because I believed it with all my heart. I gave it everything I had, spending thousands of dollars yearly for gas, hotels, food, and materials, while also making donations to help others do the same. I can honestly say I don't regret a single moment, one mile, or one dollar I spent; because I only shared the Good News of the Father's love, with no pressure or fear involved.

I didn't preach about *hell* or use it as a leverage point of fear one time in all of those years. Yes, there was a time I had been convinced by others that hell actually existed. But back then, I figured if I had just a few minutes to tell you how good Jesus really was- you'd fall so in love with him that fear or any remote thought of *not* following him, would never amount to a blip on the radar screen of your life again.

Why do I tell you these things? Not to toot my own horn or impress anyone. I tell you these things that you might see a glimpse into a guy's life who wanted nothing more than to *serve* God, *please* him, and make sure *everyone* I came in contact with was going to make it to heaven one day in the future. If this is where you're at and what you do today, I honor you, and I applaud *your passion* to do what you've been taught and believed with all your heart, just as I did. I'll keep saying it; my goal in writing this book is not some personal quest to change your mind or make you believe just like I do. I share some of my ministry history to let you know this isn't some blink of an eye revelation that happened overnight in my life. It has been a progressive awakening taking place within me since pulling over on a little gravel road in 1996, when I told God *"I want to know you."* My goal in writing this book is to merely present some things you *might* want to look at again. To ask some 'what if's' that might cause you to go back and re-evaluate (prove for yourself) what you really believe, and more importantly, *why* you believe it.

A few *what if's* can change your entire life...

In fundamental Christianity, there are many things we have been taught as truth all our lives. Therefore, since we've heard them *all our lives*, from people we have grown up with and trusted *all our lives*, we've *believed* them. We have taken for granted that they are truth, without ever really stopping to consider, *"Why DO I believe that?"* I've had questions about many beliefs of Christianity from early on. Yet I remember a certain taboo tone (and judgmental look accompanying it) from elders who explained "there are things we don't understand, but we just accept and believe them, *because the Bible says so."* This tone and *look* carried the unspoken, yet implied chains of guilt and shame that it's totally *unacceptable* (un-Christianlike) to EVER question this book I had many times seen shaken in the air and called (with the same judgmental look and tone) the "PERFECT WORD OF GOD."

I finally came to the place I could ask honest, fear-less questions regarding intimacy and union with the divine. Yes, even if they didn't look like what I was taught as the basic 101 principle absolutes and responsibilities required to first *attain* intimacy with God, along with many repetitive practices required to then *maintain* it. Everything in my life from that point on began changing for the better. Of course, my visionary encounters (or whatever term works for you) with Jesus, the Etch A Sketch, and a new Bible, definitely helped awaken a sense of permission to ask these questions of the Christ-Spirit within me.

Paul said men were given the God Spirit within that we might know the deep things of God which were freely given to us. This freedom to ask questions regarding things I didn't know, or things that just didn't make sense (as I placed Jesus beside other Biblical writings that looked so much different than him), began to open my eyes to things I had never before been able to see. Maybe because now I *really knew* there was no condemnation or judgment associated with my genuine questions toward the same God I'd pulled over on a little gravel road years ago and uttered the words, *"Show me who you really are."* Somewhere along this discovery process, I began to realize I wasn't even having to ask the questions anymore. I would wake up from a deep sleep in the middle of the night literally speaking words out of my mouth that were revelational answers to things I'd been pondering over sub-consciously. I would sit straight up in the bed and end up writing 2 or 3 pages of notes; things that just gushed out like volcanic eruptions from within my spirit.

Even *prayer* took on a new perspective in my life. I don't ask God for things anymore. Period. I know I've been enabled and infused with every heavenly blessing the God realm contains. Rituals of praying a certain way, in a specific place, for a specific amount of time- or having to 'pray through' and 'rend the heavens' to petition God to move on my behalf for a specific need, have long ago fallen by the wayside. I don't need *anything* that I haven't already been given. I'm just learning to flow out of, and participate with all that is *already* within me.

Learning to abide in this divine Oneness is actually fun. At one point, when I desired understanding on something, rather than me praying *upwardly*, I would instead turn my focus within and say *"show me."* It's humorous as these baby steps of growing awareness have taught me that I don't even have to say *"show me"* anymore. Now when I wonder or think about something that piques my interest or crosses my mind, I just smile. The smile is because I'm thoroughly convinced (and I have lots of evidence) it won't be long until this inner current of life brings the flow of further revelation about that very thing, into a present-tense state of understanding and consciousness.

So, what if... the Spirit of God within you is reaching out for your traditional Etch A Sketch ideas? What if you've been carrying around a mental 'imagemaker' that isn't *really* as clear as you thought? What if some of those fuzzy distortions are just plain wrong altogether; but until now, you've never had any reason to question them? What if your Bible might be worn to a frazzle inside and out, but because you've always been taught to study it through a *literal,* traditional lens, there might actually exist an entire treasure chest of divine goodness hidden within, that's never yet been *taken out of the box* and explored?

Some will read this book who have never studied the Bible at all. Others who will read it have studied the Bible their entire life. When we have everything we have believed, taught, and given our life to, now laid back in our lap with a suggestion that we might have missed some things, it can release a plethora of confusing, disappointing, and even *angry* emotions from within. I've felt all of them; and if you're inclined to continue on this journey with me and millions of others around the globe- you'll probably feel most of them too. One thing I can boldly say with no reservations, is that having my belief *system* offended and provoked to the degree that I had to go back and prove it for myself, is the best thing that's happened to me since I pulled over on that little gravel road so many years ago.

Check out Hebrews 12:11, written to Jews *in the process of coming out* of centuries of traditional doctrines, *into a new way of thinking*:

Now chastening (spirit training) may not feel enjoyable at the moment. In fact, it may even seem painful to humble ourselves, admitting there may be a better way than we knew before. Baby steps to maturity will require humility in our ears and heart; but if we listen, we will soon enjoy the bountiful fruit of righteous equity and inner peace this training is sure to yield. (my paraphrase)

This segment, 'Taking the Bible Out of the Box,' is to help establish the fact that even though my vision of God and scripture has changed dramatically from what I was taught 'the Bible says'; I will continue to present things from a 'biblical perspective' with the wording of scripture, because most of us were taught everything (we think) we know about God from that perspective. This book is written mainly to the church; not at all to condemn it, but because I truly, dearly, and deeply love my brothers and sisters within it.

Some will be furious that I even dared to write these things. I already anticipate that response from some. Even still, I'm convinced there's an overwhelming majority of people *with questions.* They're found in the pews, prayer rooms, worship platforms, and behind the pulpits. They've known in their heart for some time there's something *better.* They realize what Jesus revealed to men- is much better than what our doctrinal traditions describe. If your heart often pounds with an echo of love deep within, and it's screaming YES to a better way than what we've known, then this book is for you. Trust me- *you are not alone.*

The Bible (despite its various mistranslations) is exactly what it was intended to be. It isn't *right...* nor is it *wrong.* It's not a court ordered rule book to keep you from being added to some mythical naughty or nice list. It holds the beautiful backdrop of God and man intertwined as *One* by divine design. It's the historical account of one particular culture of people and *what they believed;* along with various other beliefs (some mythical in nature) from different cultures which were acquired and then blended in with their own along the way.

When we begin to see the most famous book in history for what it really is, and why, it becomes more valuable in our understanding than ever before. The Bible is a magnificent story chocked full of metaphors, symbolism, types, and antitypes. Between its covers we discover the beautiful and eternal backdrop of *divine expression* including all mankind. Yet these same treasured pages also contain a history book with pictures and lessons of what happens when that backdrop gets veiled by the ideas of man. Once we understand it for what it really is- we stop trying to prove it, defend it, or use it as a weapon of exclusion to proclaim a future judgement of others.

Our *perception* of the Bible is what needs changed; to the context of differentiating where the Jews were in the *past* when it was written, and where we are in our own moments of *present* reality. Going to theology school to obtain degrees doesn't equip us to rightly divide the scriptures. Knowing the Father's heart equips one do that. And a few history lessons *don't hurt* either. A passionate ability to quote Bible verses, and being a carrier of the Father's heart, doesn't always get delivered in the same package. As we begin to see the perfect love and meticulously interwoven design of God in man, we will also begin to realize Jesus wasn't the *only* incarnation of God in the flesh.

The Son of Man came to grab men's awareness, revealing what divine incarnation (God-life in flesh) really looks like. Here, we begin to see Jesus really was *just* like his brothers and sisters in all ways, and was never ashamed to call them *brethren*. Sure, we can view ancient beliefs and traditions as they took place in one particular culture's quest to know God over a long period of time; BUT it's vital we realize the *difference* between them (then), and us (now). This interwoven enChristed design of God IN man belongs to us ALL at this very moment in time. As we learn to *rightly* divide scripture, we'll begin to see many of the beliefs, rituals, and cultural practices in the early church, have absolutely nothing to do with us today- other than a *history lesson* of progress and mistakes they made along the way.

Can God be miraculously outside of Jesus = way?

So, the choice now belongs to us. Will we refuse to budge from what we've always been taught we were *supposed* to believe? If that's what you choose to do, I'll respect that choice while you toss this book aside. If you've seen, however, from these first few chapters, that at a closer look, scripture doesn't always *say* what we were told it did; and you now wonder what other things may have also been misconstrued from their proper context- then let's go. By turning these pages, your view of what you were taught the Bible *clearly* says, might possibly change with simplicity and understanding... *right before your eyes.*

This isn't just about the long and complex journey of an ancient culture groping around in circular wilderness thinking for so long. It isn't just about a past tribal *us and them* mindset being transformed to the reality of all in One, and *One in all.* It's not just about their culture learning the truth of a God who had no desire to be 'God' in the sense they thought. This loving, all-inclusive Source of divine nature Jesus came to reveal, was the Father's intention to BE One with, and *enjoy* real-life experiences seen through the eyes and lives of all humanity, patterned and consisting *as* I AM; ONE from our authentic origin.

There exist hidden treasures beyond imagination that are buried in the encoded depths of the ancient Hebrew texts. These consist of deep, spiritual, *mystical codes of life* which the ancient elders and sages of this planet (from many cultures) carefully passed on to generations coming after them. Many of these treasures (which will *literally* blow your *natural* mind) are ingeniously camouflaged in writings we've had in our hands all along. But we weren't taught *how* to uncover them.

Sadly, much of the church is stuck in a *literal* Bible mindset. Many beautiful people are bound to *sin* consciousness, fear of hellish eternal torment, and a distant angry deity who'll swoop down to wipe out *this world* in an end times sci-fi thriller. Until this mindset is transformed, we won't be able to see, enjoy, or mature from all the vast spiritual resources deeply hidden as metaphorical treasures *in this same Bible.*

This book is in no way intended to be a reference source for these ancient treasures. No such *manual* of life could be ever bound in one single cover. Neither do I claim to be a teacher of these *mystical* truths. I am but a young babe sitting in awe of the tiny glimpses I have seen. I have however, seen enough of these glimpses to know they do exist, like metaphorical master keys to the universal essence of all life.

My goal in writing this book was to simply record a few of the baby steps and room to room enlightenments I've enjoyed along the way. They've brought me into an awareness of a *God* much better than I was taught or believed I was part of. If any of my ramblings strike a chord within you, somehow nudging you to question things or take some baby steps of your own, then I will have succeeded in one of the most passionate desires of my heart. That, is simply for men and women to actually *think* and decide what they believe *for themselves*.

Yes, I AM willing to say certain things that might make your blood boil momentarily. But if that moment of heated frustration provokes you to go back and honestly inspect *what* you believe, *and why-* then I will have succeeded in my purpose. I think it's only fair to warn you however, if I've made you angry or offended your doctrinal beliefs so far- it's probably not about to get any better. *At least not right away.* I get it. I fully understand. Ten years ago, if I'd told *myself* what I'm writing to *you* today, I might have slapped me. Or at least gnashed my teeth in anger as I turned and stormed away from my (now smiling) heretical self. Yet there's nothing about me today, that could even imagine going back to any of what I believed back then.

> Perhaps my *vision* of the Etch A Sketch came from all the time
> I held one in my hands back in the 60's. As a child often alone,
> I spent countless hours of creative enjoyment with mine.
> Through the wise words of my beautiful mother, and the ingenuity
> and design of my Etch A Sketch, I learned an invaluable life lesson:
> If you don't like what you've created before you...
> turn it over, give it a good shaking, and start all over again!

Before we proceed... there's something I need to make clear.

In the chapters ahead, we will look at topics regarding ancient days, cultural practices of those days, and the destruction of Jerusalem in AD 70. It's actual history. It's part of the life-story of the Jews. It plays an important role in what the majority of churched people today are taught (or not taught contextually), and it needs to be discussed.

When names/terms such as Jews, Hebrews, and Children of Israel appear in this book, it's because the Bible is the story of *their* journey, *not ours*. It is recorded history found in any encyclopedia. Telling this story truthfully, without implying who it happened to, is *impossible*. This topic however, should be approached with sensitivity and care, which I have earnestly sought to do. I have several personal Jewish friends, who are among the most loving, caring, and non-judgmental people I have ever known. My life is truly richer because of them.

If certain things you read in this book appear as negative to you, be assured they are not *ever* pointed at the common people of that day; and many of them are the actual wording of Jesus himself. Jesus gave his life, in love, to all the Jewish culture; and I don't see him as ever coming against his own *people* at all. What I do see him passionately against, was any corrupted *system* thriving from ideas of separation between man and God- and those empowered by it who manipulated, misused, and helped to keep common people in alien-ated thinking so long. These religious rulers had taken what the ancient Hebrew people wholeheartedly believed God had told Moses to do- and had turned it into an industrial machine of controlling, lustful, self-serving greed.

There are some today who believe God was somehow involved in the destruction of Jerusalem and hundreds of thousands of innocent and beautiful people being murdered. I will vehemently reject any such notion as long as I have breath. Jesus revealed the Father who gives life... not takes it; especially killing people who had diligently sought to know and serve this God with *everything* they ever had.

I also reject any notion that this horrific destruction was somehow tied to a 'second coming of *the Christ.*' The Christ, in whom all consist, never left earth to begin with, or no earth could even still exist. The Christ Spirit merely needed to be unveiled and roused up in the hearts and minds of men. *That's what Jesus desired for the Jews.*

The veil of separation they lived under then, still remains over the hearts and minds of many individuals among us. May every veil of imagined separation also be torn in two, for ALL who live today. Amen.

- All is interconnected — even for those who
  question they still look for the theory
  q Everything ✓ ——
     • Quantum Field (New Age - no dist.)
                    (Christian - distinct)

        consciousness creates / interacts
        w/ matter / manifestation —

- (g racists major on distinction but
   is there — implicate order
        Explicate order
              V
                        Holographic
                        wean the
                        projection

          Show me . . .
               Who you are Jesus!
      Why you came —
          new in quantum!

CHAPTER FOUR

Heaven and Earth Pass Away

In the 2000 years since Jesus left this earth in the flesh, billions of people have also come and gone from the earth as well. Many of these dear people believed (just as I once did) that Jesus would return one day in the future, as the same *in the flesh* man who walked with the disciples on the shores of Galilee. He'd return on a swooping *last day's* judgment mission in order to fix everything that's broken, destroy our enemies, and make all things new for us Christians. *Now* we could live happily ever after in a heavenly paradise God had prepared exclusively for those who believed *just like we did*. We've been taught to spend our lives intently watching (looking up), while faithfully praying '*maranatha... come quickly Lord Jesus.*' I grew up around that 'just trudging through to the end' mentality all my life. Yet Jesus said the kingdom of God doesn't come with 'observation.' It's interesting how and when Jesus said it; and that it's the only time *paratérésis* #3907, is used in scripture. The word means: **close, diligent watching, as in looking for something in a visible manner.** It comes directly from *paratéreó*, which means, **watch closely with great personal interest, to scrupulously observe, as to hope for, or ensure a 'final success.'** That's what we've always been taught to do, but Jesus plainly told the Pharisee's *and* his disciples, *that's not at all how it happens.*

Luke 17:20-23 (NKJV)

When He was asked by the Pharisees when the kingdom of God would come, He answered, "The kingdom of God **does not come with observation**; nor will they say, 'See here!' or 'See there!' For indeed, the kingdom of God is within you." Then He said to the disciples, "**The days will come when you will desire to see one of the days of the Son of Man, and you will not see it. And they will say to you, 'Look here!' or 'Look there!' Do not go after them or follow them.**"

It's hard to twist this passage out of its contextual reality, but we have become masters at doing just that, while trudging through in a distance/delay/reward/recompense mentality. Jesus clearly tells them the true kingdom doesn't (and won't) come as something men watch for with great personal interest, looking up, scrupulously observing, and praying for something that will bring about a 'final success.'

He tells his disciples: *"There will be times you'll wish I could be here with you like I am now* (in the flesh) *as a Son of Man; but you won't see me that way."* Then Jesus goes as far as to say, *"There will be those who tell you to watch for me; teaching you to look here or look there for me, but don't go along with them or follow their ways."* Why would Jesus say this with such direct intention? Because all Jesus ever taught men (Jews and gentiles alike), was that the true kingdom was already *within* them; and their Father (same as his Father) was the One heavenly Source and Origin of all humanity.

Jesus never once talked about men going anywhere, leaving earth, or him coming back to swoop them off to an exclusive club paradise where everyone would look, act, and believe just like them. In direct opposition to that perspective, Jesus implied that men were carriers of a divine light that could never be dimmed or extinguished. He said once men got out from under their *bushel over a lamp* mentality and quit covering their true light with upside-down external measuring devices, all men could see the true light of their origin. *Together,* they would shine as *One,* like a city on a hill that couldn't be hidden.

When I have an opportunity to share my views with other brothers and sisters I've known many years, they often seem disappointed; as though I've crossed the line as apostate- one who has fallen away from everything we've ever been taught by those who went before us. My friends (at least those who still talk to me) often remind me of Bible passages like 2 Peter, talking about the day of the Lord coming and the heavens and earth passing away. I've been warned about how *scoffers* will come (and how I sound like one) saying *Jesus* isn't coming back; and if I don't straighten up, I'll have to endure the great tribulation and have my head cut off if I want to make it into heaven one day.

Let's look closer at what's caused us to think these types of things:

2 Peter 3:3-4 (NKJV)

knowing this first: that scoffers will come in the last days, walking according to their own lusts, and saying, "Where is the promise of His coming? *For since the fathers fell asleep, all things continue as they were from the beginning of creation.*"

2 Peter 3:10-13 (NKJV)

But the day of the Lord will come as a thief in the night, in which the heavens will pass away with great noise, and the elements will melt with fervent heat; both the earth and the works that are in it will be burned up. Therefore, since all these things will be dissolved, what manner of persons ought you to be in holy conduct and godliness, looking for and hastening the coming of the day of God, because of which the heavens will be dissolved, being on fire, and the elements will melt with fervent heat? Nevertheless according to His promise, we look for new heavens and a new earth in which righteousness dwells.

It's the same type of 'new creation' language we see Isaiah use in **Isaiah 65:17 (NKJV)**

For behold, I create new heavens and a new earth; and the former shall not be remembered or come to mind.

It's also the same language Jesus used in Matthew 5:18, and John used in Revelation 21:1.

Matthew 5:18 (NKJV)

For assuredly, I say to you, **till heaven and earth pass away**, one jot or one tittle will by no means pass from the law till all is fulfilled.

Revelation 21:1 (KJV)

And I saw a new heaven and a new earth: for the **first heaven and the first earth were passed away**; and **there was no more sea**.

But is this earth *really* going to pass away?

Psalm 104:5 (NLT)

You placed the world on its foundation **so it would never be moved**.

Ecclesiastes 1:4-7 (NKJV)

One generation passes away, and another generation comes; **but the earth abides forever**.

Isaiah 45:18 (NASB)

For thus says the LORD, who created the heavens (He is the God who formed the earth and made it, **He established it and did not create it a waste place, but formed it to be inhabited**), "I am the LORD, and there is none else."

Due to ongoing in-doctrine-ations of literal scripture reading, *and*, in continual defensive efforts to portray this ancient historical journey book as being the infallibly perfect word of God, we've come up with all kinds of science fiction scenes, books, and movies to try and explain the opposition of these verses against each other. Yet, as we've seen in earlier chapters, **language in scripture depicting darkened heavenly bodies, stars falling from their place, mountains crumbling to the** sea, etc., were *never* about events (then, now, or in the future) involving the literal planetary bodies, mountains or seas. They are symbolic descriptors of rulers, kings, and/or established sources of institutional power being exposed, shaken and removed from their places of control. When we go back and actually study the beliefs of *their day* and the intricate design of the temple in Jerusalem, our eyes are opened to truth. We can see the temple *system* was being used by religious leaders to manipulate and control people by perpetuating a consciousness of sin, separation, distance, returning, and repaying. As the puzzle pieces are contextually joined together, then the prophetic scriptures meant for that day and age all suddenly start *making sense*.

The Hebraic view of the temple *structure* was **'the place where heaven met earth.'** They *literally* believed this. The architectural design and artistry used throughout the entire temple (and the priestly garments) were seen as a *symbolic* embodiment of the cosmos that was meant to represent the story of creation passed down by Jewish tradition. As we will talk about later, there are other cultures much older than the Jews who have their own version of the creation story; but the Jewish version is just the one most of us grew up *being taught*.

We find the 'sea' being described in 1 Kings 7:23-26:

1 Kings 7:23-26 (NKJV)

And he made the Sea of cast bronze, ten cubits from one brim to the other; it was completely round. Its height was five cubits, and a line of thirty cubits measured its circumference. Below its brim were ornamental buds encircling it all around, ten to a cubit, all the way around the Sea. The ornamental buds were cast in two rows when it was cast. It stood on twelve oxen: three looking toward the north, three looking toward the west, three looking toward the south, and three looking toward the east; the Sea was set upon them, and all their back parts pointed inward. It was a handbreadth thick; and its brim was shaped like the brim of a cup, like a lily blossom. It contained two thousand baths.

A bath was the largest liquid measure in the Hebrew culture- with estimates of being anywhere from 4½-9 U.S. gallons. Depending on which scripture you read (1 Kings 7 describes the Sea as being 2000 baths, while 2 Chronicles 4 has it holding 3000 baths), you'll find those capacities varying by several thousand gallons.

We find the 'heavens' area (Holy of Holies) being described by the author of Hebrews:

Hebrews 8:5 (NKJV)

who serve **the copy and shadow of the heavenly things**, as Moses was divinely instructed when he was about to make the tabernacle. For He said, "See that you make all things according to the pattern shown you on the mountain."

Hebrews 9:3 (NKJV)

and behind the second veil, the **part of the tabernacle which is called the Holiest of All**

Hebrews 9:23 (NKJV)

Therefore, it was necessary that the **copies of the things in the heavens should be purified with these**, but the heavenly things themselves with better sacrifices than these.

Flavius Josephus, (AD 37/38 – AD 100) [whose father was a priest] was a scholar and famous historian who personally spent much time in and around the temple. Here we'll see some of his famous writings which include the colorfully artistic details of the temple design and its *universal* representation. (ANTIQUITIES OF THE JEWS Book III, 7.7)

For if any one do, without prejudice, and with judgment look upon these things, he will find **they were every one made in the way of imitation and representation of the universe. Moses distinguished the tabernacle into three parts, and allowed two of them to the Priests, as a place accessible and common, he denoted the land and the sea: for these are accessible to all. But when he set apart the third division for God, it was because *heaven is inaccessible to men.** And when he ordered twelve loaves to be set on the table, he denoted the year, as distinguished into so many months. And when he **made the candlestick of seventy parts, he secretly intimated the Decani, or seventy divisions of the planets.** And as to the **seven lamps upon the candlesticks, they referred to the course of the planets,** of which that is the number. And for **the veils,** which were composed of four things, they **declared the four *elements.** For the **fine linen was proper to signify the *earth**; because the flax grows out of the earth. **The purple signified the *sea;** because that colour is dyed by the blood of a sea shell-fish. The **blue is fit to signify the *air;** and **the scarlet will naturally be an indication of *fire.** Now the **vestment of the High Priest** being **made of linen, signified the earth; blue denoted the sky;** being like lightning in its pomegranates, and in the **noise of the bells resembling thunder.** And for the ephod **it shewed that God had made the universe of *four [elements:]** and as for the gold interwoven, I suppose it related to the splendor by which all things are inlightened. He also appointed the **breast-plate to be placed in the middle of the ephod, to resemble the earth:** for that has the very middle place of the world. **The girdle encompassed the High Priest round, signified the ocean: for that goes round about and includes the universe.** Each of **the sardonyxes declares to us the sun and the moon:** those I mean that were in the nature of buttons on the High Priests shoulders. And for the twelve stones, whether we understand by them the months; or whether we understand the like number of the signs of that circle which the Greeks call the Zodiack, we shall not be mistaken in their meaning. And for **the miter,** which was **of a blue colour,** it seems to **mean heaven:** for how of gold also, is because of that splendor otherwise could the name of God be inscribed upon it? **(Bold emphasis added for visual clarity)**

Now, let's look back at 2 Peter to see what this removal of 'heaven and earth' would look like:

2 Peter 3:10-13 (NKJV)
But the day of the Lord will come as a thief in the night, in which **the heavens will pass away with a *great noise, and the elements will melt with fervent heat; both the earth and the works that are in it will be burned up.** Therefore, since all these things will be dissolved, what manner of persons ought you to be in holy conduct and godliness, looking for and hastening the coming of the day of God, because of which **the heavens will be dissolved, being on fire, and the elements will melt with fervent heat?** Nevertheless, according to His promise, we **look for new heavens and new earth in which righteousness dwells.** (bold words mine in surrounding scriptures)

What had Jesus been saying about the destruction to come?

Matthew 24:1-2 (NKJV)
Then Jesus went out and departed **from the temple**, and His disciples came up to show Him the **buildings of the temple**. ² And Jesus said to them, "**Do you not see all *these* things?** Assuredly, I say to you, **not one stone shall be left upon another**, that shall not be thrown down."

Matthew 24:15-16 (NKJV)
"Therefore, when you see the abomination of desolation, spoken of by Daniel the prophet, **standing in the holy place** (whoever reads, let him understand), **let those who are in Judea flee to the mountains.**"

The heavens, elements, and sea were destroyed (exactly as prophesied) in AD 70, approximately **4 years after 2 Peter was written- burned up in such fervent heat from within until it was all dissolved.** Let's look at Josephus' historical documentation of it found in ANTIQUITIES xi. 1.2

As the flames went upward, the Jews made a great clamour, such as so mighty an affliction required, and ran together to prevent it; and they spared not their lives any longer, nor suffered anything to restrain their force, since the holy house was perishing**... thus the holy house burnt down... Nor can one imagine anything greater or more terrible than *this noise**; for there was at once a shout of the Roman Legions, marching all together, and a sad clamour of the seditious, who were **now surrounded with fire and sword... the people under a great consternation, made sad moans at the calamity they were under... Yet was the misery itself more terrible than this disorder; for *one would have thought that the hill itself, on which the very Temple stood, was seething hot, full of fire on every part of it.**

Josephus continues in THE WARS OF THE JEWS, Book 6, Chapter 8:

But when they went in numbers into the lanes of the city, with their swords drawn, **they slew those whom they overtook, without mercy set fire to the houses wither the Jews were fled, and burnt every soul in them, and laid waste a great many of the rest;** and when they were come to the houses to plunder them, they found in them entire families of dead men, and the upper rooms full of dead corpses, that is of such as died by the famine; they then stood in a horror at this sight, and went out without touching anything. But although they had this commiseration for such as were destroyed in that manner, yet had they not the same for those that were still alive, but **they ran every one through** (killed by sword or spear) **whom they met with, obstructed the very lanes with their dead bodies, and made the whole city run down with blood, to such a degree indeed that *the fire of many of the houses was quenched with these men's blood.** And truly so it happened, that though the slayers left off at the evening, **yet did that fire greatly prevail through the night, and as all was burning,** came that eighth day of the month Gorpieus [Elul] upon Jerusalem.

It's impossible to overemphasize the power and control the temple had over the people. It was literally the largest physical structure built by human hands perpetuating *a false veil of separation* between God and man. It confined the people to an alienated consciousness, continually reminding them (Heb. 10:1-3) of their *sin* and God's *judgment*. It was their whole *world*, and they believed the entire *universe* revolved around their enshrined *system* way of doing things. Everyone else was excluded, unless they agreed to adhere to specific beliefs and practices. Even then they were seen as substandard *outsiders* who had been granted a pass to the *outer courts* only out of mercy. Of course, this *mercy pass* included certain requirements and financial stipulations that must be met up front for this so-called mercy to be in effect.

These religious leaders, as Jesus clearly and publicly pointed out, were the blind leading the blind. They were users and abusers of widows, wearing perfectly adorned robes, yet with hearts, intentions, and a righteousness that carried the same equity as graves full of dead men's bones. Jesus said as long as this kind of corrupt *system* was in *business*, the common people would continue to be *ruled* by those who sat in Moses' seat, quoting and enforcing laws *that none of them kept*. Jesus said they loved being called rulers and rabbi's, sitting in special seats at feasts, while binding men up with heavy burdens, **swearing by the temple where 'heaven' was cut off to the common people,** and devouring widow's houses. He said these *wolves* in sheep's clothing would go to any extreme to convert people to their *system* of thinking (which they believed the universe revolved around), only to make *their* lives twice as polluted as the Gehenna trash dump (or the site used to sacrifice children to the fires of Molech) that Jesus compared them to.

Jesus lovingly and patiently *(well most of the time, when he wasn't calling them hypocrites, vipers, blind guides, sons of the 'devil' or turning over their trinkets and wares tables with a whip in his hand),* tried to guide them into an awareness that the universe (other than their own) didn't really revolve around their system or beliefs.

To the average person raised in the western church, any in-depth training on this subject is *foreign* to say the least. If your experience is otherwise, then I salute your pastor. After being extremely active in church for nearly 20 years, I don't remember ever getting any real meat and potatoes teaching on AD 70, their religious world/system, or how the scriptural language we've looked at in this and the previous chapter pertained *only to the people of that day.*

Perhaps I can share some info here that helped open my eyes to many things along the way. One thing that can entirely change the perceptive tone of how we *hear* scripture, is in understanding how the word 'world' is used in the Bible. The word *kósmos #2889*, means (literally, 'something *ordered*')- and properly, as an *'ordered* system'.

Kósmos *is* seen being applied to the universal creation or world, as the terra firma/earth. It is also, in the New Testament, often applied to the *dis*-ordered system *of that age*- which masked truth and reality by covering it with things that looked or seemed right, that were outwardly attractive and appealing to the natural senses.

I'll invite (and encourage) you to read that last statement several times until the words *system, masks,* and *outwardly attractive* begin to get your attention like an oversized hood ornament on a flashy car.

In Greek writings from Homer on down (800-700 B.C.) *kósmos* is seen carrying the tone of *ornament, decoration,* and *adornment,* and is where we get our words 'cosmetic' and 'cosmetology' from. What do cosmetics do? They mask the reality of something existing underneath in ways that *appear* attractive in decorated ways, or adorned apparel to draw one's attention to what's *outside* rather than what's *inside.* We call it *make-up.* Remember how Jesus described the religious scribes and Pharisees? Cleansing the outside of a cup that was full of extortion on the inside? Majestically adorned robes and garments masking their greed like freshly painted tombs that were full of dead men's bones?

We begin to realize that in context, most of the times Jesus, Paul, and other New Testament writers talk about coming *out* of the 'world,' or separating themselves *from* it, they *were not* referring to common people committing (verb) *acts* of sin as most of us have been taught. Please don't wrongly interpret me condoning harmful behavior in a person's own life or the life of another; for I am *not* doing that. I'm merely trying to present scriptures in context of how they were written in that age *to the proper audience for whom they were intended.*

John 17:13-19 (NKJV)

But now I come to You, and these things I speak in the **world**, that they may have My joy fulfilled in themselves. I have given them Your word; and the **world** has hated them because they are not of the **world**, just as I am not of the **world**. I do not pray that You should take them out of the **world**, but that You should keep them from the **evil** *one*. They are not of the **world**, just as I am not of the **world**. Sanctify them by Your truth. Your word is truth. As You sent Me into the **world**, I have sent them into the **world**; And for their sakes I sanctify Myself, that they also may be sanctified by the truth.

In this one short passage, Jesus uses the word *kósmos* 9 times. *Now let's think about this.* According to the doctrines I was taught, the *world* was a planet full of unchurched degenerates who took part in things like drinking, drug use, gambling, sex *(with the wrong person, people, or gender),* or cheating others out of their stuff. Again, this is not condoning anything that would harm someone; it's just rightly dividing scripture. Jesus said the *world* hated his followers because they weren't of *it*, just as *it also hated him* for not being part of *it*.

Did the drunks, prostitutes, gamblers, and cheaters hate Jesus? NO, on the contrary- those who engaged in such activities flocked to Jesus. Did Jesus separate himself from them? Nope. He ate *and drank* with them in public; even going home with some- apparently spending the night with Zacchaeus, the biggest manipulative shyster in town.

Who was it that hated Jesus and tried to kill him several times on their own, before finally convincing the Roman *govern*ment to crucify him? It was the rulers of the ritualistic temple system. Jesus asked the Father to guard his followers from *evil*. Our Bibles say 'the evil *one*,' but the wording or idea of an evil 'one,' or 'person,' doesn't exist in the original language. Even still, we were taught about a villainous arch enemy (once a worship leader in heaven, but got kicked out) who now prowls around as a thief to do nothing but steal, kill, and destroy.

The word *evil* Jesus used, is *ponērós, #4190;* an adjective derived from the word *pónos, #4192;* associated with pain from laborious toil, annoyances, and hardships. Jesus wasn't speaking of some mythical fallen angel; but of a *dis*ordered (fig-leaf cover-up) system of toil and labor, striving to provide for one's self over the full provision already given in their origin. Let's look at this scripture in the Mirror Bible:

John 17:15 (The Mirror)

I do not request you take them out of the world but that you keep them from the evil performance-based system of hardships, labors and annoyances! *(The ponéros-system is the system that is referenced in the Tree of the knowledge of good and evil (ponéros) which is a system based on performance as the defining reference to human life- Jesus came to reveal and redeem our authentic value, identity and innocence as defining our lives.)*

When Jesus spoke of the 'thief' who comes to steal, kill, and destroy, he used the word *kléptēs #2812;* a *thief* who takes by *stealth* (secretly masked or covered up), rather than out in the open using force or violence. Reading the entire chapter *in context-* we discover Jesus isn't talking about some fallen angelic villain. Earlier in John, Jesus said no one before him had seen the Father. Here, he adds that all who came before him were *secretly masked thieves and robbers,* referring to the well-dressed hypocrites of a man-made temple *system,* who enforced laws they didn't keep, while preying on common people and widows.

Paul, who was once a Pharisee himself, had his eyes opened to 'Christ in you' for all men *from their mother's womb*. Immediately, he then took everything he'd learned from this toil and labor *system* of condemnation, separation, and sacrifice- and promptly threw it up on the *skubala* pile, declaring it all a big ole stinky pile of manmade *sh-t*.

Paul exhorts the Corinthians to come out from among those in a *system* built on false pretense and idol worship. In the Romans letter, he's seen passionately beseeching his readers not to be conformed (in any way) to the false *kósmos temple system* of *that age*; but to be trans-formed (*meta-morphóō*) through a re-newing of their mind, to the *awareness*, or a higher level enChristed consciousness which had actually 'belonged' to them all along. Here, Paul said they would see that THEY were the only *true temples* of God, as being *living epistles* of divine logos expression, given to all men in their authentic origin!

Paul spent the rest of his life helping remove the scales from other's eyes that he'd first had removed from his own. Everywhere he went, he told people the truth of who they really were, while at the same time effectively dismantling man's *system of cosmetic cover-up* that he was once so zealous to promote. He opened his letter to the Ephesians by telling them the Father had chosen them IN him. The word 'chosen' is *eklégomai, #1586*. It is formed from 2 words; *ek*, which means 'out of,' and *légō*, meaning, *speaking* as a *conclusion*. Paul tells his audience in Ephesus (1:3-4) that all men were *called* by the surname expression of God, IN Christ, irrevocably holy and blameless IN Light and Life, with every blessing (up front) that the heavenly realm contains. And when did God conclude all this? Paul said it was done IN Christ long before the 'foundation' of the *kósmos*.

This is a good place to take a peek at how many things in scripture have been misunderstood, and sometimes distorted- by seeing how, and when, the translators *decided* to use certain words. They also used this same English word, 'foundation,' in Ephesians 2:20. Yet in the original Greek language, and in actual *context*, we find they are two completely different words carrying *entirely* different meanings.

In Ephesians 2:20, the word 'foundation' is *themélios, #2310*. It comes from *tithémi, #5087*, which means *lay down,* as in a permanent foundation for a wall or building. It is metaphorically used for first principles, foundations, and authentic beginnings- or in describing the implementation of an **ordered system of truth.** Here, Paul describes that foundational truth, which says the CHRIST (in whom all consist) is the CHIEF CORNERSTONE. It's the same word Jesus used in his parables describing the solid rock, where men could build on a *firm foundation* that could never be moved, even when encountering life's storms. I find *themélios* 16 times in the New Testament; always being translated as *foundation,* and having no alternate meaning. **This word *themélios* is *never used in any of the 10 scriptures containing the wording *'before the foundation of the world.'***

The same English word 'foundation' is seen in Ephesians 1:4, but now, Paul is speaking of something quite different. The word Paul uses here is *katabolé-* from *kataballo, #2598*. It means *cast* down, *thrown* to the ground, prostate, or being *cast to* a *lower place.* It describes a 'down-casting' or dis-ordered **'disruption'** of the kósmos/system. Paul writes that men were seen IN Christ, irrevocably holy and blameless BEFORE they *imagined* they were *cast down,* or *alienated* from God. Man, now *dis*tortedly envisions himself *dis*connected from his Source rather than his truthful stature as a partaker of divine nature. David recognized this inner consciousness battle, and we see him having to *re*-align this ground-clutter thinking by confronting his own mind and emotions with **"Soul, how could you even *think* of being *downcast?*"**

THIS *fall of man* had nothing to do with a corrupt spirit needing to be re-born with a new one, and everything to do with his imagination becoming distortedly used the wrong way. This *sick* thinking led man into a *dis-eased* perishing existence of toil and labor. He tries to *cover himself* with his own cosmetic *make-up* system of ritualistic working and sacrificing, trying to please God by making himself appealing or attractive. The only hope in the darkness of this *sick* disruption, would be an attending *physician* bringing a *healing re-newal* to man's mind.

Looking back now with clearer understanding at the 10 scriptures using terminology of 'before the foundation of the world,' everything changes. We'll look at just 2 of them, and you can study the rest for yourself to see these weren't talking about a time before the creation of the terra firma earth. They refer to a time prior to the *downcasting* of man's right mind and vision. It describes the *disruption* of intimate participation with/in man's Source; the authentic Origin always found *perfectly intact* with/in God's FOUNDATIONAL blueprint of man.

Matthew 13:35 (KJV)

That it might be fulfilled which was spoken by the prophet, saying, I will open my mouth in parables; I will utter things which have been kept secret *from the foundation of the world.*

Now let's replace those words with the intended context:
I will utter things which have been kept secret (not seen) since the *casting down of God's authentic blueprint **in man's mind.***

1 Peter 1:20 (NASB)

For He was foreknown before the *foundation of the world*, but has appeared in these last times for the sake of you.

Again, when we replace it with the intended context, we get this:
The CHRIST was known BEFORE the *casting down of God's authentic blueprint **in man's mind**-* but has appeared (manifest) in the distorted darkness of *these days* for your sake.

Just prior to this, what did Peter say men were redeemed from?
1 Peter 1:18-19 (NKJV)

knowing that you were not redeemed with corruptible things, like silver or gold, **from your aimless conduct *received by tradition from your fathers*,** but with the precious blood of Christ, as a lamb without blemish and without spot.

This *aimless conduct* is the **perishing ponērós system of man** associated with pain, laborious toil, annoyances, and hardships. It all came about from the disruption of man's participation in the divine order of God's truth, which was established in the Origin of all.

One day man is *naked* and knows *no* shame. The next day, man is naked, *just* as he was before- but is now suddenly hiding in shame-full fear, already trying to *cover* himself by his own *efforts* to somehow be acceptable and appealing to God. This, my friends, is the foundational institution of the kósmos *system* invented in man's veiled imagination. It's always trying to cosmetically *cover up,* or *make up,* in order to attain access to a divine Source he was never (ever) *disconnected* from, *except in the downcasting of his own mind.*

From there, we see man having forgotten who he was, moving in his own efforts, yet ending up further and further from the truth. His spiritual vision had become so veiled and scaled, all he could *see* was from *his physical senses.* This lost vision created such *vux* darkness around him he could not break free. The gates of *ha/des* (not to see) had restricted him to the point *ha/martía* (not seeing his true identity) had him *missing the mark* of the blueprint intention of his life. Now, not only was he acting *out* evil (verb) acts from the *inner* evil (noun) equity of worthlessness he felt about himself; he began judging and blaming others *just as he had felt judged* and blamed in his own mind.

Centuries of distortion, loss of appreciation for life, building walls of exclusion, twisted war-like schemes involving death and ritualistic offerings, were passed down by *tradition* to generations that followed. **And death *spread* to all men.** CHRIST LIFE TRUTH had been hidden *since* the downcasting of man's mind, with a *kósmos cover up system* becoming enshrined in cosmetic (false glory) workings of the temple system. Until this laborious mindset was removed, man would be *lost.*

But Jesus came to show men the river of life hidden within them, and the truth of their *real Father's* love. Finally, their spirit eyes could be *reopened,* that they might once again enjoy intimacy in spirit and truth *without* approach offerings or buildings made by *man's hands.*

With this understanding, we begin to realize that all the things we were taught would come in our day, or some day in the future, now get dissolved in our thinking when we (finally) see that Jesus *plainly* said **they would happen to the generation of *that age* and their culture.**

Matthew 24:7-8 (NKJV)

For **nation will rise against nation**, and **kingdom against kingdom.** And there will be famines, pestilences, and earthquakes in various places. All these are the beginning of sorrows.

Matthew 24:21 (NKJV)

For **then there will be great tribulation,** such as has not been since the **beginning of the *world*** until this time, no, nor ever shall be.

Matthew 23:36 (NKJV)

Assuredly, I say to you, **all these things will come upon *this generation*.**

1 Peter 4:17a (NKJV)

The time has come for judgment to begin **at the house of God**
(the temple was called the 'holy house of God')

Matthew 23:34-38 (NKJV)

Therefore, indeed, I send you prophets, wise men, and scribes: **some of them you will kill and crucify,** and **some of them you will scourge** in your synagogues and persecute from city to city, that on you may come all the righteous blood shed on the earth, from the blood of righteous Abel to the blood of Zechariah, son of Berechiah, **whom you murdered between the temple and the altar. Assuredly, I say to you, all these things will come upon *this generation*.**

In the preceding scripture, Jesus confirms the same truth Stephen *later* spoke, just before the high priest and religious system leaders stoned him to death. In the following scriptures, we'll see (first) the religious accusations against Stephen, and then, we'll see Stephen's response to them, which clearly mirrors Jesus' own words.

Acts 6:12-14 (NKJV)   [spoken *toward* Stephen]

And they stirred up the people, the elders, and the scribes; and they came upon him, seized him, and brought him to the council. They also set up false witnesses who said, "This man does not cease to speak blasphemous words **against this holy place and the law; for we have heard him say that this Jesus of Nazareth will destroy this place and change the customs which Moses delivered to us."**

Acts 7:51-52 (NKJV)   [spoken *from* Stephen]

"You stiff-necked and uncircumcised in heart and ears! **You always resist the Holy Spirit; as your fathers did, so do you. Which of the prophets did your fathers not persecute? And they killed those who foretold the coming of the Just One, of whom you now have become the betrayers and murderers."**

Now let's look again at Jesus' words, clearly describing when this event we were taught would be some future, cataclysmic *sci-fi scene to come* upon the terra firma earth in days ahead, *actually* took place. It's always been there; we just couldn't *see* it.

Matthew 24:34-35 (NKJV)

Assuredly, I say to you, ***this generation will by no means pass away till all these things take place.* HEAVEN AND EARTH WILL PASS AWAY,** but My words will by no means pass away.

We now see these scriptures and mistranslated thoughts in context. This language depicted a literal event in *that day for their culture*, and we now realize this removal of *heaven, earth*, and the *elements*:

1) is past tense,

2) was for the people almost 2000 years ago in Judea/Jerusalem,

3) described the destruction of the stone temple and the controlling legalistic religious *system of that age,*

4) is of a historical context which had/has absolutely nothing to do with our culture presently, or at any time in the future,

5) had absolutely nothing to do with literal *earthquakes*, the actual *heavens*, the terra firma or *physical earth*, or bodies of *ocean waters*.

Friends, this is the only removal of heaven, earth, elements, and sea that Isaiah, Jesus, or Peter prophesied to come; and it all happened (exactly as they said) **within 4 years of 2nd Peter being written**. There was only *one true temple* of divine presence. That, was the expressed extension of incarnation in earthen vessels; the paternal Christ Source IN which all humanity would consist *inseparably as One*.

For those who now saw themselves reflected in this enChristed nature Jesus revealed, there would be no more orphaned thinking, no more missing the mark of true identity, and no more consciousness of *sin*. Instead of a perishing pig-pen existence resembling trash dumps and tombs full of dead men's bones, rivers of heavenly living water would gush forth from within their spirit! No longer would they be bound to rules on a rock or committed to redundant religious rituals. Their hearts would be consumed in the perfect righteousness of love's liberty, as every man, woman, and child saw each other as treasure carriers of heaven within, *and the very offspring expression of God!*

It's important to realize God wasn't responsible for the killing and bloodshed that occurred in Jerusalem. The ruling powers of religion with its exclusionary condescending views of others, made plenty of enemies on its own. Religion *and* government both desired to control the *same* area, *same* people, and *same* money. Four years of conflicts and skirmishes later, Roman armies totally wiped out Jerusalem; with hundreds of thousands of beautiful and innocent people murdered or made slaves of in the process. Jesus gave his life trying to *warn* them and *save* them from the destruction that was coming; but like other prophets in generations past, they tortured and crucified him as well.

It was this *us and them* veiled mentality of *good OR evil* which grew from the toil and labor *seed* man allowed to take root in the inner garden paradise he was meant to thrive from. Neither the Son of Man, nor the paternal Source he called himself One with, had anything to do with the murder of the Jews or the destruction which took place in Jerusalem. Solomon said 'scheming imaginations' in man's mind produced *war-like machines* in, and around *their own lives*. It was power-hungry religion clashing with governmental desires to control Jerusalem that brought about the destruction of the *City of Peace*.

Jesus said nations would rise up against other nations; kingdoms would rise up against kingdoms. Deep in the darkened midst of man's scheming war-machines, there was hidden an incorruptible seed of logos-life in their blueprint design. Even in the atrocities of man's own creative ability (as destructive as it sometimes becomes), the Original *paté*rnal logos power is always working to bring good (the only thing it knows) out of man's wilderness darkness. God didn't destroy and murder those in their own little temple world of Jerusalem; it was the Roman armies who did that. Yet in the midst of all man's death and destruction, there could be seen a resurrected awareness among God's precious Jewish children (and Roman children as well) that they could run boldly into the intimacy of divine presence they had actually never been *dis*connected from. Here, sin consciousness, alienation, rituals and sacrifice could be torn from their thoughts as they awakened to a new and living hope of 'Christ IN you, the present-tense hope of glory!' They could venture beyond former veiled perceptions of *us and them*, to see *One* Father, *One* Spirit, *One* beautiful worldwide family in which factors of gender, ethnicity, social status, or religious beliefs would never be divided *or* excluded in their thoughts again!

Ancient scripture reveals the eternal backdrop of the Father's love over all humanity, *as well as* the historical journey of the Hebrew culture over many centuries. Regarding *that* ancient journey, Paul wrote this in 1 Corinthians 10:11: **"These things happened to them** *as examples for us. They were written* **to warn us** *who live at the end of the age."* Paul was saying the Old Testament letters and traditions were full of examples (warnings) of beliefs they'd built their *world* around so those mistakes wouldn't be repeated. This veiled temple *system* and ancient customs built around *that* world was destroyed 14 years later in AD 70. That *same veil* still lies on the hearts/minds of many who keep *looking back as though* what the authors of scripture wrote thousands of years ago, was then purposely *dropped in our mailbox by God* as a perfect rulebook and model for our culture to conform itself around today.

Scripture reveals how the early followers of Jesus went from house to house, sharing all they had as One, so none lacked anything. Yet we have instead engaged in a system that looks more like Moses and a temple of rituals, than being infused with the love and freedom of Christ. I don't mean to personally offend you if you are involved in church ministry; that's not my heart. I speak as one who was a core worker in the church for 1/3 of my life, and did it passionately with all I had. Yet when we place the temple system of old beside our current system of today, there are remarkable resemblances that reveal the same type of beliefs and aimless *dead* works that are obvious in both.

The Original logos design which innocent children are born and consist in, never changes or goes away. This genesis blueprint reflects the LIFE and DNA (divine nature ALWAYS) of authentic design; but the system of man begins *methodical programming* from birth. The child will be introduced to *ideas* of being alienated from his/her eternal Source. Fear sets in as veils of imaginary *disconnect* are put into place. They'll be instilled with thoughts that *God* is one place and *they* are in another. They will be *taught* they must now *do* certain things to attain and become what they *always were* in the eyes of the Father, while being in-doctrine-ated with ideas that God is holy... *and they are not.*

They're given lists of things they must believe, confess, and follow to approach this distant God, led by people in man-made structures men have deemed as *special*. From platforms and programs, they will be taught to be *sin conscious*, how to bring tithes and offerings, along with other types of *sacrifices* requiring their personal time and service.

All this is done in an effort to please a distant deity who (they're taught) *now sees them differently* than the innocent child the parents once held in their arms. They'll be taught to *draw near to God and (then) he will draw near to you*; continually seeking a Source of divine love which had actually been right there within them from their first breath. A tender heart filled with perfect love is taken and introduced to enshrined 'holy places' created by the hands of men, where weekly ritualistic requirements will be repeatedly carried out. Welcome to *man's cosmetic temple system* of making ourselves look good to be attractive and appealing before God. **We (hopefully) haven't done this maliciously or with intentional deceit- but were *programmed* to do it by people who loved us; people who believed they were doing the right thing because it's what they were taught as well.**

Congregations will be subtly pressured with various scriptures like *'fail not to assemble yourselves together as the day is approaching,'* to keep them returning on a weekly *schedule*. It won't be explained to them this was written *specifically* to Jewish brothers and sisters who'd departed from a *kósmetic sacrificial system* and were now followers of Christ. It won't be spoken in the *context* of having been written to encourage and give hope to those who were considering going back to Judaism to avoid the intensifying persecution around them. This letter was to remind them they'd been given something *much better* than the law and prophets could have ever supplied them with, and to assure them that nothing *back there* was ever worth returning to. It was encouraging them to hold to their faith, to one another, and to the truth *unveiled* to them. The 'approaching day' of destruction they'd been warned of, was fulfilled just 2-3 years after the letter was written, and had/has *absolutely nothing to do with our culture or life at all.*

Don't misinterpret these statements as if I'm against gathering corporately for fellowship, encouragement, and celebrating the divine life we've been given. **I'm not**. For many people, that's the only real family they know, and they should be able to enjoy it. Neither am I saying there aren't churches doing beautiful things for people. There are some that do great things, changing this world with a genuine heart of love. What corrupts it all is people being beat down with sin conscious preaching, teachings of guilt and unworthiness, while their pockets are fleeced to feed an institutional machine thriving on guilt, condemnation, and fear of a mythical place of torment called *hell*. We travel to the ends of the earth to make converts- only to place them in a double dose of fear and bondage that they're alienated from God and need a fire insurance plan to avoid his wrath and eternal torment.

We have 'evangelists' telling poor people and widows if they'll 'sow a seed' (send them money) God will *then* bless them. We've got preachers saying tithe (something that in no way *ever* applied to us) takes precedent even over groceries and utility bills. I used to believe it and have actually done without things I really needed to get my 10% in the bucket. I know far too many people who have been taught God will *curse them* with a curse if they don't tithe. A passage from Malachi about 'robbing God' is taken completely out of context and used to put fear in people's lives. A common belief among many people I know is that God will actually 'tear up your stuff' if you don't tithe. Sadly, this 'God's gonna get his 10% one way or another,' is a prevalent (and truly perverted) teaching among much of the church. And this passage in Malachi often used to promote this twisted idea, wasn't even written to the common people. **It was written to priests and leaders who were stealing from common people's tithe for their own personal use.**

If this seems harsh or offensive, it's not my intention to offend or insult others, and anyone who personally knows my heart will tell you that. Certain things however, have no other way of being said than in plain ole black and white. If you've been involved *inside* ministry as long as I have, then you know everything I just said is true.

All this revolves around ideas of *separation* between God and man. History *will repeat itself* over and over as long as we sew back the distorted veils Jesus came to remove from man's *Moses mindset* of judgment and alienation. Sadly, the presence of exclusive *us and them* thinking, nation against nation in wars, killing and destruction- will continue *until* Jesus' message of unified Oneness among all men takes its rightful place as that which we know as *reality* in our hearts. Our doctrine of a *deliverer* coming one day to wipe out our *enemies* isn't much different than what ancient Jews believed about their mashiach. Teaching that *our* God will cast many into *hell*, while taking *lookalike* believers to a gated club with mansions in the sky, doesn't help heal this world- *it perpetuates its division.* And any God with *enemies*, is a 'God' men have created in their own war-machine imagination.

The ekklésia was never intended to be an institutional machine functioning on a business model inside a constructed building. The true ekklésia will always be about an offspring of love. A *spiritual* building of One big family who know they carry the Father's Origin-al surname DNA, and love nothing more than sharing it all with every tribe and culture... *as One big family inheritance.*

I'll close with what I wrote in chapter 3 about the Bible:

When we see the most famous book in history for what it really is... it becomes more valuable in our understanding than ever before. The Bible is a magnificent story chocked full of metaphors, types, antitypes, and spiritual symbolism. Between its covers, we discover the beautiful eternal backdrop of a divine family which includes all mankind. Yet these same treasured pages also contain a history book with imagery and lessons of what happens when that loving backdrop gets *veiled* by the ideas of man. Once we understand it for what it truly is, we'll stop trying to prove it, defend it, or use it as a weapon of exclusion to proclaim a future judgement of others.

Honest Question Time

Before we go any further, perhaps we should take a few moments to reflect on what we've seen in the previous chapters. The fact that you're even reading this sentence means *something* is resonating inside you to the point that you haven't tossed this book aside.

Some of the very topics we've covered thus far are the foundational ideas of *what* the western evangelical church believes; *why* it does what it does, and *teaches* what it teaches. What IF these core ideas were found to not actually exist as we thought? What then, would be the remaining basis for what we were taught as a divinely orchestrated mandate called *the great commission*- along with all the energy and money we put forth in our purpose driven life? What would change if we found out the driving *purpose* we were told existed, had actually been instituted from some huge misunderstandings which end up not *truly* being a valid purpose or commission *for our day* at all?

For those who have been in ministry 20, 30, 50 years or more, the idea of this question being genuinely posed can suck the air from our lungs and move the blood up to our face. *I understand.* I didn't end up devoting my whole life to this *commissioned purpose* as some of you may have. But as described earlier- for the 1/3 of my life I did devote to it, I was an unstoppable machine, and I can assure you that no one has ever done it from a more *passionately driven heart* than I did.

Let's recap a few of these things.

1) YOU **MUST** BE BORN AGAIN.

We saw that there's actually *nothing* to substantiate this statement. We saw the *night*-time talk Jesus and Nick shared involved something *quite* different. You alone will have to decide what *you* believe; but at least now, you can do it with an honest scripture-based evaluation.

2) YOU'RE GOING TO **HELL**... *UNLESS* YOU GET **SAVED**.

As we look at factual, credible evidence *beyond* the ideas of the Latin Vulgate and King James Bible (and other Bibles which followed their lead), it becomes quite clear that Jesus, the apostles, the early church (first several hundred years), nor the ancient Jews, believed in a divinely created place of eternal torment. Neither did a single one of the four (4) words that translators *engineered* into scripture as *hell*, have anything to do with punishment from a distant deity.

3) SOME WILL BE **TAKEN** AND OTHERS WILL BE **LEFT** BEHIND. AND THE EARTH (as we've known it) WILL BE NO MORE.

The language couldn't be much plainer for us to see that everything we've been taught about these topics as some sci-fi event yet to come, actually took place (for the Jews) in AD 70, just as Isaiah, Jesus, Peter, and the author of Hebrews described. It's also important to realize Josephus (unlike us or *any* Bible translator) was actually in Jerusalem *before and after* it happened. In his historically documented account of what existed in the temple, along with what occurred during its destruction, we see him using the same wording and terminology as those who predicted it was going to come to pass.

If we now see any of these things from a different perspective than what we've been *traditionally* taught, then shouldn't the beliefs of what we *did* based upon those traditions, also change accordingly? *Just an honest question.*

When we look at the latter epistles attributed to John, reportedly written around AD 90 (20 years after destruction of the temple), we find *no language whatsoever* warning of some coming catastrophic event people would need to be alert, ready, or prepared for. *Why?* Because it already happened (20 years prior) to those it was written to in the contextual timeframe of *their existence.* Neither is there found any talk of people *perishing* or needing to be *saved* from anything.

What we find in John's 1ˢᵗ epistle (1:5-7) is the author telling them that if they *say they walk united* (as One) with CHRIST CONSCIOUSNESS, and yet *do not walk united* (as One) with their brothers and sisters, then their vision and fruit thereof is still coming from a *vux state* of darkened orphan thinking involving exclusion and separation. BUT IF they are walking in the true Light as One with each another- just as they know they are One with CHRIST, then it's blatantly obvious that what Jesus revealed to them has cleansed their consciousness from all *hamartía* (ha/A **not**- méros/**sharing** in) by which they had previously been (in *sin*) missing the target goal of their true *kaléō* sonship.

In 2:15-20, readers are told not to love the *kósmos* system of man or anything it represents; for no matter how outwardly attractive it might *appear-* it's *still* a cosmetic cover-up full of lifeless bones. They are told the left-over remnants of that powerless *make-up system* are disappearing for good; but God's authentic blueprint always reveals a life of divine treasure that *never fades* with time. A few described with ANTI-CHRIST thinking have left them, but they're not to be alarmed. It only confirms those walking away still live *from* a separation mindset.

In 2:26-29, readers are encouraged not to let anyone deceive them in believing they need *anything* other than what they were given in the Origin-al *arxé*/logos expression (BEginning) from which ALL created came and consist. What abides in them *internally* removes any need of *external* 'teachers' to show them the truth. Anywhere (3:2) CHRIST LOVE and actions are revealed (manifest in men), these men are also revealed as One WITHIN THAT CHRIST NATURE. The epistle's last words are... **KEEP YOURSELF AWAY FROM (*KÓSMOS* SYSTEM) IDOLS.**

When we see these things in the contextual reality to which they belong, and how they were *all finished* in their entirety for the Jewish culture **in their day and age and the purpose for which they were predicted**, it raises new questions which now really need answered.

If up to this point you've felt your mind being stretched, along with *un*-usual heart issues you're not quite sure what to do with, then what we're about to look at might possibly trigger some *traditional* red alert warning alarms. *It's ok though.* Whatever time it takes to absorb these things will pass; but those heart issues you've felt burning inside you aren't going anywhere until you allow your head to catch up with them and get some important things resolved. *And you can count on that.*

We've been told we were born detestable in God's eyes and there was a place of eternal conscious torment awaiting those who were not born *again*. As we've seen, these end up being merely man's distorted ideas. Any idea of being ugly, judged, or excluded in the eyes of our divine Source was obliterated by the words and actions of Jesus toward others; with the idea of some prepared place of eternal torment revealed as just a *mythical imagination* also created in man's mind.

Keep in mind what we've seen regarding traditions of *that world* and the specific cultural religious system in place *during that age*. From *that* place, let's address some additional topics which now also take on a new light IF we actually take time to research them. I highly recommend you do just that, even if you think you're sure of what you believe. It's possible to get so deeply invested in traditional ideas, that when light shines from another room (containing truth we might not have seen), it can be easier to just close the door, rather than exploring what's waiting for us. The truth is, we often simply prefer not to take a chance of disrupting something we've grown quite comfortable with.

What are we to do with all we've been taught about being *covered with the blood* of Jesus, or him *paying it all* for us, as taking the wrath and punishment we were taught God demanded for OUR *sin debt*? **Could these possibly just be *carry-overs* of how the ancient Jews saw things in *that age* and *their culture* thousands of years ago?**

CHAPTER FIVE

Oh the Blood of Jesus?

LIFE IS IN THE BLOOD! *Right?* We've written songs about power in the *blood*. We've been taught to plead the *blood* over circumstances and situations. We've been taught that nothing can wash away sins but the *blood* of Jesus. I know, we've heard it all our lives. But *why* do we believe it? *Because the ancient Jews believed it.* They truly believed it, and it's written throughout their entire history. We've somehow been convinced that *our current* reality is shaped by *their past* history and what they believed. But where did it all originate? Where did this belief come from? Who told YOU that YOU needed a blood sacrifice to have union with God?? I'll answer that question with a question. Who told Adam he was naked- which brought shame on him and caused him to hide, trying to *cover himself* until he could figure out a way back into good standing with God? *It obviously wasn't God.* We see God pursuing *Adam* as he's hiding, trying to awaken him to reality by saying: *"Can you see where you are now, Adam... hiding in shame?"* *"WHO told you that you were un-covered?"* By taking a short journey through some historical facts, along with looking at some scriptures, we'll get a broader view of certain things that led up to these *blood* beliefs- before coming back to see how those beliefs apply *(or not)* to us currently, and where we stand in the grand backdrop of life.

David, known as 'a man of God's own heart,' declared that his ears had been opened to hear the truth that God **did not require** sacrifice or offerings for sin (Psalm 40:6). Jesus, quoting Hosea, said: *"Go and learn what this means: I desire mercy and **not sacrifice**."* The term 'go and learn' was a direct implication that *where they were* in their thinking and what they believed, *wasn't* the truth of God. It implied they had some things to learn; but they weren't going to see them by staying in the same place and continuing to do the same things their fathers had done (sacrificing) for so long. The author of Hebrews (chapter 10) quotes David, and then repeats this truth a second time. What was this truth so important the author felt it needed repeated two times back to back? It was that God never desired or had any pleasure in sacrifices and offerings for sin to begin with!

With some simple investigation, we'll find that this ritualistic blood and sacrifice thing didn't start with the Jews *or* the law of Moses, even though they had built their whole life around it. Many cultures much older than the Jews also built their entire lives around spilling blood and sacrificing things to *their gods*. Ancient people groups from all around the globe believed they must *first* give up something valuable to receive favor for health, crops, fertility, long life, wisdom, and right fellowship with their *thousands of different gods*. The actual origins of blood sacrifice are so old they're lost in the vapors of pre-history. There are archaeological excavations providing substantial evidence of the prevalence of these ancient ritualistic practices which are believed to have not only existed in pre-recorded time, but continued right on through into what we can now see and touch as documented history.

Some of these excavations have revealed human settlements dating as far back to 10,000 BC. in Mesopotamia. There's evidence causing scientists to believe the indigenous Aboriginal people which settled in Australia have been in existence at least 50,000 to 60,000 (or more) years. I know- we *were taught* the earth is only about 6000 years old; a belief needed to shore-up a timeframe to make our doctrines work. We've been taught (and have taught our kids) to shake our heads at science in disregard and dismiss older earth dates because scientists are *obviously* quite mistaken, or even worse, they're out to discredit the Bible and make Christian beliefs look bad.

First off, the Bible never makes any remote claim the earth is only 6000 years old. We came up with that number on our own by adding up birthdays, years, and certain generational stories recorded *in* the Bible. We love adding up numbers and pretending we've got it all figured out. Having all the answers is an ego thing we've nurtured from our pulpits like throwing fertilizer on Kudzu vine. If you don't know anything about Kudzu vine- it doesn't need any fertilizer to flourish on its own. The religious ego of man certainly doesn't need any fertilizer; it needs weed killer. Furthermore, scientists have more important things on their minds than making modern Christianity look bad. We haven't really needed a lot of *outside help* in that.

Too many people *outside* the walls of the church see Christians as the most egotistical, exclusive minded, judgmental separatists on the planet. Honestly, how can we blame them? Of course, we can't see it from where we are, entrenched in our purpose driven mindset. The real question is, *what purpose*, and *whose purpose* is it that's been driving us? We've dressed it up with attractive accessory language in many different ways. Yet the bottom line of what *we consider* the good news message to be is this: HELL is coming BUT we can save you from it IF you do what we tell you and believe like we do.

'Our club knows more about God than your club.' This may remain verbally unspoken; yet our tone, attitude, and inside jokes about other denominations come through loud and clear. If you've been in the ministry for any length of time, you know as well as I do, it's a mindset held by *thousands* of club divisions who think they're the ones who (wink, wink) really have it *right*. We've built our own inner walls of separation within our outer perimeter club wall. Those outside our walls aren't fooled by the GOD IS LOVE plastered all over our church signs anymore. People don't care about our signs; especially when they reflect a starkly different message than our outward tone and actions.

Whether we like it or not, most churches are like an industrial machine run on a business platform. It's a board meeting attitude of having to *prove* yourself worthy, *do* your time, *work* your way up, and one day, if *we* think you're good enough- *we* may even let you preach.

Anyone paying attention sees the bottom line of our club mentality boils down to 'it's our way or the highway.' *Highway to hell*, that is. But we have a chance to change that perception for our children and the generations to come. I don't mind telling my kids and the younger generations we were wrong. *"I was wrong"* are some of the most liberating words I have ever spoken. I don't mind telling our beautiful young people they will do well to forget our egoic examples of needing to have all the answers, or thinking we were more special or smarter than others. I tell them 'I don't know' is ok! In fact, it frees us up to partake in adventurous heavenly mysteries we couldn't have seen to enjoy from our 'we've got it all figured out' boxed mentality. When we realize all things are set up to work for our good and the universe is actually working for us and not against us- things begin changing all around us. We can surrender to the flow of each day and experientially see things falling into place all along the journey. *Ahhhhhhhh......*

Interestingly, the title 'Christian' that we've grown so protective over, actually came about because of men and women who effectively tore down walls of exclusion rather than building them. Antioch was the third largest city of the Roman Empire. It was the headquarters of the Roman garrison in Syria, and was famous for all its magnificent temples, theatres, aqueducts, and baths. Like other cities of that time, it had a large circular wall around the perimeter, a marketplace in the center, while the inside of the city was walled off in ways that divided different people groups from each another. Early church followers of Jesus began to infiltrate the city with the Good News he'd given them (which had nothing to do with being saved from hell), and Paul even made Antioch his ministry base. These followers of Jesus went about doing good to all, bringing healing to those oppressed by an orphaned, alien-ated mindset, while revealing the love of the heavenly Father.

These were merely doing the things they'd learned from Jesus, who had told them *"I only do what I see my Father do,"* and *"the things I do... you will do also."* This *Good News message* of inclusion and love was so powerful that the city walls of Antioch were no longer working as designed. The Jews and other ethnic groups had begun coming together in unprecedented ways. Not just *slipping through the walls* to be present with each other physically; they were joining in the unity of *One* with each other in their hearts and minds.

Of course, this beautiful unity of Spirit carrying One love language that all cultures could understand, was having an intrinsically opposite effect on commoners than the power players of that day wanted or needed to exist. **Here the term 'Christ-ian' was first used by the political rulers and power structure in that area.** Other rulers of that age had seen Jesus as radically rebellious to their controlling system and dominating ways of life. His *unchained* message along with its corresponding actions, was so effective against the walled systems of that day *that they killed him for it.* But these rulers of darkness didn't have a clue what their crucifixion scheme would give birth to, or they wouldn't have crucified this master mirror of the Father's glory. They didn't realize the seed of his death would reveal the harvest of not just one Christ, but would release the same *resurged* tomb-splitting CHRIST AWARENESS in multitudes of glory carriers from every side!

These mirrored glory-carriers now went about doing the same things they'd seen the rebel Jesus do, but in greater, ever-growing numbers! The disgruntled and controlling leaders soon began tagging these as 'Christ-ians,' which actually meant 'little Christs'. Yet there was nothing *little* about the system defying, wall destroying effects of inclusive love and wholeness that occurred everywhere they went.

I long for the day we begin dismantling our own inner club walls with true love and Christ-like actions. Only then will *churches* truly reflect Jesus by displaying non-judgmental love so pure and beautiful that *everyone* will desire to come participate in its healing, nurturing, empowering love, with every culture and background *uniting as One.*

Back to our earth dating process. You'll have to forgive me for growing weary of trying to defend certain church doctrines I was told I must believe (to be a good Christian), over accepting obvious things that creation itself reveals with profound evidence. Tangible, verifiable evidence that actually makes sense. I was taught the scriptures were the oldest writings known to man. You might be interested to know there are writings much older than the Bible and the Jewish history it contains. *Similar* versions of stories we've been taught were *exclusive* to the Bible, such as the creation story, the fall of man, flood of Noah, and the life and complaints of Job, were depicted in older cultures as well. Some of these accounts are recorded in ancient Mesopotamian lore like *The Myth of Adapa*, and *The Epic of Gilgamesh*; an epic poem that was put into written form as far back as 2100 BC. The first writings of Moses (in what we know as scripture) are believed to have been written at least 600- 900 years later, around 1500-1200 BC.

Knowing these things doesn't detract from the Bible or journey of the Jewish people at all; it leads to just the opposite. I'm thankful for my *many* Bibles. Some of these have duct tape covers holding torn and taped pages, having been extensively explored with passion. Despite its textual errors and various translating inaccuracies, I still consider it one of the most important books I've owned. I enjoy my Bible even more now because I see it *for what it is*, and am learning to glean from it in proper context. Understanding the Bible was written in different time periods over a span of 1500 years by at least 40 different authors (some letters not *actually* being written by who they're attributed to), makes it even more interesting to me. I realize many things the Jews believed, practiced, and journaled on parchment (or stones and walls), were adapted along their journey from other cultures. Many of those beliefs were passed down through people groups that lived *long* before them. Knowing this has given me a Bible that makes so much more sense, and also helped me more clearly understand why Jesus adamantly proclaimed *"No man before me has seen or known the Father the way the eyes of a son can."*

Even though the ancient Jews believed they were God's favorite people, *they didn't see themselves as sons.* They wandered around like orphans yoked to wilderness thinking, unaware of who they *really* were. It was a *lost* state of mind Jesus passionately desired to usher them out of, *"I will not leave you as orphans."* These people had a scattered history. We see much of it in bondage and slavery *to* others; while many of the beliefs and pre-scribed actions of Judaism also revealed a tribal outlook of exclusion which included acts of violence and taking the stuff *of* others. As a culture of people who had endured much pain and suffering, the children of Israel longed and believed for a deliverer who would come on the scene kicking ass and taking names of all their enemies. This explains how all *their* enemies coincidentally ended up in their writings as being *God's enemies too.*

Jesus didn't fit their *mashiach* (powerful political leader) template in any way. He came to his own; but they didn't *recognize* him. Their engrained beliefs of what they *thought* the mashiach was supposed to do, become easily recognizable as we look back at James and John, who Jesus called *sons of thunder.* One day, they're seen asking if they can imitate Elijah by calling down fire on people; something a political ruler/king should have shouted YES to, while commending them for wiping out others who didn't look like them. Instead, Jesus tells them they obviously don't know *who they are* yet- because if they did, they wouldn't be wanting to kill people, they would be reaching out to help them. Once again, Jesus introduces them to the living illustration of: *"If you don't know who you are... you'll live like who you're not."*

Another time, these same sons of thunder came to Jesus telling him they each wanted seats beside him in his glory. Since the Jews didn't believe in a future location of heaven or hell, they obviously weren't asking Jesus to hang out with them in some *soon to come* pearly gated paradise. They were telling Jesus that they wanted and *expected* (Mark 10:35-37) to be his right- and left-hand men, seated in power alongside him in the kingdom of *physical and political* power they believed their mashiach was sure to establish on this earth.

As we look back at the stories, it becomes obvious Jesus wasn't giving his people what they *thought* they needed. He was giving them what they *really* needed. And what they really needed, couldn't have been any more opposite of what they'd thought. Jesus had no desire for war, killing, or *blood*. He had no desire to be worshipped, lead an army, or recruit servants. He just came for friends; which he openly treated like family without any regard of their *sinful* reputations. After many centuries of prophetic words of what this 'deliverer king' would look like, all formed from *cultural mental images* based on what they *thought* they needed- Jesus comes popping out of their proverbial *messiah cake* as the surprise of a lifetime.

The famous Beatitudes teaching (Matthew 5-7) is a perfect example of this. Scripture records multitudes following Jesus from all 10 cities around that region. He goes up a certain hill which provided a natural amphitheater where these vast multitudes could hear him. A perfect place for a powerful new political ruler to start setting things straight. The perfect place for him to start pointing out to all people of various cultures that there was a new sheriff in town about to start making things right. *All things for Jews, that is.* Yet, instead of using divide and conquer language, describing how enemies of the Jews (his own people) would now be destroyed; Jesus does something *quite* different. He speaks with great love to all men and women from every tribe, ethnic culture, and religious background; always referring to God as *'your Father in heaven,'* and teaching unity and Oneness among all.

He tells them *repeatedly* not to be like the hypocritical religious leaders. This Son of Man modeled the Father/Son-life as the most loving, inclusive person the people had ever seen. Matthew records (7:28-29) that these multitudes of people were completely astonished at his teachings. It was obvious to them he spoke with a knowledge and authority that wasn't known, taught, or exhibited by the scribes and Pharisees. The multitudes of people were *so drawn* to Jesus' light and love (just like Nicodemus was) that when he came down from the mountain (8:1) they continued to follow him.

Jesus was SO different than what the Jews were looking for, that even John the Baptist, the one who was to *prepare the way* and then introduce this *deliverer* on the scene, had questions about this gentle lamb-like inclusionist. John wonders why Jesus didn't look *at all* like the roaring lion they'd been expecting. While sitting in Herod's prison, he hears about all the peaceful and restorative things Jesus was doing.

**Here, behind bars and about to die... the Baptist
begins to wonder if his entire life's work had been in vain.
Had he introduced and brought attention to the wrong one?**

John sends his disciples to confront Jesus with a straight-up question:

**"Are you *really* the One who was to come...
or should we be looking for another?"**

Jesus understood the reasoning behind the question. He knew his life was a scandalous offense to the distorted image-i-nations of man, not fitting their pre-scribed template at all. He sends John's disciples back to tell him what they've seen and heard for themselves: *"The blind see and the lame walk. Lepers are cleansed and the deaf hear. The dead are raised up, and the poor are hearing good news."* Then Jesus adds one more thing: *"Blessed is he who is not offended by who I AM."*

Have you ever noticed how Jesus made certain adjustments to the law of Moses and what the prophets had written? Oh yeah- *he did.* People were either overwhelmed with relief at Jesus' authoritative editing of the law and prophets, OR they were *offended,* growling at him (gnashing their teeth) even to the point of trying to kill him. While the religious leaders pointed to Moses' law (written in the past) wanting to stone the woman caught in adultery; Jesus, instead goes straight for the (present tense) issues of the heart. His *"let the perfect one among you throw the first stone,"* clearly left all those present no choice- but to drop their stones of condemnation and walk away.

Once again, we see the Son of Man's editing skills in action as he responds to John's question. Jesus had a loving way of confirming the various glimpses and shadows of truth the prophets had seen and gotten right. He also had a masterfully smooth way of rightly dividing these glimpses of truth from the many veiled cultural *distortions* that often came mixed in with them. The author of Hebrews described Jesus skillfully (like a two-edged sword used with surgical precision) dividing what authentically originated in the Father's heart and logos blueprint- *apart from* the veiled perceptions of man's egoic emotions, which he had no problem *slicing away.*

Spirit truth always goes straight for thoughts and intentions of the heart. It totally bypasses the ideas and rules of man, which do *nothing* but hinder the intimacy and enjoyment of Christ-minded Oneness. The religious rulers were highly offended by Jesus' life and actions. Yes, they believed the coming *chosen one* would do some good things on the surface. Yet the core of *their* deliverer's operating motive was more importantly to bring the *vengeance of God* upon their *enemies*; thereby rebuilding and restoring their cities and man-made temples of worship as Isaiah had prophesied. In a local synagogue (Luke 4) Jesus reads the healing and restorative parts of Isaiah 61, while totally slicing away the *vengeance of God* clause Isaiah's 'deliverer attribute list' included. As those in attendance waited for Jesus to finish *all* of Isaiah's details describing their awaited deliverer king, Jesus roles up the scroll, sits down and says: *"What your ears have heard today, is the fulfillment of truth these writings hold within them."*

We see Jesus do the same thing with John's disciples. He instructs them to go back and tell John what they've *heard* in their ears and *seen* with their own eyes- which was healing and wholeness to all. Jesus continually revealed THE accurate expression of the Father: *"If you've seen me, you've seen the Father."* In effect, Jesus tells them they could stop looking for this *vengeance of God* thing Isaiah had added from his own ideas- which Jesus (on more than one occasion) surgically removed, *because it didn't look anything like the Father.*

As grace and truth (reality of heaven inward) is unveiled in our vision, we begin to recognize certain distorted imagery in the minds of the prophets, versus the clarity and reality of the express image (every perfect detail) of the Father. As Jesus expressed the Father's heart, he clearly revealed what Christ-mind thinking looks and acts like.

This seems like a good place to again be reminded of what the author of the BOOK OF BETTER THINGS wrote in the first 4 verses of Hebrews (my paraphrase):

"In the past, our fathers were told various ways the prophets believed they heard God speak; but in these last days, God has bypassed any chance of error through a prophetical middleman, and has spoken to us clearly by the Living Word, in the face to face person of the Son. This Son, came to reveal the I AM truth of the Christ-life, where all things consist by the same word and same power. He reveals the perfect image and reflection of the Father in every way, that we may know and behold him for ourselves, as One. In this Christ-life alone, our ideas of sin, sacrifice, and separation are purged from our thinking once for all; for in Christ, is revealed an incorruptible inheritance of life much more excellent than the prophetical messengers beforehand knew how to show us."

As these things begin unfolding in our awareness, new imagery starts to appear (manifest) on our mental Etch A Sketch. We now see the Christ-life *in whom all consist* which Jesus came to reveal. We begin to realize the book of the Revelation (THE REVEALING OF CHRIST) is not a scary futuristic thriller with a sword-wielding, flame throwing, angry lion bringing wrath and destruction upon men. It's not about a king coming to restore things in the city of Jerusalem, nor does it have anything to do with some notorious bad guy called 'the Antichrist.' It is purely *metaphorical symbolism* which John used to describe things *already finished* through a perfect (apocalyptic) un-veiling, where the Christ-life and mindset *was revealed clearly* without any distortions.

In Revelation 1:10, John gives a pivotal key in helping his readers understand these writings in their *true context*. He says *"and I heard behind me a loud voice, as of a trumpet."* It's vital that we understand **John had to turn around and look behind him** (v. 12) **to see that which had *already* taken place!** It was the FINISHED WORK of Jesus as he victoriously 'trumpeted' *(sálpigks, #4536)* the *Christ-life*. It brought 'atomic' *(átomos #823)* transformation with *death and hádēs* being swallowed up the *moment* corrupted thinking of *mortality* **put on** re-deemed, re-surged, incorruptible Spirit truth! **(See *1 Cor. 15:47-55*).** John is told only the *Lion* of the tribe of Judah can open the scrolls; yet when he looks (5:5-6) he sees the figure of *a gentle lamb* instead!

The scrolls are filled with symbolic imagery of *accomplished* things. Things we've mistakenly interpreted as literal in action, and futuristic in timing. Once we realize this *apocalyptic* (simply means UNVEILED) REVELATION OF THE CHRIST contains *nothing* to fear, we see the 'wrath' (orge) of God isn't angry vengeance poured out on men at all. It's the Father's consuming passion removing every alienated, orphaned idea that had *veiled* man's awareness and participation in divine intimacy. The lake of fire's *true purpose* is burning up and consuming all of man's hindering, divisive vain imaginations. Restoring wholeness and Christ-minded thinking, so men can *participate* in their divine nature!

The Father of creation isn't *angry* with men as we've been wrongly taught, but is passionate about uninterrupted intimacy *as One* with carriers of the divine treasure. The word 'wrath' *(orge #3709)* means 'build and teem with swelling'; and is from *orago #3713,* which means 'stretch out- as to touch or *attain.'* *Orago* carries the same desire and passion as *orgasm*- 'to build and swell until climactic pleasure and satisfaction is attained.' I don't mean to make you blush, but I hope you don't associate *that kind* of passion with angrily destroying things. It's sad our judgmental ideas have twisted divine passion into *anger,* and it's vital to realize the *orge* of God wasn't to punish or destroy men at all! It is intentional *purification* to remove *everything* hindering the passionate intimacy of God that man was designed to BE ONE WITH.

The Father isn't on a rushed time plan for this to happen. God isn't bound by time, and as Jesus knew and demonstrated- *neither are we*. This transformational filtering process isn't based on daily decisions our divine Source makes at various intervals in our life. It is simply the authentic design placed in humanity's DNA by the Master Architect. Our Source receives *and gives* pleasure by extending all that he/she has, *with* him/her, *as* him/her, in the blueprint expression of LIFE!

So, back to blood. There was nothing magical about Jesus' *blood*. He was *in all ways*, just like his brethren. There was nothing magical about the *name* of Jesus. It was a quite common name of many who lived during Jesus' time. Jesus had no desire to receive praise or worship; nor did he intend for men to think they could 'seal the deal' with God by using his 'name' like some magical incantation in their prayers. In that day, a *name* was seen as the *reflecting essence* of one's *nature*. Jesus' *power*, was in his unquestionable *knowing* that he was One with the Father, *as in* the *same* divine nature! It was here, all people could see the CHRIST-NATURE this Son of Man revealed. They could then follow his lead *as other sons of men* who now realized (as Simon Peter did), *that they too*, could also enjoy this expressive Oneness with their heavenly Source *the same way Jesus did!*

Jesus simply enjoyed un-veiling the *Christ-mind nature* to those he longed to show *how* to walk in their Source *(kaléō)* surname- *as One*. He openly displayed what divine *offspring* looks like as they actively *participated* in that divine nature. While there was nothing *magical* about his name *or* his blood, he revealed a quality of *aiónios* Life that is totally *enchanting* (delight-full, charming, irresistibly attractive) in every possible way. Quoting the *name* of Jesus at the end of a prayer doesn't contain the power to change man's life at all; but when men understand the true *nature* of Immanuel (God with/in man as One), it releases the DNA blueprint ability to trans-form our lives *from within* in heavenly ways we haven't even started to fathom.

As we realize these vital elements of truth, we can passionately grab hold of the treasured blueprint of man's authentic Origin and nature the Son of Man came to reveal! We can see, grasp, and experience it all while living from our inseparable *God-union*. And we can do it in more enjoyable depths than we've ever before known. **The proverbial icing on the cake is that we can do it all without being attached to any alienated, orphaned mindsets of ancient cultures in the past, OR any of the tribal ritualistic practices *of their age* they took part in.**

But wait- It gets better! Once we see things in proper perspective and embrace the eternal truth of mankind's unity and Oneness with this Source Jesus revealed- we find ourselves no longer looking at others with *flesh* as our reference point. We see them (like the Father does), as the treasure carriers of divine light and love they truly are, no matter what they might (externally) look like at the moment. And as carriers of the *same* treasure in earthen vessels, we not only begin to see them as One with God- *but One with ourselves as well.*

We can now begin to understand Paul's *unity in the Spirit* message to the Ephesians in chapter 4:1-6: There is One body and One Spirit. One hope of One calling. One Lord. One faith. One baptism. One God and Father of ALL who is over ALL, through ALL, and in ALL. This repetitive idea of One in ALL, and ALL in One, should hit the bullseye of our hearts to wake us up to the Father's truth. It's here, where exclusive mindsets begin to fall off like the grave-clothes they really are. It's where we effectively become administrators of the God-kind of reconciliation. When we see someone living a life opposite of their origin because of bad, shameful, or unhealthy things they've believed about themselves; we, as ambassadors of love, can show them the Good News Truth of how their Father sees them, and their true value as chosen carriers of the divine presence.

This is where we begin to see others for who they *truly* are. It's where thoughts of war and the exclusive conquering mentality behind it begins to disappear. We learn to enter in to an inner place of shalom peace where nothing is allowed to remain missing, broken, hurting, or out of joint. A place where, *wait for it...* even the multiplied thousands of denominations (divisions) begin tearing down their own walls of exclusion. Forgetting specific club ideas and rules of membership, they come together under one *head*, which is fruitful Christ-mindedness. This is where all mankind begins joining hands around the globe. Healing restoration now empowers the broken, hurting, hungry, and dislodged, effectively releasing the *true* heaven upon a *new* earth.

Will I see all this come to pass while I'm in this temporal body? Maybe not. **But that won't stop me from knowing it, seeing it in my heart, and treating everyone around me like we're already there!**

This is what the Good News will do when the scales fall away and we begin to see the enchanting origin of our life for what it really is- holy and blameless in the Father's love. Does this mean we ignore or turn a blind eye to all the obvious actions of hurt and destruction in this world? No, it doesn't. Does it mean we tell people who commit violent atrocities that everything is perfect and they're ok just the way they are? No, it doesn't. Does it mean everyone will have an immediate heart change simply because we tell them how the Father saw them from the origin? No, it doesn't. But what someone else *does* should never change what *we do* as carriers of heavenly wholeness within!

Love doesn't re-act, *it responds*. Love doesn't see what others do first, and then re-act accordingly. Love's response always comes from a desire to see healing, restoration, and wholeness overcome what is distorted, out of place, and broken. *Love never fails.* Love is greater than even faith and hope, and will one day- be all that remains. We read those words in scripture. We quote them at our weddings and counseling sessions. *But we don't live like we actually believe them.* In my heart I see the day when perfect love becomes perfect-ed *among us*. The day when, as Father/son is One in heavenly thinking, so also, as divine partakers of that same nature, are we as *One* upon this earth.

As we hold *our* grandchildren in our arms, we smile with love's determination that they will one day share with *their* grandchildren, just how beautiful and perfect they were created in Origin-al design. It thrills me to know that one day, long after this physical body no longer holds who I AM, they will be surrounded with the fruitful harvest of LIFE that Kay and I, and our children raised them in! They will have only heard (at least from our family) about their authentic *born from above* origin and divine nature in which we all consist as One.

The quickest way to reverse what we see in this world, is to start walking in real love ourselves (not church-sign *exclusional* love), and sow it deeply into the rich fertile ground of the younger generations who will inhabit the earth in the days, years, and centuries ahead. But how can we expect that to come to pass while telling our children they were born with an evil nature? How will they not judge others when we tell them they've been judged and condemned themselves? How will they see the heavenly treasure *within* them, if they've been told they're detestable in God's eyes and deserve hell? You won't catch me telling them a God who is 100% Spirit and 100% Love had to have a flesh and blood sacrifice to pay for some sin debt surveillance log with their name on it. That's what my generation was taught, and look how that's worked out for us. We watch the daily news filling our mind with negativity of how *evil* things are all around us. While muttering a prayer "come quickly Lord Jesus," we'll *change the channel* on the TV; not realizing we're the ones holding the control *to change the world*. That my friends, is what's known as slumbering perish mode.

The actual verse this chapter started with from Leviticus 17:11, says the **life of the flesh** is in the blood. Jesus came to reveal Spirit life... not flesh and blood life. He told Simon Peter flesh and blood couldn't have supplied this fisherman's CHRIST REVELATION that sons of men could intimately hear from their heavenly paternal Source. In Cana, when Jesus' mother told him they were out of wine for the wedding feast, Jesus replied *"Why do you involve me in producing new wine now,* *my time has not yet come.*" Yet we see Jesus (who loved celebrating unity and Oneness with all) giving instructions to the servants to fill the 6 pots (number of mankind) with *water*. He then tells the servants to draw some out for the master of the celebration who tastes the wine and tells the bridegroom he had obviously saved the best for last; *and it was something much better than he'd ever before experienced.*

When it came time for the Passover meal, Jesus sends his disciples to a man in the city with specific instructions. The teacher says, *"My time has come; I will keep Passover at your house with my disciples."* As they were around the table eating, Jesus broke some of the bread and said *"Take. Eat. This is my body."* They each dipped their bread in the *same* bowl, signifying friendship, intimacy, and Oneness. **When Jesus talked about *his* blood, of which they were all to drink, he had a cup of wine in his hand.** Jesus was trying to initiate a new way of (metanoia) thinking to their minds; something **which had nothing to do with religious rituals or actual blood sacrifices.** It symbolized the *best saved for last* wine that could only come from abiding *as One* in Christ, and thinking *as One* with the Christ mindset. Knowing the disciples couldn't see the relevance of it all at the moment, Jesus tells them as he humbly washes their feet: *"I know you don't understand what I'm showing you now- but one day you will."*

It would symbolize the celebration around their eternal unity and Oneness with their Source. It would celebrate the incarnate extension of GOD IN MAN, thereby removing every orphaned thought of man's stained, shame-full consciousness and all the fruit (of its own kind) that came from it. Jesus told them each time they broke bread, drank wine, or had a meal in *koinónia* fellowship with others, to remember all he'd taught them of Oneness with the Father *and each other*. The wine Jesus spoke of represented the intoxicating goodness brought about by awareness and participation with their SPIRIT SOURCE NATURE within them. He said when others drank from this transformational (water to wine) Spirit cup of celebration, that out of the very matrix of their own BEing *would gush rivers of this same living wine-water!*

Jesus was continually unveiling this new wine message of unity to others. While teaching in Capernaum, he said, "Unless you partake of my 'body' (*spiritual* bread which neither Moses nor his writings could supply) and drink of my 'blood' (new wine of *abiding Spirit* fruit), you won't know how to enter in and enjoy the life of Oneness I long for you to see." Jesus was trying to shift their focus *from* blood, rituals, and sacrifice, *to* an intoxicating feast of unity and Oneness. It wasn't a toil and labor existence of *flesh and blood*, but a celebratory Christ-life in the *Spirit*. Yet, many could/would not receive this *new wine message* which flowed counterculture to their traditions of blood, sacrifice, and killing things to *cover-up* their sins and gain acceptance with God.

In John 6:60-66, we see one of the saddest passages in the Bible. Those in the synagogue said this was a hard message for them to receive, and Jesus knew they were offended by it. He said "It's the Spirit of the heavenly Father which gives life; not the flesh and blood of your earthly fathers, which has no life apart from the Spirit within." *"The words I speak to you are spirit, and they are real life."* At this point, many turned away from Jesus, returning to their powerless traditions of blood and sacrifice, and they followed Jesus no more. Their *kósmetic* make-up system of alienated thinking kept them so focused on attentive details of *outward* appearances, adornment, and keeping their hands and cups clean, that they didn't realize their *inwardly* perishing hearts were like tombs full of dead bones.

Just as Jesus told the woman at the well, divine life wasn't about different ethnicities having different structures in different places to encounter God in different ways. He told her that one day, they'd all realize they could flourish in loving adoration of the divine- simply by knowing *they* were the holy temple, with God abiding within *them*.

Jesus wasn't on a mission to change God's mind about man, but to change man's mind about God, *and themselves*. Jesus didn't hang on that cross to pay some massive sin debt accrued on a divine account ledger. Those ideas were spawned from orphaned minds in an effort to make-up for separation, as the *disrupted kósmetic system* of man.

God isn't emotionally or mechanically offended by you or any of your actions. There's no naughty or nice list, *and never has been*. The reality that God is not recording a lifetime evidence tape of our failures on some inescapable security camera, can be foreign and downright offensive to many. Why? Because it was taught to us from our earliest childhood memories. Programming from youth is powerful. I'm not saying it's ok to do harmful things. It's not ok; but neither is it ok to teach our kids about a *list keeping God* (as a divine accountant with a judge's gavel) to instill fear *and control* from childhood. The effects of this entrenched domestication can be clearly seen throughout history, along with the bondage to fear of death that it brings. Unfortunately, it still grips many within its clutches *even to this very day*.

Only one thing on earth has the ability
to stop man in his tracks and render him powerless.
His own imagination used apart from its intended design.

Over and over we see man's distorted thinking replayed, resulting in the same alienated mindset, resulting in the same worthless (evil) act-ions. As a man thinks, as in *imagining* himself, *so he becomes*. As man *sees* himself, so he thinks others *see* him as well. When he sees himself in judgment and condemnation that he *imagines* is from God, he also begins to see others in the same accusation and condemnation.

The sons of thunder wanted to call down fire on those who didn't look like them. That's what takes place in a mindset of exclusion. They were only wanting to do something they had seen (or heard) passed down from Elijah in a mindset of judgment and fire. These traits of condemnation and exclusion were passed down through generations as they did the *same* traditional things they had seen their fathers do over and over. **And *death* spread to all men.** Jesus erased the imagery of a ruling Lion; exhibiting the gentlest, most loving, non-judgmental Lamb-like nature they'd ever known. Jesus wasn't about calling down *judgment* fire on anybody, and he made sure his followers knew it.

He *un*-plugs their blowtorch mentality till their thunderstorm gets reduced to a gentle breeze. I can see Jesus shaking his head with a humorous look of *"what am I gonna do with you?"* on his face as he says: "Look guys, I know you're only doing what you've seen your earthly fathers do, but I'm here to show you what your heavenly Father does. And I only do what I've seen him do." Then Jesus leans over closer and says: "If you knew what Spirit you were really born of, you'd know we don't judge, condemn, or call down fire on people. We're all in this together as One- and we're here to do good and help others see themselves through the Father's eyes and love."

Jesus only did what the Father did, and *how* did he do it? He went about doing good, casting out fear, healing all who were oppressed by this *satanâs* mindset of self-accusation. He destroyed the fruit-wilting imagination allowed to harbor in the mind of Adam, which was then passed down (spread) to all men. Jesus went about doing good to ALL, *"I only do what I see my Father do"*- effectively *releasing* those who **had all their lifetime been subjects of this fear-full bondage.**

The most famous scripture in the Bible, along with the two verses that follow directly after it, are also the most *misunderstood*. We've been taught John 3:16-18 is about Jesus coming to take the judgement and condemnation placed on man *by God*. Yet Jesus said he carried no judgment or condemnation toward men at all; and he only did what he saw his Father do. Jesus was simply telling Nicodemus this: when someone could 'see' the Son of Man revealing the Father's nature, that they, *with Jesus as their mirror*, could then begin to 'see' all other sons of men were loved by the heavenly Father as well. *"Father, that they may know they are One with us, and that you have loved them, even as you love me."* Finally, men could *see* (and believe) themselves *re*deemed from a perishing cover-up system of toil and labor, *re*booted back to the quality *(aiónios)* Christ-life they were meant to enjoy!

Jesus tells Nick (v.18) others could *see* his model of incarnation life and then believe it *about themselves*. This would finally set them free from the bondage of fear and guilt man could have dominated *over* to begin with- but instead became dominated *by*, as subjects under it.

Now, man could leave the grave-clothes of fear and death behind him, walking out the authentic life of Oneness with the Father he had long ago forgotten belonged to him. And all the *self*-condemnation man took on because he *thought* he was naked or *un*-covered, would also be stripped away as he saw his true enChristed nature *mirrored* in the Light of Jesus. God has never seen man any other way than through the masterpiece of authentic design, which is all humanity partaking in the divine nature as living temples not made by man. These earthen temples would BE holy and blameless in love, carrying the enChristed Light treasure within, even from their mother's womb.

The Father didn't require blood to suddenly stop counting the sins of the Jews. There was never any sin accounted until the *law of Moses*; and this same *law of Moses* said there could be no remission of sins without shedding of blood. No wonder Paul called the law *the ministry of death*. The law was given through Moses' *perception*, which was a lens of judgment, condemnation, and ex-clusion. But grace and truth (of a heavenly reality within) came through Jesus, as he revealed the *true expression* of the Father and the quality of *Christ-nature*-life.

Jesus never thought twice about editing the lens and law of Moses. The apostles had been raised their entire life in this traditional law; yet, to our detriment, we have placed them all on quite a pedestal by claiming their writings are the perfect word of God. The apostles were people just like us; *sometimes they missed it*. It would serve us well to remember they were coming out of centuries of being programmed by traditions of rules, rituals, judgment, and a blood sacrifice *mentality*. While there are *certain* divine truths that are found in their writings; there's also plenty of evidence they sometimes *backslid* into their old ways of thinking, which also got included in those letters.

It was the reconciling love of God willing to abide even in man's darkness to help man forgive and feel better about *himself*. Just like covering Adam when he *thought* he was naked. *God in Christ* would conciliate the world back to Christ-mind truth in a way THEY BELIEVED was necessary, *by the blood*. God never required a 'sacrifice'; yet Jesus was seen (by them) as the sacrifice they *thought* (in their minds) they needed so they could *have peace* concerning God *and themselves*. Colossians 1:20-23 in the Concordant Literal New Testament is clear: **Paul says man was estranged and enemies in their comprehension**; and *that* distorted comprehension led men into evil and wicked acts. Paul then says God used a body of flesh and its death, to 'make peace' *for them* through the blood *they thought they needed,* to then be able to present men (to themselves) as holy, flawless, and unimpeachable. It was the same way they'd been seen in the Father's eyes *all along*.

Jesus desired to show men the truth of who they were. We find out along the journey that our paternal Source is willing to take all the baby steps men need, until they can finally see themselves in unveiled Christ-mind truth- and that the Father had *never* been counting what they called *sins* against them. Perfect Love keeps no record of wrong; it casts out all fear, along with all the torment fear brings with it.

The Jews *thought* they needed blood because their entire culture revolved around a bloody sacrificial system. *They believed* there could be no forgiveness/remission of sins without the shedding of blood. Jesus was willing to give them the blood they *thought* they needed, to put their orphaned mindset of *sin* behind them once for all. Jesus *never* referred to himself *as a sacrifice to God*, **but as One who came offering Good News from an already satisfied, joyful Father.** We will talk more about this GOOD WILL OFFERING in a future chapter, and how the *forgiveness* extended toward the Jews *wasn't* God killing one man to let other men off the hook. It was a *cutting away* kind of forgiveness, setting men free to enjoy their authentic design. Cleansing their own evil (worthless) conscience from dead works, and removing any, and all sin consciousness from their thinking *once for all*.

What exactly can we take away from the history and journey of our ancient Jewish brothers and sisters? We can see that God is never a respecter of persons or cultures. We see certain parallels between *their thoughts* of nakedness, fear, and separation, which are much like the traditions we've been programmed with. We can see the loving Source of all things good who desired to BE One *in* us, and *as* us; even abiding with us in the midst of our own groping darkness. We begin to see how this Father of all life will climb in our self-made boxes of confinement with us along our journey *for as long as it may take,* until we finally see the truth of who we are. And as scales are peeled from our eyes, we can clearly see this *un*-veiled backdrop of love, liberty, and provision. Here, it's no longer boxed-in perishing flesh that lives- but the I AM *incorruptible* Christ-Spirit fullness, living in us, and as us, *as One!*

CHAPTER SIX

Jesus Paid it All?

Jesus paid it all... all to him I owe....

Have you ever noticed our doctrines (and our songs) end up with us still *owing* someone in the end? First, we owed God a massive sin debt; but then Jesus came and paid it all, and now we owe him. This whole 'owing and paying theology' doesn't sound at all like the Father that Jesus revealed. It was an idea born in man's head. Have you ever seen one of those big billboards along the highway with something written on it and signed with God's name in the bottom corner?

According to our doctrines, this one would be quite appropriate:

YOU OWE ME
(don't ever forget it)
-God

This is one of the foundational ideas that most of us were taught in church. Like many of our other *Bible in the box* theories, we never questioned it because we heard it all our lives from leaders and family members we trusted and were close to. It was always in the backdrop of our classes, sermons, songs, and minds. Consequently, we lived our days from mentally entrenched thought patterns reflecting a servant's jingle of **"I owe, I owe; it's off to work I go."**

As new lights come on and we begin seeing things more clearly along the journey, we are forced (in logical conclusion) to realize the monumental differences we see in one place, now effectively changes things we've just always *accepted* in other places as well.

Once we wake up to the truth that there's no such place as a literal, physical location of eternal torment (hell) where the Father of creation will one day banish *certain* humans to, we reach the logical conclusion that we don't need 'saved' from that. As our eyes are opened to see the divine Source of all life isn't (and never was) running an accounting office in the sky, tallying up humanity's faults, failures, and *sins* on some naughty or nice list, we now realize we don't need to be 'saved' from that either. As we wake up to our true genesis, we clearly see our authentic origin as being born from above. We didn't come from our mother's womb with a faulty spirit carrying some inherited terminal death gene. One by one, the list of things we thought we needed 'saved from' dwindles to nothing before our eyes. We're now forced to ask questions needing *logical conclusion* answers. Questions like: "Why did the Son of Man come?", and "If God didn't require Jesus dying as a *payment* for our sins, then why did he die?"

You may wonder why I keep using terms like 'alienated' and 'orphaned.' You may grow tired of me continually pointing back to a mindset promoting ideas of separation, distance, and delay between the Origin-al Source and *humanity* the Source BEcame. It was, *and still is* these vain imaginations rooted in the high places of man's mind which cause all the other issues of *un*rest, *dis*ease, and *di*vision which invaded the *garden life* God designed for man to flourish in and from.

The truth is, the authentic Source of all life has never seen man as *owing* anything. Nothing coming from our divine *Fatherly/Motherly* Source is accompanied by an invoice. Neither does it come with an obligation contract or responsibility clause. It comes with no shadows whatsoever, but reveals only good and perfect gifts from the Father of all lights. The original *seed thought* of separation that man allowed to root in the matrix of his garden paradise, is actually the same root source of most of our ideas, doctrines (and even our songs) about God. This distorted root still produces twisted fruit according to its own kind. Sermons and tee shirts declaring JESUS PAID IT ALL is *not* an idea that came from God *or Jesus*. It's just another example of the harvest spawned from the 'father of all lies' (that alien-seed lie) man heard whispered in his imagination, which made him think he could ever be separated from his heavenly Source to begin with.

Our perspective picture window toward God affects how we view ourselves *and* how we see all humanity as well. That's why so much in the world still exists in perish mode around us today. The only life Adam could see from his *hiding in the bushes* perspective, was that of the flesh (dust) life around him. He could no longer see things from his Spirit Source; and this veiled vision kept him from partaking and participating in the I AM truth of the God-life BEing within him.

Orphaned thinking produces a perishing, pig-pen existence. We've been *drawn* an image of God as a disgruntled judge, and ourselves as courtroom defendants; rather than the truth of a loving Father joyfully imparting his own life into his own offspring. These twisted theories say men must do certain things to initially become sons and daughters of the *great judge* in the sky. Even if we achieve an entrance into the house as sons, the judge (that we're now *permitted* to call Father) still never removes his official judging garment. This is because, 1) we're still technically on divine probation (which can always be revoked by the judge), and 2) the only reason we got to come in the house in the first place was because Jesus took the judge's wrath on himself, paying all the debt that we, *as evil sinners*, had accrued on the court ledger.

In Romans 8:12, Paul was simply stating that those he wrote to were not 'debtors' to the *flesh*, as in not owing the flesh anything. *That's all.* He wasn't saying they were now debtors *to* something (or someone) else. I understand *thinking* we somehow 'owe' God for his goodness, and I'm one of the most thankful people you'll ever meet; yet I don't see my life as something I 'owe' our divine Source for. I see it as a joyful and passionate extension of Oneness; the incarnation of divine life extended *through* us, as in, BEing *One* with our Source. Our minds struggle to wrap around such life-giving goodness without some kind of reciprocating expectancy, or life-long invoice coming with it. That's because we were programmed (domesticated) by the ideas of man; thoughts and imaginations not yet seeing or knowing what the Father's heavenly love and intentions are really all about.

My wife Kay and I, have several grandchildren as of this writing- a couple of them being just a year old. Seeing them cradled inside our children's arms after birth, as well as holding them in our own arms and speaking blessings of life over them, provides tiny glimpses of how the Father's heart must feel toward us. The tears of joy won't stop. The parents don't look at their offspring with a *you owe me* attitude, and neither do we. We're all dreaming of the life they will *know* as they learn to participate in the love from which they were birthed. How excited we are for them to start enjoying all that was prepared and set into motion, *long before they even came out of their mother's womb.*

Misunderstanding and misapplying words and concepts like wages, debt, propitiation, and adoption (to name a few) [from ancient letters not written to us] have left us with twisted *theories* about God *and ourselves.* God is now projected as a rigid judge refusing to be satisfied with anything less than blood shed through the torturous murder of his own son, inventing a bottom line that **someone had to die.** Someone *had to pay* for all these damages; and the high court of heaven could never be satisfied until that payment was made in full. Not only that, but we say the judge was then forced to turn his back on this legitimate sinless son, all because *he looked too much like us.*

Jesus wasn't on a mission to save people from the Father, which is basically what all our doctrines allude to. He didn't say, *or imply* "I've come to save you from my Father who is going to send you to hell if you don't get saved." Yet, if we strip all the external love bells and whistles off our so-called *good news* message, that's what we're left with. Jesus didn't pay some huge debt the accounting department of heaven demanded to be paid. He was killed by religious and political rulers of that day for being a *non*-conforming rebel who dis-proved, dis-mantled, and literally de-constructed (right before their eyes) their *kósmetic* cover-up system of guilt, condemnation, and *dead* works.

These guys had no fondness for this carpenter's son who flipped the tables on their back-room financial system of devouring widows houses, and keeping common people in fear-full control by burdening them with loads they were never meant to bear. Remember Jesus' words regarding the disciples and himself in his John 17 prayer?

"The *kósmetic cover-up system* has hated them because they don't partake of it; just as they hate me because I do not partake of it."

The Son of Man had no reservations in slinging their storefront approach offerings to the ground. This mild-mannered inclusionist had no problem chasing them out of their own temple area, where they regularly took advantage of people by selling them something that would *supposedly* make them more acceptable in God's eyes.

The sad thing is, we'll flaunt our **'Jesus Paid It All'** tee shirts and shout amen's at the sermons, yet we still don't *actually believe* Jesus 'paying it all' was enough. We don't really believe 'It is Finished.' We're still peddling separation ideologies of man which amount to nothing more than rebranded Old Testament approach offerings. We're still being sold lists of things to do and hoops to jump through, to make us *acceptable* and pleasing to God. The reality is- western Christianity is merely the pseudo-child of Judaism. Maybe no blood is on our altars; yet they're approached with many other forms of *acceptance* offerings.

These are ways that seem right to the alien-ated mind of man, yet no *true life* comes out of these dead-end efforts. Jesus never talked about or remotely implied that men owed God anything. He *did* talk about his refusal to leave man in their orphaned mindset, which was responsible for making them *think* they were separated from God to begin with. He *did* tell them they were the light of the world; a light so beautifully intense he compared it to an elevated city that couldn't be hidden. He *did* tell them about learning to let their inner light shine (which he associated with good) so others around them would know unmistakably who, *and how good* their true paternal Source was.

The word Jesus used for these 'good' works was **kälos** #2570, which means **beautifully ideal; standing out as being excellent in nature and characteristics**. Jesus implied their true light wasn't meant to remain concealed within, as though covered by some basket which prevented its illumination from being seen and enjoyed by all. Bushels (or pecks) were meant to be carriers of things and were used as a *measuring device*; they weren't designed to cover things or hide them. Jesus presented this 'upside down' basket analogy to show them that men and women had been seeing themselves all wrong, through some outward measurement mentality masking the beauty of the authentic light treasure within them. The Son of Man said he had no intention of leaving them in this *upside-down* limited measure mindset.

It's important to remember these teachings took place long before Jesus died. They were in no way meant to imply a *future state* of light or sonship that would only be available to them *after* the cross. We see Jesus telling the multitudes (all local ethnicities of that day) from a hillside amphitheater (Matthew 5,6,7) that they needed to stop seeing themselves upside down as *orphans*. He repeatedly told them (at least 7 times in the beatitudes) not to look toward the religious leaders he called *hypokrités* (masked stage performers) in the synagogue as their example. He *did* say these *kósmetic system* scribes and Pharisees were nothing more than a bunch of fruit stealing ravenous wolves- *covered up* in the fresh-pressed outer *appearance* of sheep's clothing.

Fifteen times within this teaching Jesus referred to *his* Father in heaven... as *their* Father in heaven, continually reminding them they were treasure carrying sons and daughters of God. He said that as their own eyes were opened to this truth, their inner light would then radiate unhindered like a beautiful city on a hill. They would not only magnify the Father's Light as BEing their own inner Source, but would help the eyes of others to become open and illuminated (waking up) to see who they were as well! Jesus was simply trying to tell them this: **"When you see who you *truly* are, you'll live like who you truly are! Your perfectly designed ideal [kälos] acts will be the undeniable expression of predetermined workmanship given in the Father's [kaléō] surname calling; the shining excellence of divine nature placed in you as treasured heavenly offspring!"**

Paul echoes this same **kälos** truth in his letter to the Ephesians:

Ephesians 2:10 (NKJV)

For we are His workmanship, created in Christ Jesus for **good works**, which God **prepared beforehand** that we should walk in them.

Now, let's take a look at *sin* in reality...

Matthew 1:21-23 (NKJV)

And she will bring forth a Son, and you shall call His name Jesus, **for He will save His people from their sins.** So all this was done that it might be fulfilled which was spoken by the Lord through the prophet saying: "Behold, the *virgin* shall be with child, and bear a Son, and they shall call His name Immanuel," which is translated, "God with us."

You won't find any language in this or any other ancient prophecies describing Jesus as paying a debt *for* anything, but as his people being saved *from* something. That's some 'thing,' as in a noun describing a place or a thing, not a verb describing act-ions or physical motions.

So, what kind of sins was Jesus to *save* (deliver, heal, make whole) people (move away, as in a departure) *from*? Most people I know will agree that *sin* can be summed up by 'missing the mark'; a term used in archery language to describe an arrow landing somewhere other than the target goal. Here are the different variations of the word:

#264 hamartánō (from 1 /A "not" and /méros 3313, "a part, share") Hamartánō was used in ancient times of an archer missing the target. #266 hamartía (a feminine noun derived from 'not' and /méros 3313, "a part, share of") properly, not-share; loss (forfeiture) because of not hitting the target; the brand of sin that emphasizes its self-originated (self-empowered) nature – not originating or empowered by God. #268 hamartōlós (substantive adjective derived from 264-hamartánō) 'to forfeit by missing the mark or falling short of the target.'

Let's take a short treasure hunt, moving away from shallow end (literal reading) perceptions, to a place where we can dive off into some deeper metaphorical riches waiting to be discovered.

Matthew 1:21-23, we saw on previous page regarding 'saving his people from their sins' comes directly from Isaiah 7:14, and here is the following verse regarding how this 'saving' of the people will happen;

Isaiah 7:15 (NKJV)
Curds and honey He shall eat, that He may know to refuse the evil and choose the good.

The word 'curds' comes from *chêmâh* in Hebrew, which means thickened milk, cheese or butter. It holds the same 'richness of kine' context as the word *châlâb* (milk) used in Exodus 3:8.

Exodus 3:8 (NKJV)

I have come down to deliver them out of the hand of the Egyptians, and to bring them up from that land to a good and large land, to a **land flowing with milk and honey,** to the place of the Canaanites and the Hittites and Amorites and Perizzites and Hivites and the Jebusites.

Châlâb is from *chêleb,* meaning the fatness of, or richest, choicest part. This promised land place was 'flowing' with things 'chosen' in richness, and is mentioned repeatedly in Old Testament scriptures. This promised land was *there all along,* but the children of Israel were too busy wandering around in their circular wilderness thinking to discover it. **There wasn't anything actually holding them in bondage** **except* **their own mindset.** (Read that as many times as you need to.)

Even when they went in to see this flowing fatness firsthand, it was their 'I am not' *grasshopper outlook* (in their own eyes) that kept them from enjoying all that was provided and rightfully theirs. Oh, and the word 'flowing' wasn't describing a gentle trickle of substance either. It comes from the verb *zuwb,* or *zoov,* and is also used in association with the gushing discharge of sexual fluids in both men and women. The promised land was therefore to be associated with extraordinary (fatherly and motherly) fertility, as its own *gushing life* produced a perpetual, fruit-full harvest of overflowing proportions. It was right there and already belonged to them; yet they forfeited participation in it, missing the goal, while wandering in their *self-made* wilderness.

Let's look at Isaiah 7:15 one more time:

Isaiah 7:15 (NKJV)

Curds and honey He shall eat, that He may know to refuse the evil and choose the good.

Isaiah's language depicts this Son of Man who *knew* he was a son of God; and nothing could move him away from that knowledge! He ate and flourished from the CHRIST TREE OF LIFE mindset alone. Just as David reflected in Psalm 1, Jesus meditated on the Father's goodness day and night; his life flourishing in abounding fruit from being rooted and grounded by rivers of living water. His eye was single; therefore, his entire BEing emanated light from within. Unlike Adam, he said NO to *diabolical* thoughts suggesting he might need something other than what he already had. He said NO to mental *satanâs* accusations which demanded that he prove "If you're *really* the son of God." He said GET OUT to the tempting *father of all lies* carrying implications that he needed another source of authority from the *outside*. Although his external surroundings often portrayed things which *appeared* as lack, fear, or separation, he *refused to be removed* from the righteousness (equity), joy, and peace of inner garden-life he *knew* was actually his!

Jesus *knew no sin* because he never fell short of knowing who he was! He walked in freedom from any alien-ated, orphaned lies or vain imaginations. The children of Israel prayed for a *deliverer* to lead them out of their bondage. Although this lover of all men didn't look anything like the mashiach they had envisioned, this incarnate son of God desired to *save them* from own their self-made wilderness, and lead them into a life of gushing richness already waiting *within them*.

This fruit-full, gushing *life more abundant* language was spoken by Jesus everywhere he went. Where did Jesus say the kingdom of God/heaven was? He said *"it is within you."* Please don't believe some watered-down translation implying that it means 'among' you or 'in your midst,' as in 'outside' or 'around' you. The word *entós* Jesus used means *presently within* or inside. He told the Pharisees they not only refused to presently enter in themselves; but were cramping the gate, hindering those who did want to enter. Jesus said it was the drunkards and prostitutes who were actually entering in and enjoying this inner kingdom life; and they did it right out in front of the religious leaders!

On the last, greatest day of their celebration feast, Jesus totally *interrupted* their sacred ritualistic service. He stands up and cries out in a way everyone present would have no choice but to hear him. I can imagine this rebel rabbi's exhortation going something like this:

"HEY, You guys look really thirsty! When you get tired of dipping those hand drawn waters of shadowed proportions, drop your tiny man-made pitchers and come to me! Once you see who I AM, you'll start seeing who YOU ARE too! Then the heavenly life within you will GUSH FORTH from your matrix like rivers of living water!!"

This inner garden paradise had been within man all along; they just refused to enter in. Stephen told them they were stiff necked and *uncircumcised* (their head was consumed with *flesh*), preventing them from feeling and hearing the intimacy of heaven's truth. He said it was because they had always **resisted the Holy Spirit,** just as their fathers of generations before them had. *And... that's when they stoned him.*

The Bible has a lot between the covers (written by different people at various times) regarding *sin*. Our doctrines have much to say about sin, and chances are slim that you'll make it through an entire church service without hearing about it in some form or fashion. Since Jesus said no man had seen or known the Father like the Son, *and*, since we're looking at things in *context*, we will look at *sin* through Jesus' words and actions, and not focus too much on what *others* have to say.

The difference in *how* people view sin will clearly show up, and can always be traced back to *their* individual perspective of how *their* God views humanity. I was taught *sin* was missing how God 'commanded' men to live and act. Some were done negligently as *sins of omission*; meaning not *doing* something enough, or not *doing* it right. Examples were (but not limited to) **not** *praying* **enough, not** *reading the Bible* **enough, not** *tithing* **enough, not** *serving* **enough,** or **not** *witnessing to others* (warning them about hell) **enough.** The common thread in *kósmos* systematic religion is, *whatever* you're doing, **it's not enough.**

Sins could also be done on purpose as *sins of commission,* which meant they were acts done out of sheer rebellion to God's laws. Either way, whether intentional or negligent, sin in any form (we were told) was wicked and displeasing in the eyes of God. In fact, sin was so evil in God's sight, that he couldn't even look at it, lest all be destroyed out of his holy and righteous judgment. This takes us back to individual opinions and perspectives of *who* God is and *how* he views humanity. It's where things get a little fuzzy (again) in what we were taught as *truth.* The right questions *always* end up with fuzzy and imaginative doctrinal theories dancing in circles trying to explain them.

Our faith statements boldly declare Jesus was fully man and fully God at the same time. They declare Jesus didn't do anything he hadn't already seen his Father do. Yet we see Jesus spending much more time (right out in the open) with those called *sinners,* than he did with the *religious leaders.* And these weren't folks who just omitted tithing or didn't pray long enough. Nope. They were the full-blown, *on purpose,* committed sinners. You know- the drunkards, hookers, and thieving types. Jesus ate with them, drank with them, and even spent the night with them (see the section on Zacchaeus). How could this 'fully God' Son of Man, who only did *what he saw his Father do,* have ongoing, intimate, public contact with so many *on purpose,* committed sinners, without annihilating them with flames from nostrils of holy anger??

It appears Jesus knew something about *sin* we've yet to figure out. It also appears, from his repeatedly *expressed* actions, that he'd seen the Father's heart doing something we've said God could *never* do and still maintain his holiness. From all public appearances, Jesus was clearly viewing these people's *sin* much differently than as them being wicked, evil, and displeasing to God. Again, this difference will always stand out, and can always be traced back to one's individual opinions and perspective about God and how *they think* God views humanity.

Jesus didn't show much concern over outward (verb) *acts* of sin; but seemed focused on the inwardly missed target (noun) *state* of sin, and the orphaned thinking which caused people to then be led into all kinds of distorted acts running counter to their authentic origin. Over 40 times in the gospels, Jesus is recorded talking about *sin* as an object or subject in noun form. Only three times is it indicated as a verb or an outward act. One of these times is John 9:3, as Jesus passed by a man who was blind from birth. The disciples asked Jesus whether it was the man *or* his parents who sinned, resulting in the man's blindness. Jesus told them, *"Neither this man nor his parents sinned."* Jesus revealed that neither guilt, nor any other supposed penalty or indebtedness to sin was responsible for this man's condition.

"Neither this man nor his parents sinned" is yet another example of Jesus dismantling concocted doctrines of *original sin* in all men or the supposed unavoidable death penalty passed down to all men from Adam. Jesus told the man he had come to reveal the true Light in which mankind was created. After putting clay on the man's eyes, he tells the man to go to the pool of 'Siloam' (which means *send away* or *let go*), and wash away the *blindness* he had dealt with his entire life.

I often wondered if this *clay and water* story represents man's *vux darkness* occurring as his focus turned *outward* toward his *earthen* vessel, to the point his mental distortion dammed up the *inner* flow of Spirit-life awareness? What if Jesus was showing the man how to exercise his rightful dominion to send that blinded existence away and let it go, as he washed it in the spirit waters of Siloam? There he could (and did) begin enjoying the *vision and mindset* he was created to flourish in. His sight isn't all that was made new to him. **This man had never seen *anything* before**; yet his entire mental awareness and brain function was transformed instantly. This allowed him to begin recognizing and interacting normally with people, places, and things he'd never visually seen even one time through the course of his life!

Once we 'see' the truth of who we are inwardly, it begins to affect how we see and interact with things outwardly as well.

This Son of Man revealing man's divine incarnation, said he didn't come to judge or condemn mankind, but to save them. **He said he was sent as a physician to heal those with _sin_, as though he were curing a disease; not as being sent by a gavel-driving judge with vengeance to punish a crime or settle a debt.** So, did Jesus see sin in the same common (hamartía) context we know as missing the mark or intended goal? Yes, I believe that's exactly how he saw it. But how could Jesus actually believe sin was missing the mark, or the goal, and yet at the same time not judge people, and treat each and every person with such love and care? It all goes back to Jesus' _perspective_ of the Father and how he saw humanity. He loved everyone the same, no matter how they were presently _acting_. **Jesus knew the Father's target goal was altogether different than what we've been taught and believed.**

Jesus showed such love and compassion for all people because the mark they had been missing, didn't have _anything_ to do with outward acts, keeping a list of rules and requirements, or pleasing some judge with a surveillance camera and a transgressors list. These _sinners_ were the same ones Jesus referred to as his own brothers and sisters. The target goal they'd been missing all their life was the _sin_ of them not seeing themselves as treasure carrying sons and daughters of God. They'd fallen short of _seeing_ themselves as authentic offspring of the same heavenly Father Jesus called his own. And Jesus knew people who _can't see_ who they are, can't know how to _live like_ who they truly are. With heavenly love and passion, the Son of Man revealed to them _as in a mirror_, what sons and daughters really look like!

The author of Hebrews referred to _sin_ as a state of being, or a _consciousness_ in man's mind that would vanish, if _and when_ they could finally see themselves in a pure state of perfection (10:2). This vision of perfection was something their worthless _sacrifice_ mentality, along with its worthless *sacrificial* objects, was never able to provide for them. *Sin consciousness* is fruit produced from the alien seed lie in man's imagination, which focuses on *outward separation*, rather than *inner Oneness* with the Father. Look at the *sin* definition (page 188): **#266**= SELF-empowered, not originating with, or empowered by God.

The Son of Man passionately destroyed the works of this diabolical *satanâs* father of all lies which had become the voice in man's head telling him he was naked, un-covered, and needed to hide. Jesus went about showing other sons of men their true origin as *sons of God*, and how much their heavenly Father loved them. His life would end up being seen (by them) as the perfect sacrifice they *thought* they needed, helping to heal their warped consciousness. The veils that kept them from *seeing* could be torn in two, setting them free from their bloody altars and continual reminders of sin once for all. This new, perfected vision of themselves would allow them to *run boldly* into spiritual high places of enthroned heavenly grace. Here, they'd finally see that this *consciousness of sin* had never even existed in the Father's heart!

It's interesting that in every *pre-cross* occurrence the Son of Man told someone their sins were *forgiven*- blind eyes were opened, they walked, ran, jumped, and were instantly healed from any *dis-eased* state they'd previously existed in. No cross, no blood, or wrath invoked payment FOR sin found anywhere. Why? The *aphíēmi* (forgiveness) of Jesus *set them free* FROM sin to see themselves in authentic sonship. They'd no longer remain SUBJECTS of the fear of death that had all their lifetime held them in the crippling bondage of an orphaned, *perishing* existence. They were *set free* to see the truth and hit the targeted life and *conscious*ness of the Father's intentional design. Now, they could finally begin to see, participate in, and enjoy their own incarnation of divine nature, extended and consisting as ONE IN CHRIST!

The *aphíēmi forgiveness* Jesus revealed to those in this perishing infirmity (sickness) of sin, was a healing *release* to move them forward with unveiled vision *to see how* to hit the bulls-eye of their authentic origin. As we've seen previously, it's like cutting the rope which had bound a ship to a *foreign* harbor, leaving it behind to sail in wide-open seas, just as it was intended to do. It is much different than *xarízomai*; which means to show *grace* or grant the type of forgiveness associated with a judicial pardon or being released from an owed debt.

Let's take a look at another instance the true meaning of *aphíēmi* is revealed in scripture, found in Matthew 4:20:

Matthew 4:19-20
Then He said to them "Follow Me, and I will make you fishers of men." They immediately **left** *(aphíēmi)* **their nets behind** and followed Him.

Do we see anything here about forgiveness as we know it? Anything about Jesus paying a debt or a judicial pardon because God saw them as evil or couldn't stand the smell of fish on them? No, because that's not what the word means at all. **It means Jesus was giving them permission to see a greater reality about their life than the fathers of their flesh had known how to introduce them to.** It was one Son of Man desiring to show other sons of men a *more abundant* kind of life their authentic *heavenly* Father had empowered them to live from!

When Jesus cried out "Father forgive them" on the cross, he was saying, *"Set them free from the bondage that veils their sight, Father; for they don't have a clue who they are or what they're doing!!"*

The one (only) time the Son of Man *ever* used the word *xarízomai* was in Luke 7:42-43. Jesus had been invited to dine with a Pharisee named Simon. A woman with a *preceding reputation* as a sinner heard Jesus was there. Intruding, obviously uninvited by the well-dressed religious host, she falls and covers Jesus' feet with expensive oil and tears of love; and then wipes them clean with her hair. The Pharisee **grumbles to himself,** *"If this guy was the real deal, he wouldn't let this sinner woman come near him!"* Jesus then engages Simon with a scenario using a type of *debt cancellation* language he might be familiar with:

Luke 7:40-42 (NKJV)

And Jesus answered and said to him, "Simon, I have something to say to you." So he said, "Teacher, say it." "There was a certain creditor who had two debtors. One owed five hundred denarii, and the other fifty. And when they had nothing with which to repay, he freely forgave them both. Tell Me, therefore, which of them will love him more?" Simon answered and said, "I suppose the one whom he forgave more." And Jesus said to him, "You have rightly judged."

Jesus opens the conversation using a form of debt forgiveness this rule keeping finger pointer might possibly be able to comprehend, allowing Simon a highlight opportunity to 'rightly judge' something for himself. The Pharisee isn't really sure where Jesus is going with his question, any more than he's actually sure of the correct answer. The scenario involves a graceful response passed down from a creditor; and graceful responses weren't something the Pharisees were known to be famous for. Yet Simon takes a stab at it, trying to logically *suppose* the response this rebel rabbi might be looking for. Jesus then tosses him a momentary *attaboy* for an assumed answer he had given from his judgment/debt/payment background.

Jesus then shifts Simon's focus to this woman of sinful *reputation*. The setting-free forgiveness the Son of Man describes over her isn't based on an idea of creditors, debtors, accounting lists, or settling a payment. Simon doesn't understand it, *but this sinner woman does...* and she's already producing fruit from it without even having asked Jesus for forgiveness! How? Because she knew this Son of Man had a *reputation* that preceded him as well. It was Jesus' reputation of love, acceptance, and inclusion that offered true friendship and intimacy to those who were outcast by religion and the popular circles of society.

Jesus, now leaving any idea of *xarizomai* 'paid it all' terminology behind, begins describing the *aphiēmi* forgiveness this woman of ill repute is obviously *already* walking in. How? Simply by recognizing Jesus' message of freedom- *and that she was already included in it!*

Luke 7:44-50 (NKJV)

Then He turned to the woman and said to Simon, "Do you see this woman? I entered your house; you gave Me no water for My feet, but she has washed My feet with her tears and wiped them with the hair of her head. You gave Me no kiss, but this woman has not ceased to kiss My feet since the time I came in. You did not anoint My head with oil, but this woman has anointed My feet with fragrant oil. Therefore I say to you, her sins, which are many, are forgiven, for she loved much. But to whom little is forgiven, the same loves little." Then He said to her, "Your sins are forgiven." And those who sat at the table with Him began to say to themselves, "Who is this who even forgives sins?" Then He said to the woman, "Your faith has saved you. Go in peace."

What evidence do we see that this woman had been *cut away and set free* from a perishing orphaned mentality, where she'd been bound to a foreign existence? Not knowing *who* she was had caused her to give herself away to many strangers, who offered her mere sustenance in a perishing existence. She had heard (and seen the fruit) of Jesus' LIFE MORE ABUNDANT message and had decided she was *entering in* to enjoy it all! Jesus said the evidence became outwardly obvious when she saw her inner God-given worth and value. Now that she had seen how much she was truly loved; she'd begun to love much in return!

Our veiled *theology* has taught us that we are *forgiven* for case by case transgressions on a daily basis, *because that's what a judge does*. And *that* forgiveness (we're taught) is handed down as a 'graceful' response that comes *only after* the high court of heaven was fulfilled by the torturous, bloody death of Jesus, to satisfy the judge's wrath by *paying* that debt. But when we stop seeing ourselves as defendants- as objects of condemnation through eyes of a distant judge, and see ourselves (as Jesus did) as expressed offspring BEings of a passionate Father, everything *in*, and *around* our life, begins changing to reflect it.

The Son of Man didn't pay any *debt* for the Jews or mankind as a whole, for which they would then *owe him*. He acted like a heavenly *physician* to heal the downcast and dis-eased perishing state of man's mind. This rebel Jesus was the smoothest re-po man their cover-up system had ever seen, and they didn't know what to do with him. Even though they hated him and eventually had him killed; his life and death repossessed many among them with a redeemed and resurged consciousness. Jesus gave his people a clear and unveiled reflection as he taught them that they too, were treasured offspring of One Source. He lived *and died* among his brothers and sisters, revealing to them *who* they really were in the Father's eyes. Why? So they could now *stand up* as extended offspring of God; not just merely partakers of, but now *seeing* how to fully *participate* IN that divine nature *as One!*

How does this affect us today, 2000 years later? We can embrace this same *resurged* heavenly love, knowing that we carry the same ability as Jesus, and are totally free to enjoy our own journey. How? Through the life and love we've seen portrayed in an ancient culture, which cut the ropes of their bondage to fear and death. Anytime downcast thoughts of condemnation or alienation try to bind us up in a foreign harbor, we can remember the life Jesus revealed of *Oneness* with the divine Source of all. It was for *freedom alone* the Jews were made free. It wasn't because of an accrued debt paid to some judgmental distant deity. It was because Jesus showed them the mirror image of the Father *and* themselves. It was unveiled in their awareness as they saw their own reflection in him, seeing this 'life more abundant' of God *with* them, *in* them, and *as them!* Here, they could finally know once for all, *they were inseparably One with their divine Source!*

CHAPTER SEVEN

A Different Kind of Offering

If the target goal the Jews fell short of (sin) was missing the mark of intimacy, then the Son of Man would have to deliver other sons of men from that *missed mark state* by restoring righteous equity to their comprehension. According to John, Paul, and the author of Hebrews, to gain that *effect*, Jesus would need to penetrate their darkness in such an illuminated way they could *see themselves* in that same light.

Paul suggested what Jesus *became* (as sin [to the Jews]) was not a penal substitution sacrifice; but was him entering into man's perishing *mental state* of alienated existence. The Hebrews author wrote Jesus would have to (in all ways) *become* like his brethren, experiencing what they had from this orphaned state of thinking. By his death, *and co-crucifying* this worth-less comprehension, they could be REBOOTED (Peter called it *begotten again*) with a REDEEMED Christ-awareness of their own authentic origin. Here, they could once for all be released (*aphíēmi*- set free) from being *subjects* (all their life) to that bondage and fear of death. It was this same fear-full seed-lie of alienation and separation (the life-stealing *satanâs* father [source] of all lies) Adam allowed to *take root* and dominion over his mind- rather than him exercising his own GOD ON EARTH dominion over it. Let's look at some things the Bible describes as Jesus actually doing.

First, it's vital to realize Jesus said the Father would never (ever) leave, desert, or forsake him. He told the disciples, *"I will never leave or forsake you,"* and he only said and did what he saw the Father do. Just before he went to the cross, he told his followers (John 16:32), "You will all scatter, each going back to your own (who *you've* always known). You will leave me (*monos*-#3441-alone/desolate/forsaken); yet I'm not alone (desolate or forsaken), for the Father (I've known) is always with me." Paul described this as Jesus' willingness to 'become sin' (for others), to crucify this orphaned, forsaken, *mindset* right before their eyes. Yet he never actually *sinned* himself, by falling short (missing the mark) of truth in regard to his own inseparable sonship. The author of Hebrews wrote it was this Christ-knowledge of sonship (to be rebooted in others) that Jesus knew was waiting on the other side of the cross. THIS was the joy he held in his heart as he endured it.

"I refuse to leave you thinking you are orphans!"

Isaiah had seen *certain aspects* of this crucifixion *in clear truth* several hundred years before the actual event, but like many other scriptures, our *translations* of what he was trying to express pale in comparison to what was actually pouring from his heart. By the Spirit of the Father within him, Isaiah was able to climb the proverbial wall of time and *view from within,* an event that wouldn't (literally) take place for another six or seven hundred years. Perhaps he experienced what Paul described in 1 Corinthians 2:10-12, as seeing *deep* things the Source of all life had seen *before the foundation of the world-* and the *lamb slain* because of man's downcast mind and the *kósmos* sacrificial system that followed it. Isaiah's vision saw this in the distance in *front of him*, yet described it as though it had happened in the past *behind him.* How so? Maybe he experienced the 'before' pro-*vision* of God not bound by time, and the restored awareness of the Father's authentic design that could never be altered or changed. It wasn't a lamb slain that *God needed* to see men differently- it was a perfect offering *they needed* (and couldn't provide for themselves) to 'make peace' and be *set-free* from their own alienated sin consciousness once for all!

Let's look at some of Isaiah's revelation as revealed in chapter 53:
We esteemed (reckoned/figured) him stricken, smitten, and afflicted by God, *but he wasn't*. He was despised, rejected, and afflicted by men. They led him as a lamb to the slaughter; and as a sheep before its shearers is silent, he opened not his mouth. He had no kingly splendor nor any outward attractive appearance that would make us desire him. In fact, *he looked just like us.* He knew sorrows, pain, and was *acquainted* with the same grief and infirmities we were; so rather than gazing face to face *with* him, we hid our faces *from* him. Then we began to see something. SURELY (why, of course), he wasn't carrying his own griefs and infirmities; he was carrying ours! He was wounded (pierced through) out of our own transgressions (rebellion). He was bruised (crushed) out of our iniquities (perverted distortions). Why of course! How could we *not* see it? It was us (like wayward sheep) who had gone astray- having turned (all of us) to a path *facing away* from truth! Yet, the self-existent One interceded through him, reaching into the depths of perversion in us all! Those to whom he offered shalom wholeness, were the very ones landing violent blows upon his back! As the angry plowmen dug their furrows deep into his flesh- they had no idea... *those stripes would bring healing to* (LOST SHEEP OF ISRAEL) *us all.*

Here we see the true *passion of the Christ* in action; not as a bloody sacrifice to a judge who demanded it, nor as an object of torturous substitutionary wrath. We see the Son of Man actually identifying with the darkened distortions and orphaned comprehensions *of others* he lovingly called brethren. The word 'acquainted' in Hebrew, is *yada `*. It means *know intimately* or become *One* with. It's used in Genesis 4:1 when Adam intimately *knew* Eve as *One* and a seed was imparted to bring new life. This Son of Man would joyfully unveil the incorruptible Christ-seed *even in* the entombed darkness of man's mind; knowing that it would produce an unstoppable harvest of *resurged* Christ-life awareness *in others, so* the gates of *hádēs* (realm of the *unseen*) could never again prevail against them or hold them back!

This oneness with man's *'you brought us into the wilderness to die'* orphaned mindset, is what the Son of Man was identifying with when he cried out the *first* line of Psalm 22: *"My God, why have you forsaken me?"* Over 30 distinct messianic prophecies (the people had all grown up memorizing) would be lived out right before their eyes, only for the Son of Man to *then* cry out the *last* line of the Psalm, which is the Hebrew equivalent of "IT IS FINISHED!" This was all so powerful, so recognizable, and so real to them, that even a Roman guard stood in amazement saying, *"Truly, this was the Son of God!"* We will look at this subject in greater detail in the following chapter.

Of course, when I share these things with my *penal substitution* believing brothers, they will always go straight to Isaiah 53:10, "For it pleased the Lord to bruise (crush) him" as proof of their doctrine. Francois du Toit shares a Mirror Bible footnote regarding this verse:

[It pleased the Lord to "crush" him.] The New Revised Standard Version translators say in their footnotes to this verse: "Meaning of the Hebrew uncertain." The Septuagint [Greek version] of this verse, which was written 250 years before Jesus, by 72 Hebrew scholars [with access to older manuscripts than we have today] have rendered the Hebrew text as follows: *"and the Lord desires to purify him of the plague!"* This can also be translated, *"The Lord desires to cleanse his wounds!"* The word *plege* means a wound.

In Hebrews 10:5-9, we see (2 times back to back) the *Christ-voice* speaking in Psalm 40:6-8, and then reiterated by the Hebrews author. Both statements adamantly say that God did not desire, require, or receive pleasure for sin offerings. You won't convince me (just because Moses said so) that a *Spirit* God (who doesn't operate according to the flesh) commanded Moses to kill animals and offer their blood to him. You'll never convince me a *Spirit* God actually told Moses he liked the smoky aroma of ram legs and entrails in his nostrils. I'm thinking maybe Moses was the one who liked it. Why? Because none of that sounds anything like Jesus, who was the express image of the Father.

Jesus didn't participate in, nor endorse animal sacrifices. Yes, I know there will always be some who bring up the leper that was healed in Mark 1:40-44, and how Jesus then instructed him to take the offering Moses had commanded to the temple priest. Let's look at this passage:

Now a leper came to Him, imploring Him, kneeling down to Him and saying to Him, "If You are willing, You can make me clean." Then Jesus, moved with compassion, stretched out His hand and touched him, and said to him, "I am willing; be cleansed." As soon as He had spoken, immediately the leprosy *left* him, and he was cleansed. And He strictly warned him and sent him away at once, and said to him, "See that you say nothing to anyone; but go your way, show yourself to the priest, and offer for your cleansing those **things which Moses commanded, as a *testimony* to them.**"

The word 'testimony' is *marturion* in the Greek. It means evidence, witness, or *proof*. By sending the healed man to the priests, is Jesus somehow implying that he is working hand in hand with the law, or that the man should participate in the law to validate Moses? I don't think this is what was going on here at all. The first **32** verses in the 14th chapter of Leviticus are FULL of rituals and requirements *Moses gave* regarding what needed to happen for a leper to be 'cleansed.' Everything from killing birds, sprinkling blood, shaving their head and eyebrows, staying out of their tent for 7 full days, killing lambs, putting blood on their thumbs, ears, and feet, burning more offerings, killing some more doves or pigeons, and on and on the rituals would go... **'such as the Leper could afford'** (14:30-31). *Read the last line again.*

Are we to believe God now saw men in a different way than they'd been seen before? Had God suddenly decided to start healing men in new ways? Was some new covenant or dispensation now in place that made things different? Oh wait, *Jesus hadn't gone to the cross yet.* None of what we're told the cross did for men had taken place. No, nothing changed; and covenants and dispensation talk are the ideas and imaginations of man anyway. Jesus, the Father, and healing were the same yesterday, today, and forever. What *changed* was this man's perspective of *his value* to God. It was then, his flesh *dis*-ease left him.

We see Jesus moving in great love and compassion (without fear), reaching out *breaking the law* to touch the man. It's this dramatic (hear the people gasp) visual experience where Jesus puts actions to his words. *"One day you'll know that just as I AM One with the Father, so also are you One with us as well."* Just like the woman who was about to be stoned- and just as the woman who poured expensive oil on Jesus' feet- this leper was touched in a way that *showed* him Oneness with 'heaven' and how valuable his life *really* was to God. This wasn't something the Pharisees or the priests who enforced the law had ever told or shown those they called *sinners*. But Jesus told people the truth of who they were- *and he didn't charge them a fee.*

What happened with the leper? Did he ask for forgiveness or jump through a bunch of hoops *in whatever way he could afford?* Nope. He didn't come to Jesus with *any* pre-scribed approach offerings. Like the woman with the oil, he knew Jesus had a reputation that preceded him. He comes to the Son of Man in the faith of already knowing, "If you're willing to act, this *flesh ailment* will have to leave me." I can see and feel Jesus' eyes welling up with tears of joy as he reaches out with a smile that says, ***"Let me show you just how willing I AM!"***

The scriptures say when this happened, the *flesh dis-ease* plaguing the man, *left him*. Jesus then tells him to take the offering *Moses required*, to show the priests (as evidential proof) that what *Moses said* was required, **wasn't at all necessary** for him to become whole, *once he saw* how God loved him. *Oh, and it didn't cost him a thing.*

Jesus didn't actually do a lot of things we have ascribed to him. He had no desire to be a lord, ruler, or be worshiped. Worship is another idea we've twisted into something it was never intended to be. We'll stand with arms outstretched *toward the sky* asking God to *come* visit our service. We plead for Holy Spirit to *come* empower us, ignoring and resisting the power of kingdom-life already within us. Why?

Because we were programmed from youth with a distance/delay mindset. We can never BEcome closer to the divine Source of Light and Life than we are right now; *we can only become more aware of it.* We can never be separated from THE CHRIST in whom all consist. Of that SAME fullness have we all received, and we are complete *within* that fullness. Nothing can ever separate the Source of life within us from that life we came from and consist in. It's *One*. The only place you'll ever be *away* from Christ is in your imagination; and there are plenty of well-meaning people out there to help you *imagine* that.

When your last breath is taken in that temporary skin suit, the **real you** will be right where you've always been, **in Christ**. The difference will be that you won't have a worldly imagination or other people's ideas and opinions hindering you from enjoying it. What will that look like? Well, whatever it is (and no one here can tell you that), it will be like everything else we've found out *in truth* about being IN Christ. It will be exceedingly, abundantly, far beyond anything we could dare think, imagine, or know how to ask for from an *earthly* point of view!

I'm not one who sets out to be offensive toward the personal beliefs of others, and anyone who *knows* me will attest to that. But since this is my book about my journey, I have no problem talking about my own beliefs, or the *lack of them*. I find it hard to fathom I ever entertained many ideas of God, myself, or others programmed into my thinking from childhood. Now in my 60's, most of those beliefs are completely foreign to me. One such former belief is of a distant deity who created everything from atoms to ants to asteroids, with passionate provision that holds them together with intergalactic harmony and consistency; **But then**, he commands men to now take away (kill) the very existence of creatures this *Spirit Source* had put life into, and set them on fire as a sacrifice that would *smell good in his nostrils* and appease his anger.

Until we realize, and are willing to *admit* the Bible was written from *ancient perspectives* (much of it written by others than to whom it is ascribed), we won't see how to glean its many metaphorical and symbolic truths which are actually relevant to our own day and time.

We can all find things in scripture to make them 'say' what we want them to, but the only ones which are actually 'inspired' by God are those seen through the eyes and perspective of our true Source, and not man. **To believe everything in the Bible is perfect and infallible just as it is written, means we have to believe everything ancient cultures believed.** I tried that for many years while striving to be a 'good Christian.' I won't do that anymore. Ever. *I know better now.*

God provided the covering Adam and Eve (hiding in the bushes) *thought* they needed to feel better about themselves; even though God's mind hadn't changed about them, nor had he *ever* seen them as *un*-covered. Some describe the cross as a heavenly scandal- whereby the Spirit Source of all life, who would never require a life [or blood] to change how he views his offspring, would now actually BEcome the enChristed offering to satisfy (once for all) what the children of Israel *thought they needed* and was required. Here, as they saw Isaiah 53 and Psalm 22 lived out right before their eyes, every detail of all they had done all those years waiting on a deliverer, along with what they'd seen on the cross, would cause an unveiling of *risen Christ awareness!* It would be FINISHED once for all. Their personal consciousness and their continual reminders of sin could be wiped away, and they could now be awakened from their orphaned, separated servant slumber to *arise and shine,* while participating in glorious equity as the authentic offspring of God they truly were!

> **"Sacrifice and offerings for *sin* were never your will,**
> **but a body you have prepared for me, to do and reveal your will."**
> **"I AM here to reveal what you found pleasure in all along...**
> ***through intimacy and sonship as One!"***

The word 'offering' (*prosphora #4376*) is used in reference to Jesus, in Hebrews 10:10-18. It comes from the word *prospheró #4374;* which ties it to *the direct presentation of* a [bloodless] oblation offering.

A contextual example of *prospheró*/*prosphora* is in Matthew 2:11:

Matthew 2:11

And when they had come into the house, they saw the young Child with Mary His mother, and fell in adoration of Him. And when they had opened their treasures, they then (*prospheró*) '**presented**' their (*prosphora*) '**gifts**' to Him: gold, and frankincense, and myrrh.

We see this carries a much different idea than other words used in describing sacrifices *for sin* (missing the mark) which involved blood. An example of burnt, or blood offerings is found in Hebrews 10:6:

Hebrews 10:6 (NKJV)

In burnt offerings and *sacrifices* for sin You had no pleasure.

The 'offerings and sacrifices' in this verse is *holokaútōma* #3646. It means a 'whole burnt offering; as in a *victim*- the whole of which was burned.' It's where our word *holocaust* comes from. Another one is the word 'sacrifice,' found in 10:1. This one is *thysía* #2378, which means 'slain or killed, as in the form of a victim.' Neither of these are applied to the Son of Man. **Jesus wasn't the victim of God's wrath, or taking man's place**, as we have been wrongly taught. Jesus *presented* a different kind of offering; a *prosphora offering*. *Prosphora* is used 9 times in the New Testament. In each occurrence, the core context goes back to a type of GIFT Jesus *offered* as he went about doing good to all; revealing the (YOU ARE THE LIGHT OF THE WORLD/KINGDOM WITHIN YOU) Christ-life **to resurrect this *same* awareness in other sons of men.**

When we look at these other *prosphora offering* occurrences in scripture, they reveal a big difference in the bloody sacrifices *from* **man to god** (which never pleased God) to gain acceptance and favor; as opposed to the *offering* Jesus presented, which was acceptance and favor *from* **God to man**. This Good News revealed man as being holy and blameless BEFORE THE DOWNCASTING OF MAN'S MIND took place.

It becomes clear that our 'gospel' (we call good news) is backward and upside down to the true message of heaven within. True heavenly clarity is seen in the message Jesus shared in the synagogue, recorded in Luke 4. Here, Jesus *masterfully edits* Old Testament scripture as he rolls up the scroll right before their eyes. In effect, he tells them what he had said (not what they'd read and memorized) was the *fulfillment* of the Father's desire. We'll come back to this in a few moments.

Prosphora is used in Romans 15:16 as Paul describes ministering this Good News *offering* among the gentiles; the favorable message of acceptance that their life *consisted in Christ* right along with the Jews. In Acts 21:21-26, Paul is encouraged by James and the elders to 'make peace' with those in the temple, after being accused of teaching Jewish brothers and sisters (living among gentiles) to *forsake Moses' ways* regarding head coverings, circumcision, and other religious customs. The gentiles were taught to stay away from all these things, including strangling or killing animals in ritualistic blood sacrifices *to worthless idols*. Following the elder's advice, Paul takes 4 men who are to pay required *temple fees* and shave their heads as an *offered gesture* of peace during the days of purification. This peace-making gesture fails however, as the Jews seize Paul, close the temple doors after dragging him outside, where they beat him and bound him with chains. It's seen again in 24:17, as Paul is brought before the Roman governor, Felix; where he describes coming back to his own Jewish nation to bring *prosphora* offerings of favor and good will to them, after his many years of preaching the Good News of 'Christ in you' to the gentiles.

Prosphora is lastly seen in Ephesians 5:2. It's surrounded on either side (4:17-5:14) with instructions to 'come out' from an old life of alienation and the worthless fruit that comes from it, and into a life of walking in love, imitating *God* (mirrored reflection) as dear children. Here, Paul effectively tells the Ephesians slaying animals and setting ram entrails on fire (or anything resembling that) wasn't something that 'smelled good' to God. He said it was the Christ-life that brought a sweet-smelling aroma (euódia #2175); simply meaning *well-pleasing* in the heavenly realm. This *euódia* would occur as they walked in love, just as the Son of Man reflected and offered the gift of *prosphora* love, awareness, and participation in the Christ-life intimacy of Oneness.

Paul writes in 2 Corinthians 2:15, that they themselves are the **euódia- the very fragrance of Christ**; and that, in and of in itself *is well-pleasing to God!* What the Son of Man *offered* to men had nothing to do with being slain, burnt, or shedding blood; but as an oblation (bloodless) offering. The Eucharist is a good example of what an 'oblation' is. It's celebrating and honoring the acceptable, favorable, well-pleasing gift of God in *co*-mmunion (the *koinónia* fellowship of something held in common) with each other. When Jesus talked about taking his 'blood,' he was holding a cup of *wine* in his hand. When he told the disciples to 'take it, eat and drink' from his 'body and blood,' he was calling the 'bread' the true sustaining life of heaven. The *wine* represented an enchanting, intoxicating CHRIST-LIFE of divine intimacy and Oneness he passionately longed to wake them up to enjoy.

We saw this effect as Nick came toward Jesus 'from the night.' The word *vux* is used metaphorically for man's *mental alienation* from God. As we saw in the first couple chapters, Nick came 'toward' Jesus (*prós*), which means *to face*, or to move with desired intention in the direction of something to have access or nearness to it. Why? Because he was drawn to the Light of God in Jesus, which Nick later discovered he also carried in his own BEing. This Light (*phós*, #5457) is, as Vine's describes: expressing *light as seen by the eye*, and metaphorically, capable of *reaching the mind*. Jesus didn't come as a debt payment sacrifice to satisfy a distant judging deity. He came to draw men out of their *(vux)* orphaned alienation to see the works of the Father within them, and awaken them to their rightful sonship! The Son of Man came *offering* the perishing lost sheep of Israel a vivid awareness of acceptance and favor; allowing them to finally start participating as *One* in the same *kaléō* intimacy he did. It was a sonship the heavenly Father had viewed as theirs all along; they just hadn't been able to see it through their orphaned images and veiled and scaled distortions.

212 · BORN FROM ABOVE

What did Jesus say as he read (and edited) what was written in Isaiah's scroll? He revealed the *acceptable favor* of heaven's goodness as he preached the Good News; which effectively opened *blind* eyes, healed *broken* hearts, and proclaimed freedom from every oppressive *bondage*. Those attending, wondered why he had rolled up the scroll without reading the last lines they'd memorized describing ideas of the 'fearful vengeance' of God. But Jesus told them they *had just heard* everything they needed to know. They had heard the true Good News which had already been established and fulfilled as far as the reality of heaven was concerned. No fear, no vengeance, no blood; only gracious words flowing from his heart which astonished all who heard them! It had nothing to do with Jesus' blood, nor of him dying like some slain sacrifice as a victim of God's vengeance or wrath toward man.

I refer you back to the chapter 'Oh the Blood of Jesus.' There was nothing magical about Jesus' blood. He was just like his brethren in every way, other than *not seeing himself separated* from the God-life within him. Once we see it wasn't his 'blood' he came to offer as some magical sacrifice, it pulls the plug on an imaginative construct that Jesus had *unique* holy blood in his veins. What good would it do other men if Jesus defeated this 'satan' with divine *super-blood* containing different genes or chromosomes than they had? No, the Son of Man was like his brethren in ALL ways *other than* missing the mark of enjoying sonship. We'll accept the fact Jesus called Peter *satan*, yet we know Peter wasn't some diabolical demon enemy. Jesus told Peter exactly what the 'devil,' or 'satan' was in Matthew 16:23. He told his disciples he was about to endure much suffering in the hands of the priests and scribes before being killed. Here's what happened next:

Matthew 16:22-23 (NKJV)

Then Peter took Him aside and began to rebuke Him, saying, "Far be it from You, Lord; this shall not happen to You!" But He turned and said to Peter, "Get behind Me, Satan! You are an offense to Me, for you are not mindful of the things of God, but the things of men."

Rather than Peter's mind being full of God-truth, it was full of *man thoughts*- alienated *lies* of distortion and separation. Paul was continually encouraging people to *set their minds* on heavenly things, and not earthly things. Jesus rebuked the Pharisees, saying:

"You seek to kill me, because your thinking is the offspring of the 'devil'- and those desires you follow. The 'accuser' *took life* from the beginning, and in it was *never* any truth. Everything spoken (involving fear and death) comes from this alien seed lie of separation, making it the *source* of all other lies! Which of you convicts me of *sin*? I'm not the orphan here. I hear my Father's words and know them within. You can't hear God because you're too busy listening to *satanas mind* lies to know who your real Father is! You live like the *devil!*" (John 8:40-47)

Was Jesus telling the Pharisees some fallen angel had given birth to them? NO. The *devil* has never fathered or given life to anything. The *satanas* dark realm lie *takes* authority as a tool by which others can be ruled, manipulated, and controlled. Those who abide in truth can see themselves as deeply loved; *having* authority to serve, nurture, and truthfully empower others from that same origin. The *diablos* lie only steals, kills, and destroys awareness of the *aiónios* quality life men are meant to live from. It's the same lie Jesus spoke of in John 9:40-10:10. He said the religious leaders were blind hirelings, institutional thieves and robbers, having distorted voices that those who could *actually hear God,* would not follow. Jesus said they hadn't seen true life or authority yet. Therefore, all they did was steal, kill, and destroy.

The Son of Man told these religious leaders that how they lived, and their attitudes toward others, was like fresh painted tombs full of nothing but dead men's bones. Jesus offered his Jewish brothers and sisters (as well as all the other current ethnic groups in that region) an inner awareness of divine sonship, which would then produce an outward life of fruitful abundance. The multitudes of common people knew and recognized (from within) that Jesus shared with them a life-giving kind of authority that the rule making religious leaders had never displayed. *That's why the multitudes followed Jesus.*

I will further submit to you that Jesus didn't *have* to die. He could have gone about doing good to all, healing those who were oppressed by this diabolical, satanas thinking; revealing their own heavenly origin to them (as with Nick) *without having to die.* The Father didn't kill Jesus. It was the angry religious and political leaders who Jesus told Peter would torture and kill him on the cross. Why? Because he disarmed and dismantled their institutional machine of fear and bondage over the people... *right out in front of them.* Even Pilate saw what was going on in the end. His wife had told him to have nothing to do with Jesus' death, for she had experienced great travail *during a trance* where she was shown the truth about Jesus. As Pilate publicly washes his hands of it all while proclaiming his refusal to have Jesus' blood on them, the enraged crowd then begins crying out as one voice: *"Let his blood be on us and on our children!"*

Again, this is why some call the cross *a glorious scandal*. These people would unknowingly cry a prophetical shadowed truth whereby the very blood they thought they were *taking from* Jesus, was actually being *given to them* by this loving, suffering servant. It would be this same joyful life freely *offered* by Jesus, that the people would later realize possessed the ability to set them free to enjoy a new kind of freedom and intimate *life* with a Father they'd never before known!

As I said in earlier chapters, there were many ancient cultures much older than the Jews who believed if their crops failed, sickness or tragedy came, or they weren't producing enough offspring, it had come about *because* they had somehow displeased a distant (and now angry) deity. They believed they must *now* sacrifice something of great worth from their realm, to appease the gods of a different realm- who released wrath (or were about to) in various negative and destructive ways upon their lives. Our doctrines imply the love, kindness, and generosity of Jesus *giving himself*, was him being punished and rejected by a distant God as a bloody sacrifice *necessary, required*, and *demanded* by this distant deity to satisfy his own anger and wrath.

This particular deity however (unlike other gods) supposedly had a *soft spot* in his heart for man. Knowing they could never come up with a sacrifice big enough to satisfy this intense anger and wrath (*he was really pissed*), he decides to sacrifice his own son who was precious to him. It was the only way this *God* could have the bloody sacrifice required for payment, which would finally put him back in a good mood *(well kinda)* and turn off his red alarm wrath switch.

Bible language referring to the cleansing effect of Jesus' blood over the Jews (and others) had nothing to do with changing God's love and consciousness of man, for that had never changed. It had everything to do with man's alien-ated mindset of sin, death, and sacrifice being washed *once for all* from their hearts and their own evil (worthless) conscience, with the pure living water of heaven's truth. Now, this resurrected Christ-life would provide the washing and resurging of heavenly awareness to awaken them to sonship. It would provide a *new and living way* (Hebrews 10:20) as their veiled and distorted vision of something between them and God *was torn in two*. How? Through the very flesh of Jesus that they tortured, spat upon, and nailed to a cross between criminals. GOD IN CHRIST would now 'make peace' and provide the freedom *kept* (guarded) in the Father's heart. Now, through the Lamb who (by them) would be slain, they could finally have *their sin consciousness* removed and be awakened to a resurrected *rise and shine* consciousness of authentic sonship!

There couldn't be any other offering for their *sin*. Why? It was *true propitiation* Jesus brought for man. **The Bible was written from an ancient Jewish perspective** (have I said that enough that it's starting to sink in?) which *saw God* as being capable of (conditionally) blessing people with good things. He was also (in their perspective) the same distant deity capable of (and willing to) release *curses* in various forms and degrees (even to the point of killing all but 8 people on the entire planet), based on how displeased and angry he was with them at the time. I'll say it again: this was not just a belief that came into being through the Jewish people and the God they *thought* they knew.

It was the same distorted thinking that possessed cultures much older than the Jews who were caught up in the same type of sacrifice, wrath, and appeasement mentality toward some *perceived* distant deity who re-*act*-ed toward people, based on *what the people had done first.*

Jesus came to grab the Etch A Sketch of man, turn it upside down and shake it totally clean of all its immature lines and scribblings of their distorted imaginations. Jesus came to show humanity a Father who didn't *re-act* based on what man did; but one who responded out of the 'before' *pro-vision* he knew was man's authentic blueprint Origin of 'VERY GOOD!' At different times in different ways Jesus taught them: "None of you, nor any of your fathers, have seen or known the true God. You've seen fragmented glimpses of his goodness, but even those have been veiled through your toil and labor lenses. I've come to show you the truth of your heavenly Father; that as I AM, you may also be with me *where* I AM. 'I AM' is the only way to the Father; and no man can enjoy the fullness of this truth... until he learns to see the Father *and himself* through the intimate eyes of 'I AM' sonship."

Jesus didn't use condescending tones of judgment, nor did he imply they were dull in hearing because they were stupid. He said their vision of God was blurred because they had *not seen* the joyous love and pro-vision from which they were *expressed* as the Father's own self-image BEings. This Son of Man was so joyfully passionate to share this that he would *lay down* his own life of confidence and intimacy, so that they could finally *take up* their true life of sonship intimacy in re-booted awareness! *"I won't leave you as orphans!"*

This Son of Man becomes *acquainted* (as One) with their alienated, orphaned mindset of separation, which had missed the target of their intended BEing, falling *miserably* short of their authentic design. As the author of Hebrews says: Jesus BEcame like his brothers in every way, even to the depths of *"My God why have you forsaken me?"* uttered by Jesus as total *(vux)* darkness engulfed their *earthen vessels.*

How could Jesus count it *joy* as he endured the torture those he longed to save, now inflicted upon him? He knew that one day, the truth of *who they really were* in the Father's eyes, would be awakened and re-surged within their own conscious awareness. "In that day you will know, that just as I AM One with the Father, so also, are you One in his love, even from before the *disruption of the world*." This Son of man took on (BEcame) their distorted vision (sin), that they might see themselves (BEcome) conciliated as One to the Father's vision of their enChristed righteousness of heavenly equity, perfection, and value!

When we take *our idea* of propitiation out from under the bloody lens we were taught to see it through, we see a much different picture. We find a picture of clarity echoing *'Surely, why of course!'* to the joy and goodness of the Father's love, as our veiled and fragmented lines of distortion are all swept away. We see that each of the times the idea of heaven's propitious action is displayed, it's through a tone of mercy and perfect love that *covers*. The very symbol of the 'Mercy Seat' on the Ark of Testimony, portrayed the covering of intimacy which Jesus openly put on display. It was heaven's testimony where the intimacy of the Father and his offspring would be seen *above*, sealing the deal of what the *Source had known* all along; removing any vision of shadowy objects of temples made with hands, or a list of rules carved in a rock.

Ezekiel wrote that God said he would remove the performance-based heart of stone in men; *waking them up* from their slumber, to restful precepts of perfect love gushing from within. It's what the picture of sabbath rest was all about. Yet man's alienated thinking twisted even that into a *command* they'd need to follow, rather than a rest-full break for them to *enjoy* apart from their toil and labor mindset. Jesus told them man's life wasn't about keeping yet another ritualistic rule called 'sabbath law.' He told them the perpetual life of sabbath-ease was created for man to live, abide, and flourish from in rest-full peace!

This secret place of inner rest and intimacy would expand outwardly to permeate every area of their life. It was this inner garden paradise from which sons and daughters who would abide in it, could *look out* and observe the perishing labor and toil of others. Even though they would behold with their eyes this wilderness existence brought about by evil (worthless) thinking of *orphanos* separation, it couldn't come near *them*. Why? Because *their* thoughts would be rooted, grounded, and established in the most-high places of their consciousness, where Christ-minded Oneness was forever enthroned *and hidden in God!*

Have you ever experienced something that hit you as being so joy-full that you didn't just smile with your face, but you laughed deep from your belly? Perhaps you've seen a child or someone do something that made you explode from within with a crazy kind of cackling laughter? Maybe you even had tears actually coming out of your eyes to the point you had to stop and try to catch your breath? Often times after such an unusual belly-laughing episode, we pause for a moment to enjoy a deep, inner happiness that up until that moment, we hadn't realized was missing in our life for way too long. It's that place where all of a sudden it hits us... "Wow! *I really needed that!!*"

I hope right now you're nodding your head at a memory that still makes you crack a smile. A memory you'll never be able to erase, that will *always make a bright spot* in an otherwise seemingly dark day. It's this kind of hilarious joy, my friends, that we find in the root of *propitiation* the Son of Man shared with others. The word propitiation (*hilastérion* #2435) in our Bibles, is surrounded by a group of words that all take you back to the same place, which means to *conciliate*, be propitious, and be gracious. Please take the time to look these words up for yourself. You'll find them listed from #2431 through #2436. It isn't just the *action* revealed in this group of words that's important; It's the *beautiful tone* through which they are displayed! The true tone of these words is *always* attractiveness, beauty, cheerfulness, and joyful willingness! None of these are meant to satisfy the anger, wrath, or a sacrificial payment plan of some distant and disgruntled judge.

Unfortunately, 'debt payment' is the tone usually portrayed in most of our common concordances and study guides. That's due to them being written by people viewing things through the same perspective lens of separation and sacrifice our ancient Jewish brothers and sisters had.

The actual meaning of the propitiation that Jesus brought to men, can be found in the very first word of this group; a word from which all the others should then follow suit. The word is *hilarós* #2431. **It means propitious: that which is disposed toward someone because the one disposing it is *already* satisfied. It describes one who is cheerfully ready to act because they are *already* approving, fully persuaded, won over, and fully inclined.** The root meaning of *hilarós* (you ready for this?) is where we get our word *hilarious* from! Here's an example:

2 Corinthians 9:7 (NKJV)

So let each one give as he purposes in his heart, not grudgingly or of necessity; for God loves a (*hilarós*) cheerful giver.

Why would Paul say this is the kind of giving God *loves?* Because it's really the only kind of giving *heaven* knows. Notice Paul makes a point to say it's done from *the heart*. Notice he also says it is *not done out of necessity*. What's my point? God's heart never changed toward man, man's heart changed toward God. And the reason man's heart changed toward God, was because his thinking changed about *himself*. Man saw himself *naked*. He saw himself *un-covered*. Man's heart change came from one single *seed* of self-accusation in his mind, which then produced a whole crop of self-judgment and self-condemnation. God didn't desert man; he pursued him. Was God so pissed at Adam that (out of necessity) he had to kill something to be able to look at him through *innocent blood?* There's no indication of anger whatsoever from God in Genesis 3; but we've sure added it in there *between the lines.* All I hear is hurt in a Father's heart of what his children will now endure, due to *them* seeing things through an entirely different and distorted lens than originally given. *"Oh son... WHAT have you done?"*

"WHO told you that you needed covered?" We see the Father's heart entering into his children's pain to give them what they *thought* they needed, even though *he had no need or necessity* of his own to do it. We've painted fragmented and distorted pictures of this same God who gave them everything- now *cursing* the very things he once called good. But God didn't curse anything. He simply tells them how things will now respond to them because of their toil and labor viewpoint of separation from their Source. For as a man thinks about himself in his heart- so his world becomes around him. What does the Father do?

He *willingly* protects. He *joyfully* provides. He *lavishly* covers.

God rejoices over you with gladness.
He renews you in his love.
He exults over you with loud singing
and spins around in joyful dancing!
Zephaniah 3:17

As our dear friend, Lydia du Toit, comments about this verse...
God must know something about you
that makes him ecstatically happy!!

This, my friends, is the cheerful, hilarious message of
acceptance and favor as it has always
been known in the Father's heart;
and THIS is the Good News...
that Jesus un-veiled to all humanity!

CHAPTER EIGHT

Why Have You Forsaken Me?

One of the most detrimental and *confusing* doctrines we've come up with is that the Father turned his back on (deserted) his own son on the cross. We've written songs about it to sing along with our blood songs. We tell people it proves how much God *loves us* by doing it. We say that in order for God to first forgive, receive, and bless us, he had to first pour out divine judgment and wrath on *someone* to pay for all the sin debt tallied up on man's *naughty or nice* surveillance videos. Someone HAD to pay it all. And that someone was Jesus.

Toward the end of his life Solomon recognized and wrote about an amnesia which occurred in man's mind regarding his true upright and righteous origin. Forgetting who they were, they took on a militant (accusatory blame, condemnation, and retribution) mindset, which then led them into all kinds of evil war-like actions that followed. Let's look into Solomon's revelation:

"Behold, one thing I have found to be true; God made all men straight, upright, well pleasing, and righteous- BUT they contrived, invented, and weaved together a divisive 'war-like' machine within their own vain imagination." (Ecclesiastes 7:29 dcv)

This is my paraphrase of Ecclesiastes 7:29 from studying it in the Hebrew wording and definitions. And yes, the term *war-like machine* actually appears in Strong's Hebrew #2810, for the word's *inventions* or *schemes* in this verse. It's interesting that in 2 Corinthians 10:4-5, Paul uses the terms *weapons/warfare* as he describes what must take place to counter-act and pull-down strongholds and vain imaginations that exist in man's mind, exalting themselves in direct opposition to the truth and knowledge of God. What are those vain imaginations? The same ones described in Colossians 1:21 that caused men to see themselves as alienated enemies of (at war with) God IN THEIR MINDS, which *then* led them into all kinds of wicked works. As a man thinks and *imagines himself... so he becomes.*

The Son of Man came to seek and save <u>that</u> which caused the *lost* sheep of Israel to be lost; and <u>that</u> was the awareness of their authentic origin. It would require a literal *re*deeming, *re*conciling, and *re*booting of death-defying, life-raising magnitude to set the record straight in their minds. To present man to himself (show valid proof of how he was made) HOLY, BLAMELESS, and ABOVE REPROACH (unimpeachable), just as he had been in the Father's eyes all along (Colossians. 1:22).

According to the 2nd chapter of Hebrews, Jesus had to *in every way*, become like those he would rescue and redeem. Man's amnesia had progressed from merely forgetting who he was, to being *overtaken* by deceitful imaginations and delusions. His thoughts had become so distorted, that his outward fruit no longer resembled *anything* close to his authentic origin. I've wondered if the description of the Son of Man having to enter into man's darkness to become like them in every way, might actually be what Isaiah was metaphorically referring to in 52:14? Man's outer appearance had been twisted into such a distorted, disfigured reflection of their own worth-less thoughts to the point they no longer even resembled the Father's intended design. Now, to free his brethren from every bondage they'd become subjects of, Jesus, as the captain of their salvation, would have to *in every way* BEcome *like them* in the depths of their darkened and distorted state.

Isaiah 52:14 (NLT)

But many were amazed when they saw him. His face was so disfigured that he seemed hardly human, and from his appearance, one would scarcely even know he was a man.

The gospels of Matthew and Mark both record that between the 6th and 9th hour as Jesus hung on the cross, great *darkness* covered the whole land. The word translated as darkness is Strong's #4655, skótos, which is used literally for physical darkness, and metaphorically for spiritual, moral, and *intellectual* darkness. It's a darkness that arises from error, ignorance, blindness, and rebellion. Now go there with me and picture this scene: The Son of Man is hanging on a cross between two criminals, being crucified by religious and political leaders of that time. In 1 Corinthians 2:7-8, Paul states the rulers *of that age* (which Paul had authority to speak about since he formally was one) didn't have a clue what was about to take place *for men* through this Son of Man's death, burial, and ultimately *an enChristed resurrection*.

1 Corinthians 2:7-8

But we speak the wisdom of God in a mystery, the hidden wisdom which God ordained before the ages for our glory, which none of the rulers *of this age* knew; for had they known; they would have never crucified the Lord of glory.

Paul sees this as the Architect's plan falling into place. The original blueprint had never changed; yet the glory of man had not only been forgotten, but had been distortedly veiled by the very men it had been given to. Still, the hidden wisdom of God had no intention of allowing its divinely expressed BEings to remain in their self-induced toil and perish mode. The love and determination of the Father now comes shining through, not willing (intending) that *any* would perish. The religious and political mafia were right on schedule doing their part in plotting to crucify Jesus, just as the Father had known they would.

They had schemed up *their* plan and their device of crucifixion as they nailed this Son of Man (who not only claimed to know God, but to be One with him) to their man-made torture rack known as the cross. The cross was intended to be a horrific drawn-out procedure of agony; a deadly device and process that only a distorted war-like imagination could have thought up and designed to begin with.

But Jesus had already given his disciples a glimpse into this mystery master-plan. It would be the un-veiling of man's authentic blueprint design as *One* with the fullness of God. Paul saw it as a plan kept (guarded) safely in the Father's heart to be revealed at just the right time. It wouldn't just be Good News for the Jews, but for the entirety of ALL men, just as the angel proclaimed to the shepherds it would!

This master *carrier* of glory (who knew who his true Father was) would now take man's vain, worthless thinking to be crucified and swallowed up by a special tomb of death once for all. But physical death had no power to hold this son who *knew* who he was. Death would give way to true life, bringing the resurrected revelation of the Father's predetermined glory upon, and IN man, out of their tombs of *hádēs* darkness! The Father's self-image BEings in flesh would now be *once again* put triumphantly on universal display as carriers of his glory, just as they had been in the original blueprint all along! This was GOD IN CHRIST repossessing his original gift (his own likeness) from a past cultural mindset, to now see themselves as earthen *living temples* of enChristed glory not made with the hands of men! Jesus had slipped in some clues regarding this *repo mission* to his followers:

John 10:16-18 (NKJV)

"And other sheep I have which are not of this fold; them also I must bring, and they will hear My voice; and there will be one flock and one shepherd. Therefore, My Father loves Me, because I lay down My life that I may take it again. No one takes it from Me, but I lay it down of Myself. I have power to lay it down, and I have power to take it again. This command I have received from My Father."

IF the religious and political rulers of that day had known what was about to take place when the *tomb-stone was rolled away*, they would have never allowed Jesus to even get near a cross! Paul called it the *mystery of the ages*. The only part men would play in the salvation of their own mindset and the redeeming reconciliation of all things, was *them* nailing Jesus *to their own cross* of crucifixion.

They couldn't see the JOY set before Jesus was that he knew their alienated, self-orphaned wilderness wandering would be *co*-crucified right there with him. Not only that, but out of the tombs of death, this enChristed re-po mission would lead a procession of triumphant sons and daughters now resurged with enlightened life and a rightful glory that had been theirs all along! It was *God in Christ* saving man's mind **from** the power of darkness (há/dēs realm of the unknown), conveying their thinking **back to** the un-veiled blueprint of their divine origin!

It would be the Father catapulting men's minds from entombed darkness, bringing them forth rebooted and begotten again as *One* in a RE-NEWING of CHRIST-MINDEDNESS, the *resurged* knowledge of man's perfect workmanship and intended design! Jesus told Simon that this revelation of men *knowing* their heavenly Source *as One* would be so illuminatingly power-full that the gates of hades (realm of darkness and the unknown) would never be able to prevail against them again!

In order for Jesus to successfully save these heavenly self-image BEings to the core, redeeming, and rebooting their awareness to who they *truly* were; he must first plunge into the lowest depths of man's own darkness and become like what man had become, *in every way*.

Suspended on man's torture device in a darkness engulfing man's *entire earthen vessel* his form is now so disfigured and twisted that he no longer resembles the true incarnate likeness of God in man. In this place of Jesus' humble willingness as the *servant* of men, he gives himself to death, even the death of the cross. Yet this suffering servant possessed a heavenly *(hilarious)* joy set before him, which knew the results of this event would soon *re*deem, *re*surrect, and *re*boot man's mind *back to* a place of knowing who they'd *truly* been all along!

At a point of mental/physical exhaustion from the depths of distorted, un-recognizable alienation, darkness engulfs this earthly mindset as the Son of Man cries out mankind's thoughts. Thoughts *similar* to the desperate lyrics we read earlier from the Sons of Korah *blues song*:

"My God, my God, why have you forsaken me??"

Now most of us have been taught this was where the Father had to turn his back on his son, not only deserting him, but actually pouring out furious judgmental wrath and punishment *upon* him. We say it was necessary that the Father *look away* from his son (because we were taught that God can't look upon sin) so justice could be served, and the righteous, holy requirement and full payment for man's sin debt could finally be satisfied. But wait- doesn't 2 Corinthians 5:19 tell us that God was right there IN Christ reconciling the world to himself? Didn't Jesus tell the disciples they would all scatter and leave him, but he would not be alone because the Father would be there with him?

John 16:32 (NKJV)
Indeed the hour is coming, yes, has now come, that you will be scattered, each to his own, and will leave Me alone. And yet I am not alone, because my Father is with Me.

Viewing these scriptures that say the Father *didn't* leave Jesus or turn his back on him present quite a different picture than what we've been taught. It raises more questions that must now be answered. The words *"My God, My God, why have you forsaken Me"* are taken from the opening line of Psalm 22. We've always been taught this was just part of the plan for God to turn his back on his son, so he wouldn't have to turn his back on us. But if we would have kept reading a little further in Psalm 22, we would have seen something we didn't hear in any of those fiery sermons from the pulpit. In fact, in verse 24 we see that the **Father did not hide his face** from the afflicted Savior as he hung on the cross, but *was there with him* as he cried out.

I was taught to trust and give my life to a God who *willingly* turned his back on his own son. That never made sense to me, but I found myself teaching it from time to time because I was told it was what we were supposed to believe. I am now persuaded that Jesus was actually uttering this widely known Messianic Psalm of their culture so they would know there wouldn't be *another one* coming. Jesus uttered the first line of the Psalm, "My God, why have you forsaken me?" from a place of man's darkness that covered their entire existence. **These words were the Son of Man releasing the cry of mankind from *their* wilderness emotions describing what *they* had believed about God.**

This cry of accusation toward God was actually the root belief that had led men into a perishing life of labor, toil, darkness and *sin*. It was the father (source) of all other lies; a murderer from its inception. It's when 'Adam' began to see himself as *un*-covered and *dis*-connected from his Source. This alien seed-lie caused man to then enter into fear as he now saw God as a judge, *rather* than a loving Father. Bondage to this death-seed began to prevail over Adam's vision as he moved from knowing the Light of *glory mode*, into the darkened *hádēs mode* of a perishing existence. This rooted perish-seed continued to prevail over man till it produced a harvest that fearfully dominated and negatively affected *everything* he set his hands to in the landscape of his life.

This mental death-seed and the actions growing from it, were then passed down from Adam to others; and the traditions of men kept it going until it had spread to ALL men. Jesus, openly crying out these words on the cross was proof that he had, in *every* way, BEcome like his brothers and sisters in their darkened state. This scene was the *beginning of the end* of man's diabolical deception and the power of darkness held over them for so long. It was the precursor having to *first* take place and be crucified once for all, to *then* deliver men into a re-surged awareness of their inheritance in the Light, where they could clearly *see themselves* as the true glory-carrying offspring of God!

Everything the first Adam touched was affected by this death-seed mentality. Everything the Last Adam touched flourished in life more abundant. This flourishing God-life revealed the accurate blueprint of man's Origin and design. Paul said all creation was up on tip-toes in anticipation, waiting to be redeemed from the effects of man's mental corruption and bondage. Even creation itself knew that it would one day be *re*deemed and *re*surged in the life-giving effects of Christ. The sons and daughters of God would now be restored, rebooted, and *roused up* to shine, awakened to their authentic, glorious liberty!

Over 30 distinct prophecies from Psalm 22 were fulfilled while Jesus was on the cross. The Psalm ends by saying his righteousness would be recounted to the coming generations and declared to ALL people, "THAT HE HAS DONE this!" This 'has done' in the Hebrew language, was the same completed proclamation of "IT IS FINISHED", which were the victorious last words from Jesus' lips on the cross.

So here we see Jesus utter the *first* words of the Psalm, and then cry out the *last*, but not until everything else in this prophetic Psalm was lived out right before their eyes. Think about when someone starts singing the first line of a song that everyone around you knows. What happens? Everyone starts singing the *same* song in their head. This is what happened that day to reveal to those waiting on a 'deliverer,' that Jesus was showing them what *this song was all about*. Every prophecy they'd been taught from youth in regard to this 'suffering servant' to come, they now not only *listened* to, but *watched* being fulfilled upon the cross. It was so powerful that even one of the Roman guards, upon hearing "IT IS FINISHED" stood in utter amazement and proclaimed: **"Truly, this really was the Son of God!"**

The Father never deserted his son on that cross; and who in their *right mind* would trust a Father (or a God) who'd turn his back on his own son? Man's true paternal/maternal Source will never do anything apart/separate from its offspring BEings. GOD IN CHRIST was giving life *to* man, *for* man, and *as* man! Jesus told the disciples before the cross: "You will *all* scatter, yet I will not be alone, for My Father is with Me!"

True fathers don't desert their sons and daughters. *Ever.* But that kind of unconditional love doesn't fit man's orphaned mindset of a distant deity poised to judge and condemn; a belief Jesus repeatedly said *and proved* wasn't true. Jesus adamantly said, "I will *never* leave you or forsake you, *and I only do what I see my Father do.*"

Psalm 22:24 (NIV)

For he has not despised or scorned the suffering of the afflicted one; he has not hidden his face from him but listened to his cry for help.

Again, this brings up questions which need to be answered. If the Father didn't *really* turn his back and forsake Jesus, which scripture (and Jesus [the Living Word] himself) plainly tells us didn't happen, then *what do* all these things mean that happened on the cross?

What if- this great *skótos* darkness (metaphorical spiritual, moral, and *intellectual* darkness from *error, ignorance,* and *blindness*) was what Paul described to the Ephesians as having covered man's whole *earthly* mindset'? On the cross, Jesus represented this *perishing state* of mankind and the *lower realm* mindset which had consumed them.

Ephesians 4:18-19 (NKJV)

having their understanding darkened, being alienated from the life of God, **because of the ignorance that is in them, because of the blindness of their heart**; who, being past feeling, have **given themselves** over to lewdness, to work all uncleanness with greediness.

What if- the alienation Paul says in Colossians 1:21, existing in man's mind (the Greek says man's *comprehension*) was the same thought (comprehension) of alienation Adam took hold of as he hid from his own Source in the garden? What if Adam, who was originally created upright and righteous, had a distorted seed-thought planted in his mind which *grew* to blind his recognition of the true attributes of God and his *true* self, as BEing God's image and likeness on earth?

Romans 1:20-21 (NKJV)

For since the creation of the world His invisible attributes are clearly seen, being understood by the things that are made, even His eternal power and Godhead, so that they are without excuse, because, although they knew God, they did not glorify Him as God, nor were thankful, **but became futile in their thoughts, and their foolish hearts were darkened.**

What if- the death Romans 5:12 says entered the world through the futile and alienated thinking of one man, then spread (was passed down) to the thinking and mindset of all other men who followed in those same footsteps through programmed and powerless traditions?

What if- these thoughts now taking root in their hearts, became so *distorted* and *disfigured,* they produced a harvest *of their own kind*; not bearing *any* recognizable resemblance to their authentic Origin, nor bearing *any* abounding *life-fruit* from abiding in *that* Origin?

What if- as they **BELIEVED** so they **BECAME**?

As Solomon wrote: **they contrived, invented, and weaved together a divisive 'war-like' machine within their own vain imaginations.**

What if- man lived so long comprehending himself as *alienated* and as an *enemy* of God, eventually producing outward actions and fruit so deplorable that it prompted Jeremiah to write the following?

Jeremiah 17:9 (NKJV)

The heart is deceitful above all things, and desperately wicked; Who can know it?

What if- Jesus crying out "My God, my God, why have you forsaken me?" wasn't about the Father turning his back on his son at all; but was from that same place of alienated darkness this Son of Man had to *enter* to fully become like other sons of men he called his brethren?

What if- it was *this mindset* of alienated separation men carried so long, that *caused* all the rebellion, anger, and twisted distortions of *sin* that Jesus carried to the cross to be crucified? What if it was to *bury* all man's 'I AM NOT' thoughts of toil, labor, and striving to cover himself to get *back* to a God he was never *realistically* separated from?

When we begin to see this in the contextual truth of what it meant to *people of that day*, the scriptures actually start making sense, something most of our constructed doctrines never have. Every Jew present at the cross, and all those who had heard the stories from childhood, had recited and memorized critical passages from the law and the prophets which included the Messianic prophecies of the redeeming Savior, *which also included* Psalm 22.

It's in the backdrop of this understanding that the scales begin to fall away. We awaken to see this was *never* about the Father turning his back on Jesus or man-kind even for a moment. To the contrary, it was the un-veiling of the Father's committed union and loyalty to the *sons and daughters*. It provided the mile-marker of conciliation they needed to help them experientially witness the passion of the Father's heart and unbroken fellowship *with*, *in*, and *as* man. It's in this open display of unified love and Oneness, we begin to see the cross wasn't about Jesus paying a massive accumulated sin-debt in the form of a bloody sacrifice demanded by some great judge in the sky. Nor was it about a Father deserting or punishing his own son(s), *any of them!*

The cross was the universal proving ground visually illustrating it would be *impossible* for the *patérnal* Source of mankind to leave or forsake their offspring BEings without actually forsaking his/her self! This Love would even dive to the depths of man's alienated orphaned mentality to *crucify* the distorted mindset that had kept the heavenly sons and daughters in tormenting fear and bondage so long. It was this one-way conciliation of man being *begotten again,* that would redeem them from their own tombs of death, rebooting them to the Origin-al flourishing life of light, love, glory, and enChristed mindset!

Continuing Journey Reflections

As I stated at the end of chapter 3, even though my vision of *God* and scripture have changed dramatically over the years, I have presented things within this book from a scriptural perspective, because that's how most of us learned what we know (or what we *thought* we knew) about God. As we've seen in the past chapters, when we look at the actual meanings and phrases of scripture in the original language, we find that much of what we were taught as being *sound doctrine*, often doesn't portray what the scriptures really *say* (in true context) *at all.*

Born from Above is an honest book for honest thinkers who are no longer afraid to ask honest questions. At some point along the journey, we realize there's *no* eternal torment, *no* naughty or nice list, and *nothing* for men to be *saved* from, other than our distorted thinking. During this process we begin to see the things written about *end times* and *last days*, were, *in reality*, completely fulfilled long ago. Out of all this we also begin to see that these biblical letters were written *by* those living *in that day, to* a specific group of people who also lived *in that day.* There is no remaining prophetical significance of *any* of these letters yet to be fulfilled *in our day*, or in the days ahead.

The previous chapter portrays certain Old Testament prophecies that resemble certain likenesses to the 'Messiah' the Jewish people prayed for and waited on. But was Jesus really *that* Messiah? Well that depends on 1) your own ideas and opinions, and 2) who you ask, or who helped you *form* those ideas and opinions. If we ask those in the evangelical church that question, we'll most likely get an enthusiastic YES! Yet if we ask our Jewish brothers and sisters around the world (the ones to whom the prophecies were written to, for, and about), the overwhelming majority of them (and all their ancestors of the past) would answer a resounding NO! If there's no angry God keeping a naughty or nice list, no prophecies left to fill, and no tormenting hell to be *saved* from, why would *Christians* need a coming Messiah anyway?

My life no longer revolves around defending the doctrinal views many of us were raised under. As I've stated earlier in the book, my desire to *belong*, or be part of a popular group huddled around certain beliefs, was superseded long ago by a desire to *know the truth*. For me, that involves being able to respectfully see other views alongside what I was taught. This honest approach means that I'm willing to lay down a previously held belief for another one, *if*, in the light of historical facts and evidence, it makes more sense. For me, sci-fi grand finale scenarios got *left behind* long ago. It may seem difficult to let go of certain things at first; but once we take those first steps of truth *over* tradition, every step from there on gets lighter and easier, confirming itself over and over (at least it has for me) that we're on the right path.

I have presented Isaiah 53 and Psalm 22 from a 'Christian' view. In fairness to our Jewish brothers and sisters, *most* of them believe these 'suffering servant' passages are describing Israel, and have *absolutely nothing* to do with Jesus. I think it's important to remember whose personal journey the Bible actually describes. As sacred as Christian beliefs and traditions may be to us, we must also see the significance and beliefs of our Jewish friends (and their ancestors) who treasured these scriptures as their own story, long before Jesus was ever born.

Can you see how one's cultural background and the traditions our elders trained us in *forms* our perspective? We might be taught there's only *one* way to see something, only to later realize *that's just not true.*

This delivering mashiach the people of Israel longed for (and still do) was never about a *divine* savior, but a *human* political and military leader. A great judge who'd redeem the Jewish people, reestablish the temple, Jewish law, and its court system. It's interesting to me that the Jews adamantly say Jesus is NOT the mashiach who is *yet* to come; while most Christians believe that Jesus was definitely the Messiah, BUT he didn't finish everything he needed to the first time around. He must return one more time to actually say, *"It is finished."*

The church today might say our Jewish friends just *misunderstood.* Our Jewish friends might say the same about the church- and that Christians highjacked the story of the Jewish *mashiach*, having edited and adapted it, turning it into *their own* cultural deliverance story.

Christians have been taught to believe the life of Jesus *reflecting* the Father the first time around, *wasn't enough.* He will have to return one day in the future to finish *other* Messiah duties. It's sad some of the things we've been taught this coming *king* will supposedly unleash on humanity (on behalf of a wrath-full deity) the next time he comes.

Personally, I see both of these views (no offense meant to either) as based on *futuristic ideas* revolving around distance, delay, reward, and retribution. *This God* will accept a certain group of people who *do* or *believe* things in specific ways; and those who *don't belong* or jump through the right hoops, will be *excluded.* I walked away from all ideas of *gods of exclusion* long ago, and my heart could never go back.

One of the most treasured landmarks of my journey is when I saw the immense value and love placed on my life, to the point I realized the Source from which we all came, had to see us ALL as One and the same. When my eyes and heart *truly* stopped regarding others by their flesh, culture, or religious beliefs, everything else in my life changed along with it. How beautiful it is to know I can sit beside *any* man or woman alive and experience true spirit/heart fellowship with them.

I'm no longer afraid of other cultural beliefs; I'm very interested in them. I've received elements of truth, love, and wisdom from people of different backgrounds and religions all around the world. I might not walk in *agreement* with all I hear, but what joy it brings knowing I can respect and learn from others, sharing important *issues of the heart,* without trying to convince or convert them to my personal *theology.*

At this point in my life, it would be impossible for me to ever again subscribe to any traditional ideas or doctrines built around:

-A *deity* that is *apart* from man in another distant location.

-A *god* demanding that entwined BEings (of the same divine Source) must *first do* or believe certain things to *then be* accepted or belong.

-A *god* of exclusion who favors one group or religion over another.

-A *superhero* (human *or* divine) coming to *rescue* partakers of a divine nature who already carry every power and ability they could ever need.

It's sad how angry people become while defending (even viciously attacking others over) doctrinal perspectives such as:

-Was Jesus really the *Messiah*? -Was he really born of a *virgin*?

-Was the physical *body* of Jesus *literally* raised from the dead?

-Are there distant, *literal* places called *heaven* or *hell*?

Us not liking these questions doesn't make them *invalid* questions. I personally now realize if I've allowed myself to believe that different answers to *any* of these questions could *actually* change my life now *or* in the future, then I've got other issues than merely being offended. Entering into divisive arguments or strife-filled debates over these topics with others (which NO ONE can actually prove), was dropped by the wayside a long time ago for me. Why? Because the Jesus parables and stories, along with my personal visions and spirit experiences, have permeated my heart with the *consciousness* of my true identity. They have redeemed and resurrected TRUTH in me out of the distorted images and traditions of men, so *nothing* could take it away!

From places of *honest* study and research, one will eventually be confronted with the question of (you might wanna sit down for this) IF Jesus was even an actual person, OR, if these stories were merely passed down as metaphorical *healers and awakeners* of man's inner self. I personally believe Jesus was real, but even if it was later proven differently, it wouldn't change *anything* within me. My consciousness was *roused up* and has *ascended* to an enChristed mindset. Jesus never desired to become man's hero, but to show men *who* they were.

In my honest opinion, the biggest reason we want and *need* a Jesus of the *flesh* to be real in a literal, physical sense, is because we desire and depend on this same *flesh man*, Jesus, to one day deliver us to a *literal* location called heaven. I've yet to see where the scriptural Jesus promised any such thing. I think we've misconstrued his words and created *our own* distant subdivision with gold streets and mansions. Why? Because for the most part, our thinking and consciousness is still consumed with the flesh and things which appeal to us *physically*.

What if- Jesus wasn't 'THE' *awaited one* the Jews looked for? As we've seen in various places in this book, he didn't look, act, or do *anything* those waiting for the mashiach thought he would. This Son of Man looked altogether *different* than the 'anointed one template' he should have fit into. Even John the Baptist, who was to introduce this coming king, questioned if he *really* was the chosen one *or not*.

What if- Jesus actually *was* a carpenter's son who grew in *wisdom* of certain things, thereby ascending to higher levels of *stature* in those things? What if early on, Jesus *saw* that his spirit was One with the Source of all life in the very Origin, existing as One with that Source as 'I AM', even *before* Abraham came on the scene? What if Jesus simply lived out of what he *knew*, and taught others that when they knew it, they would do the same things they'd seen him do? What if knowing this freed Jesus to remain totally humble in the flesh, not worried by cares of *tomorrow*, but knowing as he lived *from* this inner kingdom life of *today*, everything he'd ever need would flow *out of* that Source?

What if- all Jesus ever wanted to do was show men *they too* had been born from above withIN this same Origin of all Light and Life, thereby waking them up to live from their own authentic genesis?

What if- this Origin of Life blazed with such passion in his heart, he was even willing to lay down his own *flesh* life to un-veil it all to them?

What if- this Son of Man wanted others to see this so clearly, that *one day* when they could no longer see the burning passion in his eyes or walk with him *in the flesh*, they could live from this *same* intimate *Spirit Life* realization, as it burned within their own hearts as well?

Whether the Jesus stories were literally/physically true or not, can *never* change the *literal effect* they continue to have in and around my life. Like Paul (who rarely even spoke of *Jesus in the flesh*), once I saw my enChristed Spirit origin from my mother's womb, I realized I could participate and flourish IN that Source, with no need of *anything else*.

There's an ancient proverb that goes something like this:

When the student is ready, the teacher will appear.

When the student is *truly* ready, the teacher will disappear.

Isn't this, *in effect*, exactly what Jesus did? He shows up on the shores of Galilee one day to common fishermen, saying, "Come on, follow me; there's much I want to show you!" He pours into them day and *night*, saying, "I know you don't understand what I AM doing for you *now*, but *one day* you will. And in *that* day you will *know* that we are One." Jesus' voiced desire was, "That they may BE *with me*, where I AM." Three years later Jesus says, "It's better for you *now* that I go away."

I'll be forever thankful for the Jesus stories and parables revealing a deeper love within my heart. I will never forget my *visions* of Jesus right there beside me on a park bench, nudging me like an old friend. *Above* and beyond these, I'm thankful for the Christ-voice I began to recognize within my spirit, which I now know had been there all along.

Now... I listen. *Now...* I participate. *Now...* I truly live.

I no longer regard anyone (even Jesus) *according to the flesh,* and I live by the SAME SOURCE he showed all other men was *in them* too.

It's time for us to move on.

CHAPTER NINE

We Know Him Thus No Longer

2 Corinthians 5:16 (NKJV)

Therefore, from now on, we regard no one according to the flesh. Even though we have known Christ according to the flesh, yet now *we know Him thus no longer.*

This verse carries a spiritual precedent of life-changing proportions; not just to those being delivered from a separation/sacrifice mentality thousands of years ago, but to anyone studying and receiving wisdom from the life of Jesus today. This is one of the keys (maybe even the master-key) to unlock the inner floodgates and enjoy the gushing life Jesus was so passionate about all men participating in. Paul wrote they were to no longer regard Christ according to the *flesh*, just like they should no longer regard any other men according to the flesh. We have been taught this particular statement applies *only* to those who have been *born again*, and only IF they are in Christ.

IF is the key word in our doctrines, having the emphasis placed on it in our minds. It's just how it was instilled in our thinking by those who passed it down to us. That's certainly nothing negative toward those who went before us, because *that's* how it was passed down and instilled by those who taught it to them. This is exactly how traditions are passed down; by well-meaning people sincerely trying to do the right thing, along with a desire to honor those who taught them. But what IF the original thought that was believed by the first person who passed it down wasn't correct? Also, if someone who is a *teacher* has misunderstood something in error, or in a different way than it was originally intended or expressed- won't that teacher *also* continue to pass down that same error in their teaching of others as well?

You've probably heard stories similar to the one about the ham being prepared by a mother for a holiday meal. The woman did all the prep work making the glaze, cutting the pineapple slices, and getting the cloves out for her renowned entrée, which would soon be enjoyed by the entire family about to arrive for the holiday. The woman's little girl watched intently as her mom carefully walked through the proper procedure for this famous dish. Before placing the ham in the baking pan, the mother took out a large knife and carefully cut about 2 inches off one end of the ham. Then, placing it in the baking pan, she finished decorating it with the traditional glazing, pineapples, and garnishes before sliding it into the oven.

The mother then begins cleaning up the prep area. She's enjoying a sense of satisfaction and accomplishment that her daughter had paid such close attention to every detail of the instructions that had been traditionally passed down from her mother to her *and* all the sisters. It was these same instructions they then passed down to their children, just as they had been taught. As the mother reflected on how beautiful this experience had been for her personally, the young daughter asks: *"Mommy, why do we cut the end of the ham off before we cook it?"*

The question catches the mom completely off guard. The more she thought about it, she began to realize she didn't actually know *why*, other than she had always seen *her* mother do it, which was how she and all her sisters had been taught it was *supposed* to be done.

As the story goes, the little girl's grandmother was on her way with her own mom, the *great grandmother*, to enjoy this holiday meal. The little girl couldn't wait to ask grandma about the cutting of the ham tradition, and she ran and jumped in grandma's arms as she came through the door. *"Grandma, grandma... why do we cut the end of the ham off before we cook it?"* The little girl's aunts now chimed in: *"Yeah, mom, why DO we cut the end of the ham off before we cook it?"* Grandma thought a minute and realized she actually didn't know *why*, but as a child had seen her mom do it and thought that's just how it was supposed to be done.

The little girl's grandmother walks into the living room where great grandma, now quite old, was sitting in her wheelchair talking and telling stories to other family members. The whole family was thankful she was able to get out of the nursing home and spend the holiday with them. By this point, *everyone* now wanted to know *why* they'd been cutting the end of the ham off all these years.

"Mom," grandma gently squeezes great grandma's hand resting on the wheelchair, and says:

"When I was little, I remember seeing you cut the end of the ham off before you put it in the pan to cook it." *"Why did you do that?"*

The frail but coherent great grandmother, puzzled by why her daughter would ask such a question almost 70 years later, replies:

"Well, probably because it was too long to fit in the pan, silly!" *"Why else would anyone cut the end of a perfectly good ham off?"*

The mouths of every adult in the room drop open momentarily, before erupting into spontaneous laughter over what they'd just heard!

While this is a funny little story where no one gets hurt, there's a very important lesson we can all learn from it. This grandma had seen the great grandmother cut the end off of a ham almost 70 years prior, and it had stuck in her head as important. She never really gave it any thought, but now, somehow convinced it was the right thing to do, taught all her daughters, who had in turn, taught all their daughters... *you see the point.* Jesus said it was good to be like little children, and that the inquisitive nature of a child wasn't afraid to ask questions. Neither do they think about it offending someone from generations past if they simply want to know *why* for themselves.

Let's take just a deeper look at these verses, and see if we might have possibly missed some things along the way.

2 Corinthians 5:14-17 (NKJV)

For the love of Christ compels us, because we judge thus: **that if One died for all, then all died**; and He died for all, that those who live should live no longer for themselves, but for Him who died for them and rose again. Therefore, from now on, we regard no one according to the flesh. Even though we have known Christ according to the flesh, yet now we know *Him thus* no longer. Therefore, if anyone *is* in Christ, *he is* a new creation; old things have passed away; behold, all things have become new.

As we pull our gaze away from one specific tree we were trained to stare at, we *now* see there's a whole forest in view. It was an area man had been taught they'd need to labor and sacrifice their way into, only to *now* realize it had all been done *for* them, by the God they were *told* was angry and distant from them. Remember, this was written to ethnic groups surrounded by the kósmetic temple system of man their entire life. It was a system of separation revolving entirely around the *flesh* and the self-effort of *doing* to attain. Paul, a former ring leader who once passionately promoted this system, was now telling them to *forget about the flesh,* and just enjoy their inner BEing in the Spirit!

Therefore *if.* IF *what?* If any man is in Christ, *right?* Of course! This statement found in 2 Corinthians 5:17 indicates that any man found IN Christ is a *new* creation. But what are we to do with the thought of *therefore?* Therefore what? 'Therefore' correctly means 'and,' or 'because of this,' denoting a continuation of something already stated or pointed out. A *therefore* means this line of thought can't be contextually received as a stand-alone idea, because it is a *continuation* deeper into (or *from*) something *previously stated.*

How many people could you walk up to and begin a conversation by saying *"Therefore,"* without them looking at you like you're crazy? They'd look at you as though something was missing, and most likely ask *"therefore WHAT?"* Which is exactly what one should always ask when seeing a *therefore* in scripture. It's grammatically incorrect for this verse to exist with no prelude explanation of what it's *there for,* and it leaves one with an *incomplete* picture of what's being conveyed. So, we have to go back to the previous statement in v.16, which also begins with 'therefore,' indicating we must go back even further to the previous statement in v.15. Since v.15 begins with the word *and,* we have to go back even further still, to the verse preceding it.

Verse 14, in itself, is still a continuing part of extended thoughts back to back, connected by conjunctions. Many people don't realize Ephesians 1:3-14 was written as one long sentence containing around 240+ words. Following it, verses 15-21 also contains over 160 words in one single sentence. Seeing this writing style, we can view verse 14 as a FOUNDATIONAL SPRINGBOARD for the reconciliation discourse which follows, to then *flow out of.* This statement (v.14) is strong enough to support other attached addendums, eventually leading up to the verse we so often quote, "If any man is in Christ, he is a new creation", and all other comments (14-17) are *meant to remain directly tied to it.*

2 Corinthians 5:14 (NKJV)

For the love of Christ compels us, because we judge thus:
that if One died for all, then all died.

Here is a statement which is fully worthy and proper in context to stand all by itself. Yet it's such a foundational cornerstone in, and of itself, that it's capable of supporting the weight and layers of further revelations which are also true *because* of it. The words 'compel' and 'judge' play vital roles in making this the stand-alone powerhouse it is. *Compel* means to hold, and it isn't with a tone that comes from mere suggestive persuasion. It actually means to be gripped or held in such a manner that prevents any possible way of escape. The word 'judge' means to examine, question, and inspect thoroughly. This is done with the intent of *determining* and then *pronouncing* an official decree regarding the issue, now reached at the conclusion of the examining and questioning. With this judging and decreeing in mind, a correct translation in our language could be rendered something like this:

The love of Christ has tightly hemmed us into one view,

for after inspecting it from every possible angle,

we've firmly concluded there's no other way to see it.

One died; and when he died, he died *for* all, and *as* all.

Can you see it? This is the true foundation Paul knew had to be examined, judged, and declared as the cornerstone, before he could ever use *new creation* language. **Read it very carefully.** Notice there are no stipulations that must first be applied to make this closely examined and rightly judged statement *become* true. It is true on its own. Period. It might help us to say it out loud: "IF One died for all, then all died. ALL died." But wait. Doesn't the word IF indicate a question? Well it can in certain *questioning* contexts, but as we are about to see, not here. Paul plainly explains to the Corinthians (and other sacrifice mentality cultures of his day), that this statement had been placed under rigorous scrutiny and examination. It had come out with confirmed, *conclusive* results leaving no other option or any other way it could be seen than *this*. So, IF all the questions have been removed, why is an IF still attached? Because the IF is not presented as a question, but as a *conclusion*. Let's look at an example:

You're on a cruise ship out in the middle of the ocean. You find the most amazing dessert bar you've ever seen, with *all* kinds of delicious items on display. You ask the attendant the price of a specific item. Realizing you may not be familiar with cruise line policy, he smiles and politely explains, *"If you're on the ship, everything is included in the package."* Is the attendant *questioning* IF you are on the ship or not? No, he isn't. He's quite sure you're on the same boat he is out in the middle of the ocean. This means his *"If you are on the ship"* isn't a question he doesn't know the answer to. It's a conclusion of something he's already quite sure of, and he continues on from his conclusion by informing you *that you're entitled to everything connected to it.*

Paul somehow anticipates the religious mindset of man about to explode from this *almost* too good to be true good news. As they scurry to add *their ideas* of what men must do to complete *their end* of the deal, he throws in verses 18 and 19 to stop them in their tracks.

2 Corinthians 5:18-19

Now *all* these things *are* of God, who has reconciled us *to Himself* through Jesus Christ, and has *given us* the ministry of reconciliation, that is, that God was in Christ *reconciling the world to Himself*, not imputing their trespasses to them, and has committed to us the word of reconciliation.

Paul posts this concluding declaration for ALL to see, effectively saying: **GOD DID ALL THIS FOR YOU, and the only part you played was nailing the enChristed One to the very cross that set you free!**

Ever wonder why the letters attributed to Paul contain no details of Jesus' birth, his lineage, or parents? You won't find anything about his early days, how John baptized him, or him enduring the wilderness temptation. In reading all Paul's letters combined (which make up a third of the New Testament), we would never know Jesus told a single parable, cast out any demons, healed the sick, or raised the *dead*.

We wouldn't have a clue Jesus made the best wine ever tasted, drove the money changers out of the temple, or taught anything about the kingdom of heaven. We wouldn't know Jesus blatantly interrupted the sacred ceremony on the greatest day of the feast of tabernacles. We wouldn't have any details of Jesus being on trial, Pilate's speech about Jesus being innocent, or the governor publicly washing his hands of the whole ordeal. We'd never even know Jesus was scourged and humiliated while onlookers mocked him and pulled out his beard. In fact, if Paul's letters were all we had, we wouldn't know much of anything about Jesus' life in the *flesh* at all, other than his death and resurrection. Paul's entire *post Damascus* road ministry had virtually *nothing* to do with the natural life of the man Jesus. It had everything to do with the *Christ-life Spirit and nature* Jesus revealed as being an entire kingdom of heavenly life consisting within all men.

The apostle told those at Corinth and Philippi he had determined *all* that was important to him was being *found* (himself) IN Christ, and enjoying the worth (equity) of righteousness that was un-veiled and revealed in Christ-life resurrection power. Yes, there are vast and inexhaustible treasures we can glean from the many *Jesus stories* of his time on earth. We will never stop seeing heavenly truths from his stories, parables, and outward actions as he un-veiled and displayed the Father's heart before men's eyes. Don't think I am undermining that truth or saying anything along those lines, because I'm not. *Ever.* What I am saying is that the collective *church* is just now beginning to see what Jesus was *really* on a mission to do. It's why Paul spent little or no time concentrating on *anything* other than this *r*evealed and *r*esurged Christ-life awareness within himself and others.

As I said before, it's been really easy for us to pass right over what Paul was actually saying in the addressed scripture of this chapter. We're still too busy still regarding the *natural man* Jesus and his life according *to the flesh*, rather than setting our focus inward, and on the Christ *Spirit* Life revealed in a *resurrected unveiling* of man's Origin.

The book of Acts starts where Luke's gospel ends, recording this scene:

Acts 1:8-11 (NKJV)

"But you shall receive power when the Holy Spirit has come upon you; and you shall be witnesses to Me in Jerusalem, and in all Judea and Samaria, and to the end of the earth." Now when He had spoken these things while they watched He was taken up, and a cloud received Him out of their sight. While they looked steadfastly toward heaven as He went up, behold, two men stood by them in white apparel, who also said, "Men of Galilee, why do you stand gazing up into heaven? This same Jesus, who was taken up from you into heaven, will so come in like manner as you saw Him go into heaven."

Most of us have a picture programmed in our imagination from youth of Jesus floating up in the sky, his robe and hair blowing in the wind as he goes *back up* to a members-only gated community with gold streets and many mansions. He will check his *earthly* robe at the gate, put back on the robe of glory he took off to come to earth and walk among sinners to then sit back down on his majestic throne right beside his Father. At some point in the future (which he doesn't personally know the timing of), the Father will lean over and say, *"It's time to go, Son. They've had their chance and time is up. Your white horse and sword are ready. Don't forget to show 'em the tattoo on your leg as you unleash my wrath on those who didn't choose me, and then cast them in the lake of fire!"* I was programmed with these kinds of images too, but what if we lay aside colorful sci-fi manuscripts for a few minutes and actually look at what's being revealed here?

"He will *so come* in like manner as you saw him *go into* heaven." We've been taught this is describing a *flesh* person, the man Jesus we've grown to love and adore, who'll come back in the same *form* and imagery of that *person*. It's not. *Far from it*. This wasn't about Jesus departing earth after 33 years in the same form in which he entered it.

Jesus was born into this world (in the flesh) in a simple dwelling where even the animals felt comfortable. He was born to parents as common as any human could be. There are a few different stories about Jesus' early life. Yet there is no credible evidence or any details about where Jesus was or what he was doing from the age of 12 until he appears on the scene with John the Baptist around the age of 30. Jesus knew his existence (in the flesh) was the *expressed extension* of the Father of all life. However, in this life of the flesh, he still had to *grow* in the wisdom and understanding of it all, into a more mature 'stature.' This same exact wording is used to describe Samuel growing into maturity in 1 Samuel 2:26. It is also used concerning the growth of believers in Ephesians 4:13-16.

Although it took Saul many years to realize he had been *called* (in kaléō surname origin) from his mother's womb, it was not so with the *boy* Jesus. At 12 years old, he was already growing in grace and wisdom, knowing that his life here was 'about the Father's business' (Luke 2:40-49). Mary and Joseph were shocked by his actions, not understanding what he meant about being IN-volved with the 'things of the Father.' Young Jesus seemed equally surprised at their lack of understanding regarding why he questioned religious leaders, or what 'things of the Father' he was talking about. Even though Jesus was obviously already tapping into the spiritual reality of enChristed origin *within*, he still 'subjected himself' in humble obedience to his *flesh* parents as he *continued* to increase in that knowledge. (Luke 2:51-52)

Once we see what was happening with Jesus as a boy in the temple, we begin to realize an obvious parallel and same willingness to humbly subject himself (in the flesh) that Paul describes in Philippians 2:5-8. Jesus didn't consider it (robbery) as him taking something *from* the Father. Nor did he consider it as being 'wrong' to know he was *equal* with the expressed likeness *of* the Father. Jesus wasn't just becoming increasingly aware of his spiritual position as *One* with the Father, he also knew this life of intimacy and Oneness which *bound him* to the Father, could never be taken from him.

The words 'I must be about' that young Jesus used, carry the idea of 'it is binding,' or being bound (as One) to *all* the Father *is* and all the Father *has*. That's why he said, "I only do what I see my Father do" and "No man can *take* my life; I *lay it down* on my own, and I pick it back up on my own. This is because I AM One with the Father."

Paul writes that Jesus willingly humbled himself, as the taking on of (becoming in all ways) the 'form' of men. The word *form* here, is *morphé, #3444*. It implies an outward expression and embodiment of the essential inner substance, even to the degree that the *current* form becomes in total harmony with the inner essence. This *morphé* was Jesus, of his own will, residing in man's *darkness* to rescue them from their perishing state of orphaned thinking, right where they'd fallen miserably short of the truth of their authentic *kaléō* calling. This was a Son of Man who *never sinned* because he *never doubted* he was a Son of God. Yet Paul said he 'BEcame' *sin*, as in *embodying* the mental essence of those perishing in their self-made wilderness of *orphanos* thinking. He was tempted every possible way to take on the *satanas* accusatory mindset of 'I am not.' Yet, even in man's darkness, this Son of Man overcomes every *diabolical* accusation demanding *proof* of his Oneness with God. Jesus effectively declares, "Nothing can disrupt the Source of all; neither can anything seduce a son who knows he's *One!*"

This *morphé* form Jesus remained in went deep in the flesh he had subjected himself to. His enChristed nature within knew his *Oneness* could never be *apart* from the Father, yet he *embodied* the depths of man's orphaned cries, taking them all with him to the cross: **"My God, why have you forsaken me?"** Jesus knew *men* would all leave him, but he also *knew:* "I AM not alone, for my Father is always with me!"

What was the relentless passion that bound him to do this with such joy? He knew he would enter the distorted, disfigured, *embodiment of sin* and its orphaned, perishing state. BUT he also knew there would soon be roused up *for all to see,* a resurrected, resurged, and rebooted **state of enChristed awareness** that all other sons of men might then live from, gushing fearlessly and abundantly *from within* themselves!

This Son of Man BEcame (took on) *sin* (*morphé* orphaned thinking), that his brothers and sisters might BEcome (*morphé* awakened to) their expressed treasured equity and worth of perfect love, and their surname *kaléō* calling as authentic offspring of God!

This was how Jesus ROSE from the *hádēs tombs of the unknown*, bringing men with him. It was him revealing the Risen Christ, along with other sons and daughters of God in this newly *resurged* state of enChristed awareness. Their authentic genesis had been so forgotten and removed in man's thinking from generations past, that to them **it was actually like them becoming a new (as in *restored*) creation.** It was a *Spirit-life-form* none of them had known or witnessed in their earthly fathers who'd passed along their powerless traditions.

Paul said as men saw themselves being presented (already) holy, acceptable, and unimpeachable in the Father's eyes, their *renewed* mindset (Romans 12:1-2) would result in a *morphé* trans-*form*ation of their own! They would no longer see themselves according to the *flesh* or in a worldly (separation, sacrifice, religious requirement) way, but as BEing transformed (metá-morphé-oo) within a clear and powerful Christ-IN-you *re-newal* and *present tense* living hope of God's glory!

Anything **seen** having physical form is temporary, or finite. All *formed* things in the flesh pass away, but that which is true life and awareness of who 'I AM', is **not seen**. And just as its Source, *it cannot pass away*. If you need a *scripture* to prove that for you, then here you go:

2 Corinthians 4:18 (NKJV)

While we do not look at the things which are seen, but at the things which are not seen. For the things which are seen *are* temporary, but the things which are not seen *are* eternal.

Here we awaken to the truth-full mystery of *Spirit* realm things being more real than any of the temporal things of *flesh*. And yes, that means even the flesh of Jesus. *Flesh is flesh, no matter who it's on.*

I know, our western theologically IN-doctrine-ated minds have been programmed to vehemently reject any idea that Jesus isn't actually going to burst through the clouds on a white horse one day and rescue us from a world gone bad. As I discuss this with people, they often bring up stories after the resurrection such as this one:

John 20:26-29 (NKJV)

And after eight days His disciples were again inside, and Thomas with them. Jesus came, the doors being shut, and stood *in the midst*, and said, "Peace to you!" Then He said to Thomas, "Reach your finger here, and look at My hands; and reach your hand *here*, and put *it* into My side. Do not be unbelieving, but believing." And Thomas answered and said to Him, "My Lord and my God!" Jesus said to him, "Thomas, because you have seen Me, you have believed. Blessed *are* those who have not seen and *yet* have believed."

This *type* of Jesus story points to truth that while men may reside in *temporal* jars of clay, the *eternal* treasure within isn't confined, restricted, **or regarded *by* that flesh**. Jesus continually showed men living illustrations that one could have a father of *flesh*, but their real Source was in the *Spirit realm*. Jesus always referred to himself as the 'Son of Man' to reveal (as with Thomas) 'you can have an outer body, yet simultaneously live out of a higher Spirit realm of God-truth!'

Likewise, when Simon Peter recognized THE CHRIST in him, Jesus said: "It wasn't your *father of flesh* (who taught you to catch fish) that showed you this. It was your heavenly patérnal Source (same as mine) who blessed you with this *Spirit* revelation from within!"

Saul of Tarsus didn't *see* 'Jesus' in the *flesh*, but heard THE CHRIST VOICE from within. Later, with this new *Spirit* consciousness, Paul tells the Colossians to 'set their minds' higher, on things above, where CHRIST is, where their *real* (Spirit) life was hidden- IN CHRIST... in God.

Jesus had no desire to become a theological goalpost of attainment, but rather to reveal man's enChristed Origin to them *from within*.

The manner in which Jesus *ascended* was not the Son of Man according to the *flesh,* but as the Risen Christ according to the *Spirit. This* was how *the Christ* would return (appear/manifest), not by the flesh, but by the Spirit. It's exactly what Jesus told them on his way out of here; that when they came to a place of *upper room* awareness in the high places of their thinking as One, the *Spirit* would gush from within them in a *living force/form* they had never before experienced!

It's important to understand the Bible is a historical journey record of the Hebrew people and the early church. It's also a treasure trove of metaphorical, symbolic imageries that are parabolic descriptors, and not always meant to be literal. Misunderstanding this fact has caused people to see things recorded in scripture as literal, inerrant, and, as we've seen earlier in the book, in a fantastical sense of sci-fi thriller proportions. These high-pressure fundamentalist teachings over the past 100-200 years have further perpetuated theories like a secret *rapture.* This event will supposedly involve *certain* people (who believe *certain* things) being covertly whisked away to the same club paradise Jesus is believed to have disappeared into as he floated up into the sky. As we begin to view these scriptures in their metaphorical significance, sci-fi depictions such as these *in a literal sense* begin to fade away, just like the books and movies written about them.

1st Corinthians 15:40-49 describes a *natural* man according to the sensory realm of the flesh (*earthly* things), and a *spiritual* man in tune with *heavenly* things. The natural man is created outwardly from the dust as an earthen vessel which can expire. Yet within that vessel is hidden a treasure of real life with Christ in God, *that can never die.* This is the Christ-life revealed in resurrected awareness that men may know, that *just as* they have borne the image of an 'outer dust man,' so also do they bear the image of the *heavenly Spirit man within.*

There was a *rapture* that took place in early church days alright, but it was in the *form* of a new creation consciousness that took man's focus off of flesh, and was *raised up* in unveiled *Spirit-vision of Christ.* That same enraptured consciousness needs to be *caught up* in the thinking of the church today. It's where the mindset of *corruptible* flesh is crucified (as seed going into ground) and raised back up in an abundant harvest of *incorruptible* life of the Spirit! It's where fear, death, and bondage to the seed-lie of separation is swallowed up by the victory of *true*-life awareness that can never die. It is ALL symbolic imagery of a re-newed and trans*morphéd* MIND OF CHRIST! It's what Paul planted in the garden of the Philippian's thinking as he wrote:

Let this (same) mind be in you which was also in *Christ* Jesus!

Of course, we've been taught Jesus was always the same because he was God's Son. Yet, Mark and Luke attest to a much *different form* in which he appeared to his closest friends after the *resurrection.* It was *so different,* they didn't recognize *him* with their natural eyes, but as they heard *his* words, their hearts *burned from within!*

Mark 16:12 (NKJV)

After that, **He appeared in another form** to two of them as they walked and went into the country.

Luke 24:16 (NKJV)

But their eyes were restrained, so that **they did not know Him**.

The Greek word 'eye' [*ophthalmos #3788*] is a 'viewer,' and is used figuratively for 'the mind's eye.' 'Restrained' [*krateó #2902*] means 'to seize,' or in this case, means 'prevented.'

Understanding these things, one can now view this verse in the metaphorical sense as saying something like:

"It was their mind's eye preventing recognition of *the Christ*."

Even though Jesus' disciples walked with him on the same road, they didn't know (regard) *him* in the manner they'd followed him in for 3 years. Luke uses the word *epiginóskō* (from *epí*, which intensifies *ginóskō*; to *know* through personal relationship). Yet as they walked along their journey with this *stranger*, the words they *hear* ("the words I speak to you are spirit and life") carry a special *fire-starter effect* echoing from within their own inner matrix!

Luke 24:31-32 (NKJV)

Then *their eyes were opened* and they *knew* Him; **and He vanished from their sight**. And they said to one another, "Did not our hearts burn within us while He talked with us on the road, and while He *opened* the Scriptures to us?" (*Christ* takes scripture out of *their* box.)

As Jesus washed the disciple's feet, he was symbolically preparing them for the *journey* he knew would soon confront them from within. *"You don't understand what I do for you now, but one day you will."*

"Did our hearts not burn within us?" asked those whom the Christ *confronted* on their *journey* to Emmaus. Emmaus has ties to the Hebrew root-verb יָחַם *yâcham*, meaning *hot*. It is used for physical heat, but also as *mental arousal,* or the act of *conceiving*. Where did the Christ meet these disheartened disciples? Luke 24:13 records this encounter took place 7 miles from Jerusalem. 7 meaning completeness and perfection; and Jerusalem, the place of wholeness and peace. Why bring this up? As a reminder that Christ-truth (man's anointed Origin) will always confront men on their own personal road of restrained darkness. It burns in their heart as a flame of passionate awakening to their authentic kaléō calling, which was *conceived and consists* within the *heart* of the Father. For these disheartened disciples who had lost all hope in the darkness of Jesus' crucifixion, it was on a journey to their own conceptional *resurrection* of peace and perfected wholeness.

For a tormented Pharisee named Saul, it was a *crossroads* where he'd arrived to face his own 'bloody sack-full' (meaning of 'Damascus') of persecuting and killing early believers. Here, Saul (a name derived from the same root word as *Sheol)* was confronted in the midst of the inner darkness he'd battled within for so long. He was now overtaken by the illumination and fire of heaven, burning and calling his name as the Christ 'appeared,' or *manifested within.*

Saul hears a *voice* asking, *"Why do you keep coming against me?"* Saul, (the name also means inquires of God) then asks:

"WHO are you, Lord?" The voice answers,

"I AM... the Yahweh salvation you keep coming against!"

The Christ voice says, "This hasn't been easy for you, has it, Saul? You've been kicking against the promptings you've had from within, battling *against* all those doubts and apprehensions over what you've been doing for so long." As we saw earlier in the book, the voice Saul hears doesn't come in a tone of judgment, but in a tone of love, as he's spoken to *as a son.* It comes in a tone of compassion that understands the struggle this man has faced for so long. Why? Because this voice belongs to the *Christ within* who had been with him from his mother's womb, even in the midst of his own inner Damascus darkness.

This voice hadn't come to condemn Saul for what he'd done along the way, but to awaken him to the truth and authentic origin of who he *really* was, from the very beginning. This voice wasn't looking at the sackful of blood on Saul's hands, it was assuring him that the burning truth he'd felt in his heart for so long, would *never* leave or forsake him. Saul recognizes this familiar voice he'd pushed away too many times. At this point, he surrenders to what he's now convinced is the voice of truth from within, asking, *"What do you want me to do?"*

Other scriptures also reveal imagery of *Jesus* appearing and then vanishing from their *physical* sight. They all point to a transformation; images, morphé's, forms, and appearances that were merely their *Spirit viewer* being awakened (aroused) to guide them into all truth.

It was all meant to remind them of what *Jesus*, who they first knew by the *flesh*, had prepared them for ("the words that I speak to you are *Spirit and life*") in their journey of transformational *metá-morphé-oo*.

These episodes opened their eyes to realize they'd once known Jesus according to the flesh, but they knew him *thus... no longer*.

This can all be traced back to when Simon recognized THE CHRIST as *manifest* in the Son of Man. Jesus awakened him to the truth that *all* sons of men could hear from their heavenly Father, confirming the foundation of their *ekklésia* (*ek*-out of, *kaléō*-surname) calling. It was preparing them for the day they would no longer know the enChristed One as they had in the *flesh*, but a personal manner of *knowing Christ* from their own *internal* genesis. It would be the day they would know, *that just as Jesus was*, so also were *they* the incarnate expression of One patérnal Source, as offspring spirit BEings of God! **Perfected love is knowing: As Christ is, *so also are we* in this world.** (1 John 4:17)

Many others would also soon encounter this same fiery effect in an *upper room experience* as they came together in the harmony of One mind, *the mind of Christ*. Mary Magdalene, one of Jesus' most loyal followers who remained with him at the cross (who I believe perhaps knew Jesus' heart better than anyone else) experienced the same type of *Christ encounter* in a way that was (at first) *strange* to her:

John 20:11-14 (NKJV)

But Mary stood outside the tomb weeping, and as she wept, she stooped down and looked into the tomb. And she saw two angels in white sitting, one at the head and the other at the feet, where the *body* of Jesus had lain. They said "Woman, why are you weeping?" She said, "Because they have taken away my Lord, and I do not know where they laid Him." 14 Now when she had said this, **she turned around and saw Jesus standing there, yet did not know that it was Jesus.**

Do you see it? Mary looks for the *flesh body* she'd known Jesus in. She feels a *presence* in her midst... yet *not seeing* what she longed for.

Remember what Jesus told his followers in Luke 17:20-23? The Pharisees had just questioned Jesus about how the 'kingdom' would come (manifest). Jesus tells them it wouldn't be *anything* like they've been 'looking to see,' as in an *outer realm observation*. Jesus then turns, speaking intently to his disciples who followed him in the *flesh*:

"The time is coming you will 'desire' (*epithyméō* #1939; *intense passionate longing*) **to 'see'** (*optánomai* #3700; *look at, behold*) **one of the 'days'** (*hémera* #2250; *a 'natural' day*) **you've known me as the Son of Man... but you will not 'see'** (*be able to view*) **it. Many will come saying, 'look here' or 'look out there' in outward observation, but do not go after anything that can be observed from *'out there.'* Remember: the kingdom life I revealed to you comes from within. Nothing 'out there' can give it; for *it's already within you!"***

Now let's go back to Mary at the tomb:

15 Jesus said to her, "Woman, why are you weeping? Whom are you seeking?" She, [*supposing Him to be the gardener*], said to Him, "Sir, if you have carried Him away, tell me where you have laid Him, and I will take Him away."16 Jesus said to her, "Mary!" She turned and said to Him, "Rabboni!" (which is to say, Teacher). 17 Jesus said to her, "Do not cling to Me, for I have not yet ascended to My Father; but go to My brethren and say to them, I am ascending to My Father and your Father, and to My God and your God."

Jesus *only* spoke in parables, but would then later explain them to his disciples as they had *ears* to hear them (Mark 4:33-34). Rather than uncovering vast scriptural treasures of symbolic truth, we've instead covered them even deeper with our literal, fundamentalized mindset.

What if we allowed western theology/vacation Bible school images to fall away from their traditional literal perspectives, and permitted our *Spirit*-man to *ascend* in an un-veiled *higher way* of seeing things?

When Jesus used the descriptive word *Father*, he wasn't referring to a *distant* entity with a specific male gender. He was referring to the divine Source from which proceeds every beautiful attribute associated with life itself: male, female, nature, the heavens, seas, and animals. This *Father* Jesus often spoke of as being One with, is *patér* #3962. It describes One who not only imparts life, but *remains* committed to it.

Jesus declared the Father as the *progenitor*; intentionally bringing into expressed BEing, that which the Generator's authentic likeness was passed on to. It's the same root source words like *pattern* and *paternal* come from. This is the Source which can never be *limited* by specific details of gender, culture, or position, but One which entirely encompasses them all in the unlimited blueprint Origin Source. It's where every intricate detail of imaginative beauty is found in its authentic state. John, trying to find a descriptor in *their* language for this pattern-all Source, settled for 'logos.' What does a logo do? It's an authentic and original image which expresses the very nature of the company, product, or service originating and flowing from it.

When translators opted to insert 'word' as the descriptor for 'logos' in scripture, it wasn't (in my opinion) the best idea they've come up with. Logos, literally means 'an original template being imparted outward/forward with the full expression of itself.' It is NOT a 'word,' nor is it a 'reflection.' Reflections alter and change with movement. While it does *in a sense* reflect, that reflection is because of an *inner Source* likeness manifesting outward, and not coming from something outside on a surface level. While a 'word' *is* a form of an expression, it pales in comparison to the *extension* of all the logos actually contains.

Just as Jesus expressed the *fullness* of the *Father*, John said of that same *fullness* had ALL received. Paul said 'don't let the vain kósmetic traditions of man rob you from knowing you are *complete* in Christ!'

So, *where* does John 20:15 reveal Mary? At Jesus' *tomb*. What is a tomb? It's where things of *the flesh* are laid to rest. Jesus told them there would be days that those who loved this Son of Man who told them all about the *Father*, would long intently to *see him like that* just one more time. For Mary, *this* was one of *those* days.

As Mary weeps, she hears a *voice* which first asks why she's crying. At first, she doesn't know who the voice belongs to, but then she hears "**MARY!**" Knowing there was only One voice that could affect her heart like this, she *turns* and responds "**RABBONI!**", meaning 'Teacher.'

The voice of Christ within always sounds like the *real* Jesus, for the *real* Jesus (not cosmetic hair spray TV Jesus) only said and did what flowed from his *paternal* Source. Jesus said that *after* he was gone, another 'like him' would (manifest/be aroused) that would comfort, teach, and guide them in *Spirit Truth*. Jesus said (John 14:16-17) this *Spirit Teacher* would abide with them 'forever' *(aión #165; meaning age/space of continued time)* when he *no longer* would. He said the *kósmetic* world *system* wouldn't hear this voice, just as they'd refused to hear Jesus. Yet his followers would hear this Spirit voice *within*, just as they had learned to tune *in* to Jesus' words *of Spirit and life*.

Mary listens to this voice she supposed was the 'gardener' (Jesus said the Father would *tend/prune* the branches to bear more fruit).

"You can stop crying, Mary. Stop clinging to what you've known in the flesh. It's time to let go of that. It's time you and my brethren ascend with me, that you may BE where I AM. I'll never leave or forsake you, for in the paternal Source *we will always be One!*"

As with Simon Peter, Saul, and the Emmaus disciples, it was the *Spirit* of truth that now had Mary's attention. It was the inner garden *voice* bringing them face to face with the Christ within, where all the veiled ideas and scaled distortions of *flesh vision* would now finally fall away. And though they had once known their beloved Jesus in the flesh, they now realized... *they knew him thus no longer.*

Here, a resurrected awareness of the Christ-life in which all consist could now begin *ascending* to its rightful place. It would guide them into wholeness and truth from the *Spirit-life* garden within their heart, *back* to a *re*deemed and *re*stored mindset made new *all over again.*

The words 'I' speak to you are Spirit, and they are Life.

There's an 'I' within the garden matrix of your heart
that knows the way, and will guide you into all truth.
I AM

And when your view is single (One)
your whole BEing will be filled with Light and Life.

None of Jesus' earthly life or *miracles* were on Paul's spiritual radar. Even Jesus said he didn't need to stay on earth any longer. He said men focusing on *him* was actually detrimental to his mission, which was waking (rousing) men up to participate in their authentic Christ origin that had been forgotten long ago. The Son of Man said he had much to show them, but they weren't ready to bear the magnitude of it all because they focused *on him* (in the flesh), rather than living *from* the *spiritual* kingdom he displayed. He referred to it as *kingdom* life within them, ready to gush like NEW WINE RIVERS of living water once they finally *knew* it. Jesus' whole life revolved around getting men to look at him *only to see* the Father's heart and nature, so they would *then see their own lives* as BEing partakers of that *same* divine nature.

Jesus spoke of his enChristed Origin often, in detail. He repeatedly took the focus off himself and what he did, always pointing back to the Source from which the true power came. The people then, not unlike today, were busy watching *him* and making him famous for what he did among them. Consequently, many of them didn't grasp his true passion of doing it in love, only to show them *who they were* and just how much power they too *had hidden within them.*

We've been painted a picture of a man called Jesus who possessed supernatural abilities in a human body. It's *easy* to see how Jesus had become such a popular leader. He was a champion of the common people, a liberator of the poor, defender of the helpless, and upholder of the truth. He brought healing to those who were blind, and set-free those who'd been held captive. He released a pure love that disarmed fear, oppression, and healed broken hearts among the masses, but never once did he take any credit, as though *he* were the Source.

The gospels tell us that Jesus' *fame* spread rapidly throughout the regions and preceded him everywhere he went. Yet fame and attention as 'THE ONE' was never something Jesus desired. Jesus never once said "I will heal you." The divine power of heaven worked through him in mighty ways, but Jesus never took credit for any of it. Jesus repeatedly took the attention off himself by saying, "I myself can do nothing, but it's the Father (the Origin Source) that *does* the works."

Jesus helped people see what *he* knew about the Father, and assured them, "All things are possible to those who believe!" He told them things like: "according to *your* faith, let it be done to you," or "*your* faith has made you whole." He said that when they understood their patérnal Origin as he did, *they too* would do the same things he did. He talked about needing to go away for their benefit, but he said a Spirit teacher would manifest (be aroused) within them, showing them all truth, as well as empowering them to then walk in it.

Jesus showed men that the life of *flesh*
was in the blood and had an ending place.

He also un-veiled the Christ-life of the *Spirit*
in redeeming, rebooted, resurrected power
which didn't depend on flesh or blood,
and could *never* be taken away!

What *we've done* with Jesus' life is much different than what he intended. He had no desire to be lord, ruler, king, or be worshipped. He had no desire to have yet *another* exclusive religion named after him. The desire to control others and the veiled mind of man *did that*. The Son of Man only desired to heal those with veiled (blind) eyes so they could *see* the truth about the Father, themselves, and others. To empower those who were crippled in their thinking, so they could get up and run free on their own. To unchain all those held captive by a governing religious *make-up* system that kept them striving, working, and paying to become something *they already were*. He simply desired to show people how to stop living an orphaned life of perishing pig-pen existence. How could they do it? By following his walk of inseparable sonship as he revealed the Christ from within. The *same* Christ that was in them. Paul finally got it when he saw the Christ had been in him from his mother's womb. He said nothing about following the *flesh man*, Jesus, but: *"follow me, as I follow the Christ."* It was this Christ (within the matrix/womb) that spoke to Saul, removing his scaled and distorted *viewer* so he could see who he *truly* was.

'The veil of the temple was torn in two.' Many Bible scholars believe this was written about 30-35 years after Jesus' death, and then other gospel writers leaned on *Mark's* writings to construct their own. Many of us were not taught that Mark never actually 'knew' Jesus, nor was he a chosen disciple (Matthew 10:2-4). Luke didn't know Jesus either, but reportedly gathered his information from the apostles. Neither of them was at the cross when Jesus was crucified. Mark was a traveling companion of Paul and Barnabas, and for a while traveled with Peter as well. Although it's not been substantiated, many scholars think Peter may have dictated the *gospel* of Mark for him to write. Why bring all this up? Though Mark didn't know Jesus (in the flesh), nor was he at the cross, he wrote of something which occurred *because of* the cross. And if he did in fact get it from Peter, well... we know that Peter wasn't personally at the cross to experience it *in the flesh* either.

Try as you may (and I have), you'll not find a single account or any historical record of the veil being damaged, repaired, or replaced at the temple in Jerusalem. Sure, I know the detailed teachings (having taught them many years) about how tall and thick the temple veil was, and how it would have been impossible for anyone but God to tear it in two. The truth is however, that after Jesus' crucifixion, things went on *exactly* the same in temple practices as they had for hundreds of years prior to Jesus being born. Nothing within the man-made stone temple changed at all, *until it was destroyed by Titus in AD 70.*

So, if Peter wasn't at the cross, and Matthew, Mark, or Luke weren't at the cross, and the temple practices carried on exactly the same for around 37 more years after the cross... *what* could Matthew, Mark, and Luke have meant by their words, '*the veil was torn in two*'? Could it be they were describing the *effects* of the cross in retrospect? Is it possible they were looking *back* to the eye-opening experience they'd matured in the wisdom and stature of, now living *from* this redeemed and rebooted Christ-Spirit truth within themselves?

In our *literal* Bible upbringing, we've missed a huge part of what the scriptures were actually meant to say, over mere tidbits of truth we skimmed from a surface level through our pre-scripted doctrinal lenses. Again, I'm not bashing anyone here. I'm speaking as one who was right in the middle of it and saw it the same way for many years.

This *veil being torn from top to bottom* doesn't describe a fabric curtain in some stone building. Remember Jesus' talk with Nicodemus about being born *(anóthen)* from above? This 'top to bottom' tearing of the 'veil' was done by the same *anóthen* 'from above' Source that man's Origin-al genesis consists in. It had nothing to do with a stone temple or a literal curtain hanging in it. It was about the *true temple* which houses the extending presence of divine Origin, *which is man.* It was a *personal* removal of man's distorted *Adam* consciousness, the law of Moses, and the bondage of fear, guilt, and separation all those things brought. It was *people* being set free from perishing pig-pen thinking, to *see* themselves as authentic offspring BEings of the Divine.

The veil being *torn* was a beautiful metaphorical image of man's eyes being *inwardly* opened to truth, which would bring a power-full, literal, abundant life into *outward* open manifestation. The scriptures validating this have been right in front of us all along, but our treasure detectors weren't activated to see those hidden depositories and dig them out. Just as we saw in Saul's life (who studied the scriptures thinking *they* gave life), he needed his vision actively *de*-scaled to see the truth. Likewise, all who feel separated from their Source today, need their vision *un*-veiled to see the truth of Oneness as well.

Hebrews 10:19-22 (NKJV)

Therefore, brethren, having boldness to enter the Holiest by the blood of Jesus, **by a new and living way which He consecrated for us, *through the veil*, that is, His flesh,** and having a High Priest over the house of God, let us draw near with a true heart in full assurance of faith, **having our hearts sprinkled from an evil conscience and our bodies washed with pure water**.

2 Corinthians 3:14-18 (NKJV)

But their minds were blinded. For until this day the same veil remains unlifted in the reading of the Old Testament, because the veil is taken away in Christ. But even to this day, when Moses is read, a **veil** lies on their heart. **Nevertheless, when one turns to the Lord, the veil is taken away. Now the Lord is the Spirit;** and where the Spirit of the Lord is, there is liberty. **But we all, with unveiled face, beholding as in a mirror the glory of the Lord**, are being transformed into the same image from glory to glory, just as **by the Spirit** of the Lord. (Bold emphasis is mine)

The veil is *personal* in the eyes, face, and vision of individuals turning *inward*, to *face the reality of* THE CHRIST. Stephen, in Acts 7, helps us see Holy Spirit didn't come *anew* at Pentecost as we were taught, but BEcame manifest (roused-up) in men's *resurrected* Christ awareness.

The Spirit was always in man, but man *resisted* it in generations and kósmetic traditions of long ago that were then passed down to others. The veil is man's imagined *separation* from God, *ripped in two* after seeing all Jesus finished. The cross was a precursor (of temporal flesh) to redeem (in Spirit fulfillment) the truth of man's authentic genesis, now gloriously rebooted (begotten again) in this resurged awareness of man. Man-kind just needed to *see* the truth of who they really were, so the rivers of living water (which had been in them all along) could be *un*-veiled and *un*-corked for this intoxicating NEW WINE truth to come gushing from within them, *just as Jesus said it would*!

Those at the cross, and the first 'Christians' after this *resurrection*, believed this to be *much more* than a *normal* Roman crucifixion. They saw Jesus as the DIVINE, hanging on the cross up close and personal. It was an unveiling of grace and truth, revealing *heaven* wasn't far away at all, but was actually right there *with* them, *like* them, and *as* them... in the very midst of their orphaned darkness, pain, and suffering.

We see this personal *tearing* of man's veiled ideas even having an effect on a Roman guard. He wasn't a Jew, nor was he a Christian. He wasn't raised in the scripture or the law. Yet he became a *believer* that day as he witnessed the love Jesus poured out on that cross to prove there was a much greater reality of truth than men being separated from God. This guard experienced an unveiling of his own that day, as something *rose up* like a confirming echo from within him that said, *"Truly, this was the Son of God!"*

Believe what you want, but I'm convinced this guard, *like Saul*, had his own Damascus (sackful of bloody past) experience with *Christ* in these moments. He saw Jesus' response to a thief on the cross beside him. He heard Jesus tell this thief of a *paradise* that was already his. He'd most likely heard of Jesus' teachings telling the Jews and gentiles alike, that they all, *like him*, had a *heavenly* Father. I'm convinced that right here, a new and living hope *rose up* in his spirit which personally unveiled what Jesus lived. And just as he knew *Jesus* was the son of God, the Christ-Spirit within him echoed, *"You're a son of God too."*

It's *only* this face to face Christ encounter *within* that tears away all our veils. It's where we behold ourselves as in a mirror, expressing the authentic blueprint glory of our *patérnal* Source. What the Father *always* knew about man now becomes vibrantly clear, replacing every accusatory lie that fueled man's vain war machine mentality. Scaled vision is removed once for all, along with man's mind being cleansed from a fatherless, *orphanos sin consciousness-* which for too long had kept them *missing the mark* and intended goal of offspring intimacy!

"It's better for you that I go away"

As beautiful and comforting as the life of *Jesus* was, he knew people were focusing more on him and what he did, rather than what he wanted them to see about themselves. It's possible to honor someone and the Source they flow from without idolizing them. Yet it's easier (and more comfortable) to focus on the one in front of us, rather than what the one in front of us is pointing to *within* us. Jesus continually shifted the focus off himself and back to the *patérnal* Origin: "It's not I who do the works, but the Source within me." He shifted the focus off himself back to *other* sons of men: "It's *your* faith that makes you whole." Jesus' desire was to show men the same Source of love and power revealed in his life, was *their* Source of love and power too. **"There's only ONE Father, and you are all brethren!"** (Matt. 23:8-10)

Was the fullness of God in bodily form overwhelmingly obvious in Jesus? Absolutely! But it's no less true of other sons and daughters of men who also carry the incarnate life of God in their earthen vessels. The difference is Jesus *knew* it and lived *from* it. He said when others knew it like he did, the things they'd seen him do, *they would do also!*

It doesn't detract (in any way) from the life of Jesus (the person) for our focus to shift to *that* which exemplifies the Christ (Spirit) Origin he spent his life un-veiling. "In that day you will know you are One, just as I and the Father are One." There are no levels or ranks in *One*. If separating levels or ranks exist, *then it's not actually One*.

If I deny my own 'I AM Oneness' (Christ Source Origin) of being the same as *that* which Jesus displayed and enjoyed with the Father, then I've denied his Good News message to man from the *(patérnal)* Origin of all. Jesus didn't come to bring men *into* this heavenly family, but to unveil, awaken, redeem, and resurrect man's awareness of THE Source from which *the whole (patriá) family of heaven and earth is named.*

Our gaze has been so entrenched in a 'looking upward' for a *future* cataclysmic second coming of *Jesus*, that we pass right by, not looking inward, *or* outward to *see* the intricate heavenly handiwork filling this earth with CHRIST LIFE, love, and glory that surrounds us all *right now.*

Many are still focused on what Jesus did on earth while praying to *him*, asking *him* for things, and depending on *him* to get them through life's tough situations. Jesus never taught, encouraged, or endorsed any of this. Yes, we saw how Jesus *the man* did things in the flesh, but *we know him thus no longer.*

Jesus won't return to rescue us today;
***but* the Christ-voice he taught men to hear**
and gave his entire life to reveal within them,
carries every blessing and heavenly power for us
to re-create a global landscape of Light and Love.
May our hearts blaze with words of Spirit and Life
and may those NEW WINE RIVERS Jesus spoke of,
gush unhindered from the core of our matrix.
Awake (be aroused) you who are sleeping
and the Christ will give you Light!
May we finally know
I AM
is all
we ever needed to know, and
may we never lose the wonder of it all.

CHAPTER TEN

The Patĕr-nal Blueprint

Things were different for the early believers after this *resurrection*. Their idea of life as separated servants of a distant judge was now being transformed as the un-veiled truth of intimacy had centered the bullseye of their hearts. The echo of divine truth that had always been within them wouldn't, *as Stephen said the generational fathers had done,* be resisted any longer. They were awakening from the slumber of generations past where manifested intimacy and Oneness with God had been *un*-seen. Perfect love was moving them from an *existence* of fear, death, flesh, and blood that once bound their thinking. They'd been roused up to shine in a revelational consciousness of Spirit Life as *One* with their Source. Jesus called it *life more abundant*. They could no longer be manipulated with fear and control by institutional thieves and robbers. Neither would their once *un*-seen and *un*-known Origin be held captive by the restrictive *gates of hádēs* ever again.

The *ekklésial* enlightenment Jesus described to Peter as he realized the truth of his heavenly patérnal Source, was now serving as the firm foundation for the spiritual house of *koinónia* fellowship to build on.

Saul had heard this *ek kaléō* calling from within, realizing it was his from his mother's womb. Simon Peter realized sons of men could hear from their Father in heaven. So also, did others feel this burning Spirit Life from within as they I-dentified with their redeemed genesis. Now coming together in *upper room* unity, a once *downcast* consciousness was experiencing the *metá-morphé-oo* of total transformation.

It was BEcoming One with this awareness that empowered these untrained and common people to do uncommon and powerful things. Even the scribes, rulers, and high priest marveled as they perceived these uneducated *ordinary* men had BEEN WITH Jesus in co-knowledge of THE CHRIST. This 'been with' (*sýn* #4862) statement, goes much deeper than the disciples merely being in the *proximity* of Jesus. It confirmed they'd grasped the resemblance of their *sons of men* lives in mirrored reflection of Jesus- just as he'd unveiled THE CHRIST to them! Their acts proved they'd seen the truth about themselves *face to face*, and their veils of distorted fear and separation were falling away. They were no longer bound to their former consciousness of orphaned and perishing *sin* mode. They were *abiding* in a conscious *co-knowledge* of the same gushing fountainhead of CHRIST-LIFE that Jesus revealed to them! So, what happened at Pentecost?

Jesus' instruction to the disciples (Luke 24:4) sounds like this in the Greek: **"Behold, I am delegating the Father's promise upon you. Now you be seated (abide) in shalom wholeness and peace** (Jerusalem means place of peace) **till you should be putting on ability (power) from** *on high*." The term *on high* means elevated place (*hupsos* #5311); a position exceedingly and abundantly above (*huper* #5228). It's this same enlightened *high place* of comprehension Paul prayed ALL would come to understand through their enChristed inner man. It was this same EXPRESSION of the 'Father' (patér #3962) Jesus revealed, from whom the whole 'family' (patriá #3965) of heaven and earth is named!

Words like *parousía* (come/coming) and *phaneroó* (appear) have been misportrayed in many of our concordances as something coming from *afar*, or as in Christ *coming back* after being gone to a distant location. Likewise, has the term '*endued* (enduo) *with power from on high*' been distorted, as though it came from the distance 'out there' and made a *new* arrival. This power *comes* from the highest Source of power. Yet it isn't a *new* power that comes from afar, but a 'putting on' in one's awareness the kingdom *patriá* life that Jesus said already existed within, and living *from* the present tense manifestation of it!

Scriptures about the 'coming' of the Lord *or* the 'arrival' of Christ, aren't saying to look up and watch for something out in the distance. They're describing a *manifested* occurrence of a personal, immediate presence NOW BEing un-veiled and fully grasped in one's awareness. Paul wrote Colossians 3:4 to be read and received something like this:

When Christ (who IS our life) **appears** (is presently expressed), **then** (at that same time) **you will appear** (BEing presently expressed) **with** (him) **Christ IN** (that same present tense) **glory.**

This wasn't about the Christ *returning* from some space mission in the distant heavens. It's simply saying we are *always One*. It means that as Christ *reveals us* as an incarnate extension, *so also* does our life (from this same glorious Oneness) *reveal* and express the Christ!

The core of Acts 2 in the original language isn't painting street address imagery of a bunch of guys and girls hanging out together in a specific second story apartment. It says the fulfillment of the day of Pentecost came upon them **when they were *all alike* in the *same* place. It means of One mind with the *same* focus.** There's a difference in a group of people all being gathered in one room together, as opposed to people who are unified there as *One*. Jesus told them there was a day coming when they would *know* they were One with the Father *and* One with each other. That's when things would start manifesting from *within them* in power-full ways they had never before seen or known!

So here they are, *as One*, when out of heaven (ouranós #3772 as the abode [kingdom] of God [by implication happiness, power, eternity]) something began to *manifest*. Where did Jesus tell them the kingdom abode of God was? He said it was already *within* them. In fact, Jesus told them not to listen to anyone who implied the kingdom would come or appear from 'out there' somewhere. **Suddenly** (*aphno* #869), **something comes** (*aphanés* #852 [not previously manifested] in conjunction with *phaino* #5316, [to enlighten, appear and shine]) **from within them**. It was like a mighty breath or wind (*pnoe* #4157; the root of *pneuma* #4151; the flowing current of Christ-life Spirit breathed into humanity). In John 7:38 Jesus referred to it as SPIRIT RIVERS of living water. He said it would flow (gush) from all who'd believe the truth of 'I'mmanuel: God IN man, while recognizing that God was IN them too!

Jesus didn't say this manifestation of force-filled power would come from a distant location. He said it would gush like a fountainhead from their own belly (koilia #2836), which is the matrix/womb of the divine he said was *already within them*. This fountainhead implication Jesus used, meant once it manifested and started flowing, that no barrier, *even the gates of hádēs* (man's previously *un*-seen Origin) could ever prevail or restrict its flow again! These higher-level thinkers in unified agreement with their resurrected awareness would be the **first buds of the great harvest**, *which was what Pentecost was all about!*

These *first-fruits* would be the sons and daughters of God coming in recognizable open manifestation as described in Romans 8:28-30. Paul didn't imply these sons and daughters would need a *new* identity that had not previously existed. He said all creation had longed for them to **put on** their true *kaléō* identity *un*-veiled in resurrected Christ awareness! They would finally come into their long awaited, rightful, and open manifestation as extended offspring of God! This enChristed awareness brought an *echoing love language* of unity and Oneness which all men and woman intrinsically understood as their own, regardless of age, gender, or any cultural differences! (Gal.3:28)

Let's talk a little bit about *fire*. It's interesting that these higher consciousness *tongues of fire* are of the same beautiful origin of fire used figuratively in scripture as the *consuming fire of God*. This *fire* transmorphés all it touches *into light and likeness* with itself.

Remember, the Light doesn't come to *expose* what we have been taught were 'sinful acts' in men. It comes to *reveal* the treasure within men, by *removing* what the Father knows is the root source *behind* the distorted acts. **That source of distortion will *always* go back to a mindset of alien-ation which led man into those acts to begin with.** When Jesus told the Pharisees, "You are of your *father*, the devil," he wasn't implying some *fallen angel* was their literal father. He was saying their *outer fruit* actions were the harvest of the *satanâs seed lie* of separation they had allowed to be inwardly rooted in the garden of their matrix. This *Jesus vs. devil / good guy vs. bad guy* scenario men have created can only exist in an alienated mindset. Yet the scheming war-machine villain we've conjured up to blame for our self-produced drama has *never* possessed the ability of 'fathering' anything.
The refiner has no interest in the worthless, contaminating dross as he stokes the fire. His only interest, and the whole reason for the fire, is to reveal the beauty and purity of the gold by removing every impurity which does not contribute to or confirm the gold's worth!

These tongues of 'fire' (pýr [*pur*] #4442) appearing on each of them in this united upper level thinking, was validating proof of their vision and hearts being cleansed (*pur*ified) from *foreign* elements. The *dross* of an alien seed-lie had kept this Spirit manifestation from gushing out in generations before them who were *bound to powerless traditions*.

Isaiah 6:6 speaks of a **live coal** (*ritspah #7531/feminine of 7529; a hot stone*) which was taken from a heavenly alter where the *pur*ifying fire of God burns continually. It was then touched to Isaiah's own lips, which he now recognized as having uttered *unclean* language.

Isaiah 6:5-7 (NKJV)

So I said: "Woe is me, for I am undone! Because I am a man of unclean lips, and I dwell in the midst of a people of unclean lips; For my eyes have seen the King, The Lord of hosts." Then one of the seraphim flew to me, having in his hand a live coal which he had taken with the tongs from the altar. And he touched my mouth with it, and said: "Behold, this has touched your lips; Your iniquity is *taken away*, and your sin purged."

The term *unclean lips* Isaiah uses here is quite significant. The *unclean* means contaminated and/or polluted. The *lips* in this phrase signifies a language, speech, or talk using vain [worth-less] words.

Look at the *fiery* results of *(pýr #4442)* and the *pur*-i-fication that took place. First off, Isaiah was not *physically* touched. This fire he experienced was not a *literal* fire that burned him. It was *symbolic* for the cleansing and removal of contaminated, worthless speech being *taken away* from his language. This *holy setting* in Isaiah's vision was seen as THE PLACE of exclusive superiority and eminence where ALL things were pure, sacred, and undefiled. Isaiah understood the *One* he was looking at as high and lifted up, to be the 'Lord' (adon #113) and 'heavenly Master' over all. The Israelites believed (because Moses said) that no man could see 'God' and live. Yet Isaiah *sees the Lord* sitting on the throne in 'THE holy place' as a thunderous voice cries out:

"Holy, holy, holy; the whole earth is filled with his glory!!"

As truth of a *glory filled earth* is *un*-veiled before his eyes, Isaiah realizes he's been speaking a contaminated language among an entire people group who all had the same polluted, *worthless* language. He isn't punished for being a 'sinful' man in the presence of this holiness. Instead, this divine holiness *pur*ifies the *polluted lips* of his earthen vessel, removing the worthless (dross) language he'd spoken before!

This beautiful picture (aligning with the Father's nature) goes right along with the *lake of fire* we have too long misunderstood in the REVELATION OF THE CHRIST. This fire was never to physically *punish* God's extended offspring. It was to burn away every hinderance that kept them from seeing, enjoying, and participating in the true worth of their authentic *patriá kaléō* identity! The nature of man's blueprint Origin was set into motion to *passionately* work all things for man's good. This *orgē action* is in motion until every shred of contaminated dross-filled skubala gets burned up and consumed in the purifying fire of intimacy! As we've seen earlier, the word we've been taught to fear as *wrath* has many similarities to our word *orgasm*. Hopefully, fear, suffering, or punishment aren't attached to *that* word in your life.

As with Isaiah's vision, this teeming passion from which man's life was expressed coming forth from the logos Origin, was set into motion to overflow like a fountainhead gushing with goodness from within. This *working for the good* is continually refining the worthless dross from our thinking and our speech, to *reveal* the authentic treasure we house in these earthen vessels. The refining doesn't come physically, but from within the Spirit matrix of our heart, where all the true issues of life flow from. It's here, that as a man thinks and sees this truth in his heart, so that truth BEcomes literally, and physically *manifested* in a life much more abundant than he or she has ever before known!

Because our thinking has been *trained* from a judgment mentality, we've seen (with veiled vision) symbolic treasures hidden in scripture as literal, physical actions coming in the form of retribution. Due to this, we have entirely missed the divine beauty these scriptures hold, which is *complete*-ly of a *restore*-ative and *pur*-i-fying nature.

Take for instance, the word *brimstone*. We've been taught it reveals divine judgement (in a negative sense) upon man. When we take off our pre-scribed lenses and war-machine mentality to see the word in its intended context, we find something quite different and beautiful. It's been there all along... *we just couldn't see it.*

In the purest form (and each of the 7 times in the New Testament), it is actually *theíon*, #2303 - properly, sulfur ('brimstone', i.e. **burning rocks/stones**) i.e. sulphurous, is so named for the distinct sulphur smell **left by lightning**; (figuratively) fire of heaven, displaying divine, awesome, and unstoppable power.

Remember the live coal (burning stone) touched to Isaiah's lips? It wasn't there to punish him, but to purify his language with the refining (all-consuming) *treasure-revealing fire* of God!

It was the same effect in Luke 10:18 when Jesus said he witnessed **'satan fall like lightning'** from *heaven*. Jesus wasn't talking about some fallen angel being cast out of a distant location of divine domain up in the sky. The disciples had just returned from a field trip Jesus sent them on without *any* of the things they thought they'd normally need, as in money, or physical supplies of any kind. This excursion caused them to realize everything they could ever need to operate in true *heavenly authority* was already within them, *as long as* they went about believing and seeing things *from the same view* Jesus did.

The Son of Man was making a joyful remark that this field exercise was *pur*ifying (casting out) 'I am not' *satanâs* thinking, and was falling from the high places of their consciousness. Here, they began realizing *no diábolos enemy existed* that could have *any* authority over their lives in *any* way. It's exactly what Jesus meant when he said once they realized they were sons of men who could hear and operate from the Fatherly Origin within, the gates of hádēs (darkness, accusation, or *fear* of the unknown) could never again restrict them in *any* way!

This *pur*ification of *language* is what we see take place on the day of Pentecost. Their long-held consciousness of exclusive 'us and them' thinking was now falling from the high places in their minds. They had come to an upper-room awareness where they saw themselves in the true unity and Oneness with the Father that Jesus had told them was definitely *coming* to them. Suddenly, out of *heavenly places within* comes gushing forth the love language of their patérnal Source: One Father, One Spirit, One love in whom *you are all patriá family!*

This *pur*-i-fying fire now caused the language of *One* to gush from within them in a clear and beautiful way! Even though many cultures were there among them, each person now legibly understood this love language of *One* like it had been their own native tongue all along!

This *fire* of undistorted truth also awakened a BOLDNESS causing others to marvel at these common *earthly* people doing *heavenly* things. A life more abundant is now put on open display which reflects the same enChristed nature as Jesus. How? Because of a resurrected and rebooted co-awareness of their authentic patérnal Origin!

Acts 4:13 (NKJV)

Now when they saw the boldness of Peter and John, and perceived that they were uneducated and untrained men, they marveled. And they realized that they had been with Jesus.

Did this boldness make them pushy and arrogant? On the contrary, they gave of themselves freely to others, to the point *no one among them lacked anything*. They'd learned on their field trip that lack had no authority to exist in their lives. Neither did the disciples any longer have a desire to call down an Elijah *judgment fire* on others. Now, just like Jesus, they took no offense with anyone, but desired to share the Father's healing, cleansing, *puri*fying *love fire* with everyone!

Seeing the Blueprint Changes Everything

Having been a superintendent over commercial construction projects for many years has helped me to form my own *personal imagery* of the Father's blueprint vision. There were different stages of time you might visit one of my building sites and walk away with extremely varying impressions. If you came while we were digging the trenches for the piers and foundation, you might get bored and wonder how long it was going to take before you could actually *see* a building.

The amount of time involved in making everything straight and stable, along with every accommodation for water, electric, sewer, etc. that a properly functioning building will require, can become quite time consuming. It can seem overly tedious and drawn out, especially for those lacking experience of how something of this magnitude is actually done. It can be easy to forget it's the foundational stage which involves the most important part of the building. Though not *visibly* seen, this foundation will be solely responsible for supporting multiple levels and wings of the entire complex. It will be expected to endure time and any outer elements to come. If the foundation isn't secure, everything built on it will be subject to fail. Once we see our authentic Origin as rooted, grounded, and secure in the Father's love, we'll know it can support all the weighty things of heavenly glory resting upon it, while withstanding any temporary storms of life that come our way.

There might be other times you would visit my site and wonder: *Are they building something here... or tearing something down??* There are certain times it's actually hard to tell. Perhaps you can relate if you've been through some *deconstruction* periods in your personal theology. There were times I would pull up to the gate in the morning and think, *"This place looks like a freakin' war zone!"*

Yet no matter what it looked like through my eyes in the current snapshot of time, I could *always* slip inside my office trailer and flip to the final page of the blueprint. It was the one place available to me where I could always re-adjust my vision and behold the architect's *signature* design. I could see things clearly, just as they were intended. I could behold the same undistorted picture the architect had *always* seen in his heart. A completed state of perfection openly displaying every needed provision and accommodation utilized along the way. This final page would *always look the same*, revealing every function in proper place to facilitate the building's beauty, integrity, and design.

This imagery is like men and women slipping into the secret place *within*, even when all hell is breaking loose around them. Sure, they can look and see various pestilences and arrows of destruction laying waste *out there*, but these *called ones* know it can't come near them. They *know* the foundational logo of Oneness originally placed within them. They refuse to let alien voices of accusation draw them from within their inner garden paradise, where rivers of living water gush forth and produce lasting fruit of the *God-kind* in every season. All creation has been waiting on the Father's surname offspring to not only know and possess, but to *participate in* their divine nature of empowered joyful dominion over every area of their life. The mind of man tends to get bogged down in temporary details along the journey. Yet the mind of Christ is fully assured that every intricate detail and functionality of the plan *will come together at just the right time.*

Having become friends with some gifted architects over the years, I realized they carried a *much different vision* than I could see when they pulled up on the job. Perhaps it was a phase involving wiring shafts or specialty conduits, or how to get newly revised power source lines through odd places in floors and walls without compromising the structural integrity of the building. These things add much pressure if you're staring at a 'finish by' date on a calendar. Yet the architect *knew* that whatever was necessary to assure these transitions taking place would be provided for and accomplished to achieve the end goal.

No matter what a *momentary snapshot* may have looked like *that day*, the designing architect knew there would be accommodations to facilitate forward progress in that phase of the plan. They refused to get bogged down in any moment of what it might *look like* right then. NOTHING could distort or erase their passionate anticipation of the day when everyone else would get to see and enjoy what they had seen from the moment of conception in their heart. This was *their baby* that carried *their name* and *their logo,* and they had no intention of settling for anything less than the fullness of *their original design!*

I've seen sub-contractors frustrated and angry when they couldn't see *at the moment* how things could ever work out. Yet once we sat down face to face, our eyes would be opened to perspectives not yet seen. This new unified view we began seeing *together,* made the goal no longer *appear* impossible. In just one moment, the entire atmosphere could change. The architect knew the final page of finished splendor would one day be enjoyed by all. Now, *we began to see it that way too.*

We still get hung up on a *particular day* in the story of man, as the Bible records it in Genesis 3. We see Adam's distorted thinking which led to a *mental* alien-ation from the truth of Oneness with his Source. We have viewed (and taught) this *allegorical* story through our own distorted lens as though it somehow became *everyone's* starting point. A point where all human life begins: in *deficit, lack, and separation.* WE made this scene OUR *mental* starting point. Just as Adam did in the story, we start trying to cover ourselves with our own devices. This alienated mindset keeps us trying to work our way back in systematic ways that *seem right* to man, yet hold no life whatsoever in the end. **The 3ʳᵈ chapter of Genesis is not mankind's authentic genesis, nor does it even exist in the Father's expressed logos masterpiece!**

The scene depicted in Genesis 3 didn't ruin the Architect's dream, nor did it mar the pro-vision within it. Adam became *un*-mind-full of his Source. But *his* alienated thoughts, ideas of broken fellowship, or the distorted acts that came *from* it, never changed the Father's vision of him in any way. It was but a momentary snapshot in time, which in no way altered or made any less valuable what his authentic genesis contained or what the Origin-al logos blueprint would always reveal.

The final page of the Father's dream will *always* display man's authentic genesis life as BEing extended divine treasure, consisting IN the immovable, unshakable, FOUNDATION OF CHRIST. Having our Christ mind *renewed,* allows us to finally view the framework of *everything* through the finished plans and purposes of heavenly truth, rather than some war-zone snapshot taken in a *moment of time* along the way.

It's at this point in our journey where we begin to see things through the Architect's eyes and we're no longer viewing life through an unclear perspective. We stop approaching our days like a struggling laborer in a darkened elevator shaft, trying to work his way through multiple obstructions to somehow attain a distant, higher level. As we turn to the Christ within, our unveiled face to face encounter with the paternal Source of all life clearly reveals there was never anything lacking in the Father's master plan at all. *We just needed to see it.*

We've poured concrete around doctrines formed out of the ancient shadowy glimpses of Moses, Elijah, and others we *thought* were truth. Yet Jesus came wielding a heavenly jackhammer, saying:

"NO MAN *before me has truly seen or known the Father.*"

Jesus chips away and dismantles all of our distorted *Godologies*, pointing back to our enChristed logos Origin. All so we *can see* the Father's blueprint and *un*-veiled reality of Christ-life within. As our veils are removed, we see the TRUE FOUNDATION of life we can trust and enjoy from a new understanding of 'faith.' This faith doesn't busy itself stretching into the distance trying to bring something good into our present reality. True faith *rests* in a realization of what we know from within, that the divine design of this blueprint masterplan has *already* provided every heavenly thing we could ever need along our journey.

This authentic Source of perfect love views everything created from itself as VERY GOOD. Once we see this truth, how could we *not* want to participate and fully enjoy this heavenly surname of our divine Origin? **Not just belonging _to_ us. Living _in_ us, _as_ us, choosing to BEcome us.** This Source wakes us each morning in echoes of our authentic genesis and hearts blazing with love! How excited we now are to surrender to all this day of abundant life holds in store. Yes, and surrender *we will.* For our unveiled eyes now behold this Source so complete, it carries its own perfect love and power to *work all things for good* in our lives!

In that day you will *know* you are One.

Perhaps it's *that* day for you.
If so, and you've seen your true reflection
in Jesus, the Mirror,
don't ever again walk away
forgetting what he revealed.
~I AM ONE~

So... What Now?

There are multitudes around the globe, who, once the light comes on in that first room, they begin seeing truth so deep, so real, that they can never deny or *unsee it* again. For those who have been in church ministry much of their life, it can feel like a vacuum effect, *sucking out* that which we so long invested into *with everything we had.*

There isn't much to compare with the emotions that come when you feel like you've given your whole life to something you've believed and diligently driven yourself in commitment to, only to now wonder (like John the Baptist) if it had all been just a total waste of their time. *Discouraged. Hurt. Angry. Betrayed. Empty. Ashamed.* Just a few of the emotions that can come pushing us around like a tidal wave we long to get away from. Many have called it *the great deconstruction.*

Some have walked away from everything, carrying their emotions with them, mad at God, and mad at everyone else. Others, having actually *seen* the truth, will resist it. After all, it takes courage to stand in front of people we have preached to diligently for 20, 30, 50 years, and tell them *we now know* we were wrong about some things. Those choosing to hang on to prideful traditions rather than learning, letting go, and moving forward in what they've seen *in their hearts*, continue to carry the luggage of all these tidal wave emotions. Trying to conceal what our heart has *seen* will eat at us from within *everywhere we go.*

There are others however, who, having seen enlightened truth so beautiful, will reach out and embrace it with joy. These are *relieved* to know God is infinitely better than what we were taught *and* what we taught others. It's these, like Paul (Acts 9:18-22), who leave behind the *scales* once restricting their vision. They immediately go back to their churches or ministries and begin teaching the unashamed truth of Christ *within* from their mother's womb. These men and women of courage are unafraid to boldly proclaim this *almost too good to be true Good News*. They will also gain greater respect, admiration, and love from their congregations and classes than they've ever known.

People want *truth*. People want real *love*. People... are *ready*.

As people are freed from thoughts of being estranged from God, along with ideas of *sin*, fear, torment, and bondage to death, they will *together*, leave the grave-clothes of veiled distortions behind on the corporate skubala pile. These will have *no part* in their journey ahead.

They will also realize, not one single thing in their journey along the way has been wasted. Any remaining pride and ego will be completely swallowed up in joy. They now see the experiences in their past have actually been working toward something better all along. They had merely *believed* before, but now they can *know from deep within*.

The more we all turn to *Christ within*, the veils of past distortions fall away one by one. It will be these who no longer just *believe*, but now personally and experientially *know* this glorious truth which can never be taken from them. They will *know* how the Father has seen them all along. They'll experience the transforming truth of how (and where) they see *heaven*, how they see *themselves*, and how they now see *others* all around them. This landscape altering love no longer sees others according to mere *flesh*, and no longer knows *Jesus* according to *his* flesh. Awakened eyes now behold every man, woman, and child as originally as authentically consisting IN CHRIST. All are now seen as incarnate carriers of patérnal DNA in treasured earthen vessels.

Imagine the present-tense wholeness that could manifest if we refocused the multiplied billions of dollars we spend each year trying to 'save' people from a *hell* that doesn't exist. What if we invested that, *and ourselves*, in those living in *hell* among us? The *hurting, sick,* and *broken. What if* we actually loved our neighbors as we love ourselves?

"As you've done to the least of these, you've done to me." ~Jesus

Imagine a world where the dividing walls of man were no longer put up, *but torn down.* Will it be easy? No one is saying it will. But hands that reach out in initiating love toward the hands of others they *once* saw as different (or as enemies) *can't* fail. **Love. Never. Fails.**

Exclusion, hunger, racism, wars, and anything that even smells like division, could be burned up in the climactic joy and *pur*ifying fire of *heaven.* Here, the divine echo of love and truth which was *un*known, squelched, and *prevailed* against too long, will gush as a fountainhead from the matrix of ALL life. And each and every one, in every tribe and culture, could hear love's truth of *One... as in their own native tongue.*

This is a picture of *true* heaven, bringing its landscape to a *new* earth.

Can it really happen?

Oh yes, it can,

and I believe it will.

In fact, it already is.

How will it happen in our lives individually?

It starts with the person right in front of you.

Look at them through love,

and if you can't see them

through the eyes and love of Christ,

keep looking... until you do.

Thank you for reading Born From Above.

And now that you know your authentic genesis...

don't ever forget who you truly are.